Gerald Warner Brace

Writer, Sailor, Teacher

Gerald Warner Brace

Writer, Sailor, Teacher

by
Charlotte Holt Lindgren

 HOLLIS
PUBLISHING
COMPANY

To Don—with love

ISBN #1-884186-08-4

The following publisher has generously given permission to use quotations from a copyrighted work. From *Travels with Charley* by John Steinbeck. Copyright © 1961, 1962 by The Curtis Publishing Co., © 1962 by John Steinbeck, renewed © 1990 by Elaine Steinbeck, Thom Steinbeck, and John Steinbeck IV. Used by permission of Viking Penguin, a division of Penguin Putnam Inc.

Printed in the United States of America by Puritan Press, Inc. of Hollis, NH.

♾ The paper used in the book complies with the Permanent Paper Standard issued by the National Information Standards Organization (Z39.48-1984).

Acknowledgments

I am grateful to the many people who have aided me in my research of Gerald Warner Brace. His daughter, Barbara Brace Seeley, has been a constant and unfailing help. His sons, Charles Loring Brace IV and Gerald Warner Brace, gave added insights and information about their parents. Niece, Brenda Gilchrist, graciously allowed me to read and quote from her memoirs and to see once more the Brace family summer home. His other niece, Julia Donaldson Barnett, and his nephew John Gilchrist shared memories. Former students sent letters and anecdotes: Burton Cooper, Evelyn Dodge, Lane Faison, John Gilgun, Donald Junkins, George Lane, and Bertha Carter Ruark. Geoffrey Austrian and George Brockway, Brace's editor at W. W. Norton, read the manuscript and gave helpful advice. My brother, David Lindgren, gave me facts about Dartmouth College. My sister, Ruth Stevens, and her husband Philip, made it possible for me to revisit Deer Isle. I am grateful also to the following people who gave me encouragement, information, technical help and permissions: Neva Sylvester Beck, Margaret Buffum, Tommy Chang, Julie Duncan, Harriet Lane, Charles McLane, Edward Myers, Norman Pettit and Eric Winslow. The library staffs at Boston University and Lasell College were always willing to offer assistance. Dr. Howard Gotlieb kindly granted me permission to use and quote from the extensive collection of Brace papers in the Boston University Special Collections. I owe thanks most of all to Gerald Warner Brace's friend and colleague—my husband, Donald J. Winslow—who spent many hours aiding and reassuring me.

Gerald Warner Brace

WORKS BY GERALD WARNER BRACE

(Arranged chronologically with abbreviations used in the text)

Novels

The Islands. (TI) New York: G. P. Putnam's Sons, 1936.
The Wayward Pilgrims. (WP) New York: G. P. Putnam's Sons, 1938.
Light on a Mountain. (LOM) New York: G. P. Putnam's Sons, 1941.
The Garretson Chronicle. (GC) New York: W. W. Norton and Co., 1947.
A Summer's Tale. (ST) New York: W. W. Norton and Co., 1949.
The Spire. (TS) New York: W. W. Norton and Co., 1952.
Bell's Landing. (BL) New York: W. W. Norton and Co., 1955.
The World of Carrick's Cove. (WCC) New York: W. W. Norton and Co., 1957.
Winter Solstice. (WS) New York: W. W. Norton and Co., 1960.
The Wind's Will. (WW) New York: W. W. Norton and Co., 1964.
The Department. (TD) New York: W. W. Norton and Co., 1968.

Nonfiction

The Age of the Novel. Boston University Press, 1957.
Between Wind and Water. (BWW) New York: W. W. Norton and Co., 1966.
The Stuff of Fiction. (SOF) New York: W. W. Norton and Co., 1969.
Days That Were. (DTW) New York: W. W. Norton and Co., 1976.
Days That Were, Vol. II. (DTW II) Privately Printed, 1979.

Other Printed Works

"Artisans and Models," *Maclean's*, May 15, 1936.
"The Damn'd Profession," *Writer's Monthly*, June 1936.
"Deep Water Man," *The Story Survey*, ed. Harold Blodgett. New York: J. B. Lippincott, Co., 1939.
"The Great New England Novel," *New Hampshire Alumnus*, March 1954.
"Robert Frost's New Hampshire," *New Hampshire Profiles*, May 1955.
"I Traveled a Good Deal in Amherst," *Amherst Alumni News*, Winter, 1963.
Introduction to Anthony Trollope's *The Last Chronicle of Barset.* New York: W. W. Norton and Co., 1964.
"The Essential Novel," *Texas Quarterly*, Spring, 1965

CONTENTS

Introduction xi

1. Dobbs Ferry and Deer Isle 1

2. A Young Romantic 11

3. Amherst 19

4. Epiphany 33

5. Studying Architecture 39

6. Harvard English Department 49

7. Williams College 57

8. Marriage 67

9. Travel with Huldah 81

10. Dartmouth College and a Growing Family 87

11. Mount Holyoke Women 99

12. Boston University 119

13. A Time of Tension 133

14. Recognition 145

15. Great Spruce Head Island 161

16. Academia 169

17. From the Mediterranean to Penobscot Bay 183

18. Teaching Creative Writing 193

19. Stepping into a New Age 201

20. The Sixties 211

21. Mirroring Life's Experiences 219

22. The Darkening Years 231

23. Final Years 241

24. L'Envoi 249

INTRODUCTION

Gerald Warner Brace was my teacher, mentor, and friend. I first met him in September of 1941 in a large English writing class that he taught at Boston University. Almost six feet tall, lean and tanned from a summer's sailing at Deer Isle, Maine, he was a handsome man of forty. He did not seem a typical academic. His hands were scarred and calloused from clearing brush and hauling in moorings. His suit was comfortably worn and baggy, and his unruly hair, inexpertly cut, was tinged with grey. He glanced shyly over the top of his glasses at the students when he called the class roll in a rather tremulous voice. Because the course met in Jacob Sleeper Hall, a large auditorium that held two classes simultaneously, it was only possible to hear his rather softly spoken words by giving him complete attention.

When I consider the powerful influence Brace had on my life, it is difficult to realize that he had already lived over half of his existence before I met him. We did not become actual friends until I was hired five years later to be his graduate assistant. I continued to correct his papers and type his manuscripts through the years that he guided me through my doctorate. He seemed to take the half-avuncular, half-romantic pleasure in molding my mind that an older man often feels toward a young admirer. I frequently visited him and his wife, Huldah, at their homes in Belmont, Massachusetts, and Deer Isle, Maine.

Gerald was at his happiest in Maine. He was a natural sailor brought up in a family where the sea was a way of life. His niece, Brenda Gilchrist, remembers how at home he was in a boat. "He sailed by the wind on his cheek, the signs on the water, impatient with people who couldn't do the same. He played the boat, fingering the halyards and lines like the strings of a cello, bowing the tiller until the boat sang." Like his wife I was incapable of being part of this salty world, and he was willing to accept the complete ignorance of some women about such matters, though he could be annoyed with those who sailed without achieving expertise. He delighted in taking us out in his sloop *Festina* or in his sister's boat, *The Roaring Forties,* and pointing out the settings of the novels he had written. The names of the islands resound like a litany: Eagle, Fling, Hurricane, the Porcupines, Isle au Haut, Crow, Pickering, Marshall, Heart, and Long. If the weather turned cold and foggy as so often happens in coastal Maine, he would build a fire in the fireplace and we would read or he would tell stories of what life had been like on the islands when he was a boy. At such times, he became relaxed and outgoing.

He was born in 1901, at a time when most Americans—certainly those from his comfortable social class—welcomed the new century with optimism

The author back in "the days that were"

and hope. Believing in the perfectibility of man and society, they felt certain that the new inventions and discoveries of the previous age promised a better future. A few rare individuals such as Henry Adams recognized that the continuity of history had reached its end, but no one was prepared for the swiftness of the change. Wars, scientific advances, the speed of transportation and communication, overpopulation, and man's ventures into space shook old faiths and diminished the importance of the individual. Polarization—of youth and age, rich and poor, pale skins and dark, male and female—increased, even as social consciousness rose. Women discovered their force. Men, once secure about their position in society's hierarchy, had to revise their attitudes.

The eleven fictional works of Gerald Warner Brace document a vanishing way of life which, if not totally forgotten, is increasingly misinterpreted. Brace's struggles to come to terms with modern times offer a fascinating glimpse of how life was forever altered by World War II and Vietnam. When he wrote his autobiography *Days That Were* in 1976, he looked back at his life with a certain sense of accomplishment. He had published fourteen books, and had taught for over fifty years. In spite of fears that he no longer was attuned to current thinking, he reflected with some satisfaction:

> I was once a scholar and teacher, a writer of novels, a painter
> of pictures, a sailor and boat designer, a trout fisherman, a skier and
> climber, a carpenter and handyman, a father and husband.

Although born in New York, Brace seemed the quintessential New Englander, and, indeed, lived most of his life there. He spent his school years studying at the Gunnery and Loomis schools in Connecticut and his summers on the coast of Maine and Massachusetts. While attending Amherst College he grew to know intimately the mountains in New Hampshire, Vermont and western Massachusetts; for the remainder of his life he skied their slopes and walked along their back roads. He had an instinctive empathy for the stalwart country folk who still clung to a way of life that was already beginning to disappear. It was difficult for him to explain the almost supernatural awareness he had for the region. "I saw myself hovering like some air-borne spirit above all those miles of far mountains and the islands of the coast, and at the same time I felt as though I had been given special insight into the lives and native ways of the inhabitants." So successfully would he encapsulate their lives into his novels that the poet Robert Frost, himself a New England transplant, expressed amazement that an academic born in New York could have such an intuitive understanding of native New Englanders. Brace became so thoroughly a part of that small geographical segment of the globe, that he would make it his permanent home. He married Huldah Laird, a girl from the Boston area, and raised his three children in Massachusetts. He died in the hospital at Blue Hill, Maine, not far from his beloved Deer Isle summer home.

It was in New England too that Gerald Brace was educated and taught in some of the area's most prestigious colleges: Amherst, Harvard, Dartmouth, Williams, Mount Holyoke, and Boston University. During his long career as a professor of writing and literature he helped guide generations of students, many of whom later became successful authors and teachers themselves. If his novel writing allowed him to indulge in romantic fantasies, his teaching kept him grounded in reality. Though he originally entered the profession as the only field in which he could pursue his writing interests and manage to earn a living, he became convinced that education offered the only hope to a troubled world. He wrote in the unpublished second volume of his autobiography:

> No institution has a more difficult and even impossible task to perform than the modern university, which encompasses all that is known or ever has been known about atoms and man and stars. At its top levels it is expected to profess the ultimate achievements in the sciences and the arts and to take charge of and promote all the wisdom of mankind, and at the same time it must make itself responsible for the lives and professions of all the hordes of young men and women who clamor for admission and attention and some share in what they consider to be the good things of life. In this age of incipient disaster, the universities and colleges are what we count on to show us how we may be saved. If they fail, we are doomed.

Brace had been raised to believe that it was the responsibility of those born more fortunate to help those in need, expecting that they in turn would be grateful. He was confused and dismayed in the sixties and seventies by the unleashed anger of the civil rights movement, the demands of students, and the strident voices of women activists. As a liberal he believed in their causes, but he could not understand their need to destroy all that he considered civilized.

During Brace's long career as writer and teacher, he had to revise his views of women as their roles in society changed. As a youth he idealized them. Born into an upper class Victorian household at the turn of the century, he was sent to all male-private schools. For years he believed that all women could be divided into four categories: goddesses, temptresses, society ladies, and hard working country wives and mothers, but he never felt antipathy toward them. Women were attracted to him, not just because of his craggy good looks, but because something in his shy, withdrawn manner encouraged them to try to probe under the carapace to seek out the sensitive romantic beneath. He fantasized about love, and was flattered by their attentions, yet his world was primarily masculine. The graceful lines of a sailing vessel were more beautiful to him than any female form and his highest passions were reserved for mountains and sea.

As a young man, he accepted the popular attitude that male and female were two distinct species each with separate roles. The conservative view he expressed in his first novel, *The Islands,* published in 1936 was shared by most of the critics. Maine poet Robert Tristram Coffin writing in the *New York Herald Tribune* (31 May 1936) commented approvingly:

> Brace's book proves a point I have always made in describing my own coast folks. The women-folks keep their place. Men's work is men's. Women keep out of it. This all sounds very aboriginal. But it works, and sometimes I think the reason why the savor has gone out of a good deal of modern living is because of the loss of the very salt of man's supremacy outdoors. People needn't think from this that the Maine womenfolks are unimportant. Besides the cooking, the housekeeping, the preserving and sewing, the bearing and raising of children, they educate all the future artists of ropes and oars in reticence. Their strength is about double that of other women, for they have to exert it more obliquely than their oblique men. They keep their place for the sake of running things.

Before World War II needed a female workforce to replace the men called into the armed forces, women may have made the world go round, but they had had to do it from the kitchen.

All Brace novels have New England settings, where Puritanism lingered longest. He was never comfortable writing about sex. He had been trained to reticence and propriety. Perhaps that is why his novels, once best sellers, are not more popular today. Preserved as in amber is a way of life already poised for extinction. His novels move slowly, full of rich descriptions of landscape and weather. In the accelerated pace of today with electronic media becoming ever more visual, interactive, and graphic, it seems increasingly possible that the whole genre of the novel is doomed. There is escalating interest in violence, and in overt sexual behavior. Few today have the time or inclination to savor words, even those written by a fine artist and craftsman.

A gentleman of culture and accomplishment, Brace never lost an almost transcendental love of nature. Seduced by the poetry of Keats and Wordsworth and boys' popular fiction, young Brace dreamed of great deeds and lovely ladies. Now, as romance and idealism become increasingly suspect, it becomes more difficult to empathize with an author whose most passionate responses were to nature: the sound of a woodthrush, a lonely mountain road, the smell of sea air. There are still adventurers who long to sail the ocean alone or cross over it in a hot air balloon, but even in 1976 when Brace was writing his autobiography, he was aware that the mood behind these exploits had changed. "What is lost is the illusion of transcendent mystery that used to keep beckoning us onward toward the bright fields of promise, the belief that divinity itself was somehow waiting for us there." Old age brought disillusionment, but for him, the dream never totally faded.

In his last decade he grew increasingly lonely and sad. The physical strength that had made it possible for him to walk forty or fifty miles in a day, to ski, to play vigorous tennis, to climb mountains, and to sail in all kinds of weather had given way to health problems. In addition, he feared that his novels were no longer relevant to the modern age. He turned increasingly inward. The autobiography published when he was in his seventies was a valedictory to the happier days of his youth. His attempt to write a second volume dealing with his adult years was less successful and was never accepted for publication. He found it impossible to write candidly about those close to him, and, perhaps, he hesitated to examine seriously his mature life.

He was pleased that I wanted to write his biography. He wrote long letters in answer to my questions and arranged for me to have access to his private papers. In writing of his early life, I have naturally relied heavily on his own autobiography, *Days That Were*. For further information about the Maine islands, I depended on the authoritative book by Charles B. McLane, *Islands of the Mid-Maine Coast: Penobscot and Blue Hills Bays*. The family allowed me to read the packets of letters Brace wrote to his wife and to his friends, Carl Dennett and Millicent Lewis Pettit. I interviewed and corresponded with his family, colleagues, and many of his former students, and perused the extensive collection of his papers in the Boston University archives. Yet, I realize that all my findings have been colored inevitably by my own memories and impressions.

Gerald Brace could count his many achievements, but he was aware in his final years that like the psalmist his days had become "like a shadow that declineth." He had no belief in an afterlife, the wooden boats that he had designed were beginning to deteriorate, and his books were out of print. His only hope for immortality was through family and the memories and writings of former students. There is, however, compelling reason to recall his life story. The span of his years, 1901 to 1978, covers the first three-quarters of the twentieth century, a time in which even New Englanders had to abandon much of their self-sufficiency and independent way of life. The world of Gerald Warner Brace has ceased to exist, but it should not be forgotten. The strength and values of that simpler age provide a possible fulcrum on which to balance an uncertain future.

1

Dobbs Ferry and Deer Isle

Louise Warner Brace must have had mixed emotions when she learned that she was about to have a fifth child. She would be thirty-seven years old; her husband, Charles Loring Brace II, was forty-six. Their older daughters, Dorothy and Eleanor, ages fourteen and twelve, considered themselves young ladies, and the two little ones, Charles Loring III and Elizabeth, were an active seven and five. Even with household help, life already took a good deal of planning. With the baby due in early autumn, it seemed wise not to vacation too far from their home in Dobbs Ferry, New York. A house was rented on Islip, Long Island, and here on September 23, 1901, Gerald Warner Brace entered the world. It

Louise W. Brace

was always a matter of regret to him that he had not been born in the family homestead, but he never got a satisfactory answer as to why his parents had remained in the resort town on Great South Bay, Long Island, instead of returning to their comfortable home overlooking the Hudson River.

Times were difficult in America at the turn of the century. A week before Gerald's birth, President McKinley had been assassinated by Polish-American anarchist Leon Czalgosz. Millions of immigrants were pouring into the United States and seventy percent of the population of New York City was jammed into overcrowded tenements, increasing the spread of diseases, especially typhoid. Strikes threatened to cripple the country and there had been a panic on Wall Street. The Brace adult males, Charles Loring and his younger brother Robert, had inherited from their father a deep concern for the New York poor, but they carefully insulated their wives and children from the harsher aspects of life. In Dobbs Ferry, twenty miles north of the city, the

Charles Loring Brace family lived on a three-acre estate known as Ches-Knoll in a large Victorian Gothic house from which the Palisades could be seen across the river. It was a wonderful place for a child. In addition to a coach house and stable, there was a long sloping driveway perfect for sledding in winter, and huge beech trees to climb. The house had been designed for his grandfather by Calvert Vaux, partner of his grandfather's closest friend, Frederick Law Olmsted, creator of New York's Central Park.

Charles Loring Brace II

Gerald always considered his grandfather Charles Loring Brace to be a hero. He had lived an eventful life. In his youth he had gone to Europe with John and Frederick Olmsted. In Belfast, Ireland, he had courted and been accepted by Letitia O'Neill, and in Hungary he had defended Lajos Kossuth, the revolutionary hero who was seeking to free Hungary from Austrian domination. For this, Brace was thrown into prison and might have been executed if a recently released priest, who foiled their jailors by conversing with him in Latin, had not succeeded in getting word to the American Consul.

Both Charles Loring Brace and the Olmsted brothers had been strongly influenced as young men by the teachings of Horace Bushnell, who preached good works and believed that a child nurtured in a proper Christian home would be saved without recourse to conversion at revivals. While Bushnell believed mothers were responsible for the salvation of children, he remained opposed to women being allowed the right to vote. Inspired by Bushnell's social conscience, Brace began training for the ministry. Struggling to unite his scientific and religious beliefs, he wrote such theological works as *The Unknown God* and *Gesta Christi*; but he became primarily interested in doing something to help the city's poor. In 1853 he founded the Children's Aid Society to find better environments for the street waifs. He would devote the rest of his life to this task. In addition to awakening the social awareness of society by writing *The Dangerous Classes of New York*, he set up the famous News Boys Lodging House, established schools and convalescent homes for the children of the New York lower classes, and raised enough money to send over 90,000 homeless boys to help on farms and ranches in the west.

Meanwhile his friend Frederick Olmsted was creating green spaces in the cities. As part of his belief that the spiritual and physical health of all classes of people would be improved if there was a place for them to get closer to

Charles Loring Brace

nature, he convinced the city to allow him to turn 840 acres of swampland and slums in Manhattan into what would become Central Park. Later he would design the Capitol Grounds in Washington D.C., the landscaping for the great Columbian Exposition in Chicago, and the Emerald Necklace, the circle of parks around Boston. Although both men were too busy with projects to see much of each other as the years went by, they continued their correspondence until Brace's death in 1890. It was through the Olmsteds that the Brace family first began summering at Deer Isle, Maine. In Frederick Olmsted's later years, ill in both body and mind, he had been taken to Maine. Deeply depressed and with memory failing, he did not enjoy Deer Isle, but his wife Mary and daughter Marion loved it. Although eventually his mind failed to the point where he had to be committed to McLean Asylum in Belmont, the Olmsteds continued to summer in Maine and invited the now adult children of Charles Loring Brace to visit them there.

When Charles Loring Brace senior died he left Ches-Knoll to his older son, expressing the hope that he would carry on his work at the Children's Aid Society. Charles Loring II was not driven by the same passion for social work as his father, but he had the Brace sense of duty. He gave up his position as a civil engineer in Minnesota where he was building railroad bridges, and moved from Minneapolis with his wife, Louise Warner Brace, and two young daughters, Dorothy and Eleanor, to the family home still occupied by his mother. His wife was delighted to move back to New York where she would have a large house complete with maids, cook, gardener, coachman, and even a German governess for the children.

It was at Dobbs Ferry that the three younger children were born. Since the first son had been given the Brace name of Charles Loring III, the second boy was named Gerald Warner in memory of his mother's brother who had died in childhood. Her father, an eminent New York physician, had considered it a great tragedy that he lost his only son and was left with two daughters. Although their own mother had died, Louise Warner and her sister May enjoyed their early childhood, but when Louise was twelve, their beloved stepmother, Sarah McKaye Warner, a talented pianist who was sister of the dramatist Steele McKaye, died. Louise's busy father, unable to cope with a teenage daughter, sent her to live in the Brace household. When she and Charles Loring Junior subsequently fell in love, her father was furious. He accused him of being a fortune hunter and threatened to disinherit his daughter if she should marry him. This did not deter the young couple. Although disowned by her father, she inherited a sizeable fortune from her grandfather. In New York society this, of course, was the subject of much gossip, to which the novelist Henry James was privy. This always made Gerald wonder if perhaps the novel *Washington Square* had been partially based on his parents. Certainly the Dr. Sloper of the novel behaves very like Dr. Warner, though fortunately the outcome for Charles and Louise was much happier.

It is highly unlikely that this story was the primary basis of the James novel, for an entry in the author's notebook for February 21, 1879, asserts that he took the plot from an incident told him by his friend Fanny Kemble about her brother. Henry Kemble had been courting the daughter of the Master of King's College, Cambridge. She was heiress to her father's fortune of four thousand pounds a year, but her father said he would disinherit her if she married a fortune hunter like Henry Kemble. She was willing to anyway, but when her fiance became convinced that her father would carry out his threat, Henry broke off the engagement. He returned ten years later after her father had died, leaving her the money. He tried to renew his suit, but by then she had decided to remain single. Since this is almost exactly the story as James wrote it, there seems little doubt that this is the true source. However, it is also true that James frequently wove snippets of gossip from various sources into his novels. When he decided to use Washington Square as his setting, and to make his heroine's father a New York doctor, a widower whose ambitions for the future had been dashed by the death of his young son, leaving him with an unloved daughter whom he was determined to protect, James may well have been thinking about the Warner family. At any rate, it says much about the social milieu in which Gerald was raised that he thought it might have been his parents' story.

Queen Victoria died nine months before Gerald was born, but he had a typical upper-middle class Victorian upbringing. He would always look back with nostalgia to the moral certainties and romantic visions of that age. Though he would live in a century of mechanization, technology, and rapid change, he dreamed of sailing ships and lonely country farms. When he was two years old, the Wright brothers flew a powered aircraft for the first time; before his death, men would walk on the moon. He would see horse and oxen replaced by automobiles and tractors. Even harder to accept were the social changes. He was raised in a Jamesian world where the men discussed philosophy or politics and women talked local affairs. There was gossip, of course, but it was discreet, especially if children were present. Pregnancies, divorce, sex, finances, or serious illnesses were spoken of only in private, if at all. In that male-dominated society, women wielded their power only through sons and husbands. It was not until Gerald was nineteen years old that the Nineteenth Amendment gave American women the vote. Brought up in such a society it is not surprising that he had conservative opinions about the female sex.

Very early in his life Gerald identified with the world of men. His greatest hero was his brother Charlie, seven years older. It was he who interested Gerald in sports and taught him how to throw a ball. He put great emphasis on winning, and perhaps that was the reason Gerald never liked to lose in any sport he played. His father spent as much time with the family as possible, eschewing the sophisticated social life his own father had led. He took his family skating at a private pond where only "very nice people" were allowed. He introduced them to the woods. However, his job was demanding of his time. He not only was continuing the social work his father had started, but he enlarged upon it. By 1894 he had established the Brace Memorial Farm School in Valhalla, New York, to train city boys to work on farms. Later he set up a foster home department for children who were temporarily homeless. Horatio Alger found much of the material for his rags-to-riches books from the time he stayed there. When young Charlie went off to the private MacKenzie School, usually the only male around was Patrick, the coachman. Gerald enjoyed helping him shovel the long driveway, and followed him around as he did his work. Occasionally his uncles visited them, especially his father's brother Robert. Uncle Rob also worked for the Children's Aid, and Gerald never forgot how he would sled down the long drive to catch the train for New York.

It seemed to Gerald, however, that most of the time he was surrounded by strong minded-women. Gerald's grandmother Brace spent a portion of each year in her Ches-Knoll home, though she also divided her time among her other children. She was a vigorous, independent woman whom her grandson remembered primarily for the large purse from which she doled out coins to him. Margaret Buffum, whose family also lived in Dobbs Ferry, recalled over ninety years later, having seen a lady riding side-saddle on a donkey around the aqueduct with children clustered around her. Later her mother told her that this was Madam Brace, who had been accustomed to riding on a donkey in Ireland and continued to do so in her adopted country. Certainly, one of the children was Charlie, and perhaps Gerald was there too, though he himself had only a dim remembrance of what must have been a most unusual sight in that upper class, decorous neighborhood.

As a child, Gerald was in awe of his beautiful mother. He loved and admired her, but she was very much the chatelaine of the estate—austere, moral, and upright. She did not permit either profanity or rebellion. His sisters, Dorothy and Eleanor, already had busy lives of their own. After attending a private school in Dobbs Ferry, they went off to finishing school at Miss Wheeler's in Providence, Rhode Island. When they were at home they considered it their duty to take responsibility for their little brother's good behavior, and it seemed to him that they were always bossing him. Even Betty, only five years his senior, had her own friends and social life. In addition, his father's two sisters frequently visited: Aunt Emma, always the grande dame, imperious and demanding; and the more tolerant and affectionate Aunt Leta. Then there was Uncle Rob's wife, Aunt Bessie, and Aunt May Sherwood, his mother's sister. But it was to the maids that Gerald turned if he skinned his knee or had a fight with his friends. Swiss Erica, Frieda, and Irish Maggie gave him the warm affection he craved. Not surprisingly, he would always idealize warm-hearted women whose kitchens were the centers of their homes.

Recognizing that her son needed boys his own age for companions, Mrs. Brace decided to send him to primary classes at nearby Miss Master's school. The school was set in lovely countryside overlooking the Hudson. It had been established in 1877 by the Misses Eliza and Sarah Masters for the education of young girls, but a few choice boys from proper families were admitted to the lower primary grades. Gerald played with Bobby Frazier, a classmate who was a doctor's son, but the two boys fought furiously with Gerald usually the aggressor and victor. He much preferred working-class boys who were both tough and loyal. His closest friends were the three Forsythe brothers who lived over the steam laundry of the school. Willie, Jack, and Bob were Irish Catholics and Mrs. Brace only reluctantly allowed them to come up to the estate. One day they brought some of their friends who climbed up into the beech trees. She angrily sent them away, and though at the time Gerald accepted such class distinction as the normal behavior of society, it must have subconsciously made a deep impression, for he later used it in a telling scene in one of his novels, *The Garretson Chronicle*. It was not that the boys were Irish—after all, so was Gerald's own grandmother—or even that they were Catholic, though Mrs. Brace was a strict Episcopalian and deplored the fact that her husband (who called himself a Unitarian) refused to go to church. It was simply that the Forsythes and their friends were not "gentlemen."

These early years were a very happy time. In addition to coasting on the hills and skating on the pond, there were all kinds of adventurous activities. Sometimes it was the court of King Arthur and sometimes they were Western gunfighters. It was an age of heroes, imaginary and real. The heroes were all male, of course—Admiral Dewey, Teddy Roosevelt, Thomas Edison, and Buffalo Bill, not to mention the great sports figures like Jim Jeffries, Ty Cobb, and Jim Thorpe. The most magical time of all was Christmas. Santa Claus was a tangible being who filled the stockings hung on the fireplace in the children's nursery, before arranging the presents under the big Christmas tree in the front parlor, a room rarely used except for Dorothy's piano practice. After breakfast the door would be thrown open to reveal the tree shining with real candles, which had to be extinguished before presents were opened. In the afternoon there was a big family dinner with turkey and all the fixings, and, of course, plum pudding. Christmas would always be special for Gerald, but it would never again be quite as wonderful as in those days of innocence. He could still recall those emotions when he wrote his autobiography almost three-quarters of a century later.

> Happiness could never in the world be more pure than it was for me and I think all of us on those Christmas mornings, not simply because we had new toys and surprises but because we believed in the myth and mystery of Christmas and lived for awhile in a presence of a vast benevolence that cherished us with perfect love and generosity. The day passed with a strange and timeless ecstacy. Nothing outside counted or even existed. It came as a surprise to realize that the weather was functioning as usual, that people were doing things; the world was as remote as a dream, it had no immediate reality; it was simply a sort of stage-like scene over which presided the spirits of Santa Claus and Jesus who made all good things happen. (*DTW*, pp. 56–57)

But if winters at Ches-Knoll were happy, summers in Maine were pure bliss. Gerald had only one memory of the couple of years that the family summered at North Haven, Maine. He could vividly remember his step-cousin, John Donaldson, painting a toy boat and setting it out to dry in front of a wide expanse of blue water. The recollection is prophetic, for Gerald would spend most of his life in a dream of boats. As he wrote in *Between Wind and Water*:

> I drew them, whittled them, sailed them in tide pools, watched them near and far, listened to talk about them. I hoarded pictures. I knew the names and the look of the great yachts: the *Reliance*, fastest of all Cup defenders, the *Defender* herself 'with her crew of Deer Islers' as the caption said—a detail I've never forgotten because in a small way I was a Deer Isler too. And the splendid schooners, *Enchantress, Irolita, Elena, Queen Mab*, and the *Atlantic*, three-masted, breaking all records for an eastward crossing to England—the picture of her charging to windward under full sail, all topsails set, is still as dramatic as anything I can remember. They had nothing to do with earthly life, those boats; they were pure visions, and reflected a romance not of mortal people and their concerns but rather of triumphant speed and grace and mastery of wind and sea. (*BWW*, pp. 91, 92)

Among the papers that Gerald's mother preserved was an accurately drawn sailboat that Gerald made for her at the age of six. Already he had an eye for the grace and line of hull and sails.

Deer Isle, Maine, became a popular summer colony around the turn of the century. At first the visitors stayed in boarding houses, but gradually the regulars began to build their own summer cottages. There were no great mansions such as were being constructed at Bar Harbor. The summer folk who came to this part of Penobscot Bay wanted to live as simply as possible spending as much time as weather permitted out of doors—rowing, fishing, and sailing.

Gerald's Aunt Leta Brace married Jim Croswell, who became headmaster of the Brearley School for Girls in New York. They had come to the island as friends of the Olmsteds, but in 1903 they began to build their own place at Dunham's Point. It was on a point of land reached by a rough road that led to an old mine. Though it was called a silver mine, its ore was mainly lead and zinc. It had been abandoned by the time the Croswells started building, but it was reopened about the time the house was finished. Approximately twenty men worked two shifts, using steam driven pumps and drills to take ore from 260 feet below the surface. The mine building could not be seen from the house, but certainly the noise of its clanking machinery and underground blasting must have been clearly audible. In 1908 the mine closed permanently because it proved unprofitable to have to ship the ore to New Jersey for smelting. The mine was covered over, and another cottage built on its site.

The Croswells lived on Mill Island while waiting for their house to be finished. This was the place that Gerald's family would later rent for many years. His mother might never have learned to cook or do the heavier housework,

The Brace Family Summer Place at Deer Isle, Maine

but she was an excellent organizer. He would always remember the sense of excitement and adventure as the family set forth from Ches-Knoll for Deer Isle. "There were five children, a cook and a maid, a dog, cat and canary bird, a flock of trunks, and we proceeded by train to New York, by cabs (though I remember once taking a horse car) to the Fall River Line Wharf where the romance really began." (*DTW*, p. 64). At Fall River they had to take a train to the South Station in Boston. After all the baggage was collected they would proceed to the wharf to catch the Bangor boat, either *The City of Rockland* or *The City of Bangor*. In Rockland they disembarked to take the side-wheeler *J.T. Morse*, which carried them to the North Landing at Deer Isle. Here they were met by Benny Raynes with a buckboard for the passengers and a team for the baggage. Everything had to be carefully timed, for Mill Island could be reached by land only at low tide. The whole expedition took two days. Often they would board at the Sylvester farm while the work of preparing the cottage was going on. Shutters had to be opened, the house aired, and food and ice ferried across the water.

Since Dunham's Point was less than a mile away, the Croswells and Braces were frequently together. Uncle Jim owned a catboat, called *Tureen* because of its tubby shape. Eleanor usually was in charge of that boat as the family considered her a better sailor than either aunt or uncle. Gerald's father had a twenty-eight foot knockabout, *Bettina*, and the two families frequently joined for picnics on nearby islands.

There were always guests enough to fill both houses. When close friend Julia Vaux Donaldson, daughter of the architect of Ches-Knoll died, her widower, Harry Donaldson, married Aunt Emma and the two Donaldson boys became part of the family. Julia's sister Marion was Louise Brace's dearest friend. She had married Lincoln Hendrickson, Professor of Classics at Yale, and they came with their daughter Marion. When more space was needed, some of them would stay at the Sylvester farm so that it too became an important part of Gerald's life. Edgewood Farm covered a hundred acres between the village of Deer Isle and the house at Dunham's Point. Cows were pastured across the street down by the shore and there was a huge woodlot. The Sylvesters provided the summer people with milk, butter, cream, eggs, vegetables, berries, and ice. It seemed to Gerald that they lived an ideal, self-sufficient life even though both men and women had to work very hard. Always the youngest, Gerald's own life was carefree with long hours for solitary exploration of woods and coast. Summers seemed endless and full of happiness.

When Gerald was nine this Edenic life ended. The Braces decided that the children ought to have a chance to meet new friends; so instead of returning to Mill Island, they summered at Vineyard Haven on the north side of Martha's Vineyard. The busy harbor was filled with coastwise schooners; for before the Cape Cod Canal was completed in 1914, vessels sailed up Vineyard Sound en route around the long arm of the Cape. Gerald's father rented a small sailboat with a mooring and a raft from which the family could swim. The Donaldson boys had bought a small sloop called *Scorpion* from their Uncle Lincoln, and Charlie helped them sail it to Vineyard Haven. The Hendricksons arrived on their sloop, *Vega*; so there was plenty of activity. Charlie, Betty, and their father competed in the weekly boat races, though their rented boat was not very fast. Gerald felt that he passed a rite of passage into manhood when his Uncle Lincoln took him on an overnight cruise across the Sound to Woods Hole. For breakfast aboard the boat he was allowed his first cup of coffee, much diluted, to be sure.

The summer had proved better than he had anticipated, but what hung a cloud over his days was that he knew the family would be returning, not to his beloved Dobbs Ferry, but to New York City. His father had been commuting for years. It had been determined that it would be easier for him, and would offer the girls a better social life if they moved into a city apartment. Gerald, a child of nature and freedom, dreaded the thought of being caged.

2
A Young Romantic

Mrs. Brace was worried about her younger son. Their apartment on Sixty-first Street and Park Avenue was large and convenient. She had found an exclusive private school for Gerald, near enough for him to rollerskate to classes at the Allen-Stevenson School located in a brownstone building only about five blocks away. She had been sure that her son would adjust quickly, but he was doing poorly in classes and seemed always unhappy. What is more it was affecting his health. He had constant colds and sore throats. It had already been determined that Charlie would have to be sent to a drier climate for his serious chronic sinus infections; now she had to worry about Gerald. His rebelliousness led to frequent demerits at school; so afternoons when he might have been happy rollerskating with his friends in Central Park, he had to stay in detention memorizing long passages of poetry. Most of his time was spent dreaming of Maine and sailing. Fortunately, he found a kindred spirit in Edward Janeway. The two boys spent hours poring over the pages of *Yachting* magazine and learning the appearance of all the great yachts and schooners.

The Braces knew that their son would be further upset to learn that the next summer they were going to Woods Hole instead of Maine. Uncle Harry Donaldson was a scientist at the Marine Biological Laboratories there. His sons, John and Norman, would both be home. The water was warmer for swimming and the girls would have better social opportunities. Aunt Emma knew everyone worth knowing and would introduce the girls to all the best families. To Gerald, Cape Cod—with its scrub pines, sandy soil, and humid atmosphere—was a poor substitute for Deer Isle, but that summer, in spite of his misgivings, Gerald had a good time.

Winter in New York brought back all the old misery. In addition to colds, Gerald suffered with chicken pox and measles. He was heartened, however, by the promise that the following summer the family would once again go to Mill Island. He did not know that it would be for the last time. The difficulties of moving and the problems of life on an island within an island had become too difficult for Mrs. Brace. But that last summer was perfect for young Gerald. The Donaldson boys pitched a tent just outside the house, and Gerald spent as much time as he could with them. Although he was considerably younger and probably a nuisance, they treated him kindly, as if he were a younger brother.

It had become obvious that when they returned in the fall something would have to be done to make life more acceptable for Gerald. Uncle Rob had gone to the Gunnery School in Washington, Connecticut, and he suggested that Gerald might be happy in its country surroundings. It had been established in 1850 by the abolitionist Frederick William Gunn and his wife Abigail. Since it was only twelve miles west of Litchfield, where Gerald's great grandfather, John Pierce Brace, had been headmaster at Miss Pierce's Female Academy, the two families had been acquainted. The school was still run by the founder's son-in-law, but it was not as academically outstanding as it once had been. The major emphasis seemed to be on athletics and good sportsmanship. Gerald played football on the Fourth Team made up of the twelve and thirteen year old boys. Although he never excelled in team sports, he had intense admiration for the older boys who became athletic stars.

The Gunnery allowed the boys a good deal of freedom. They were required to go on long walks but this, Gerald enjoyed. The work load was not heavy, and Gerald had ample leisure to read the stories of Sherlock Holmes and Zane Grey. The latter seemed to replicate the sort of life that his brother, who had transferred from St. George's in Rhode Island to the Evans School in Mesa, Arizona, was living. Charlie wrote home glowing letters telling how he had been to the Grand Canyon, and explored the Superstition Mountains on his horse Red Wing which he had bought for fifty dollars. It all seemed very adventurous and romantic to his younger brother. Charlie's letters heightened his enjoyment of the Western novels he was reading, often smuggled inside his textbooks when he was in study hall. Years later Gerald would write in *Days That Were*, "I never went beyond the Pecos until I was old. I haven't read a Zane Grey for forty years, but that youthful dream of Western stars and purple sage and a stallion named Wildfire still lives in my imagination." (*DTW*, p. 134).

The influence of those Western novels would remain with him. The evocations of New England mountains and coast in his novels are reminiscent of the colorful descriptions in the works of Zane Grey. They also shaped his ideas about women and the relationship of the sexes. When he arrived at the Gunnery he had been completely innocent. He had been shocked by the pornographic pictures and sniggering comments about sex that he heard from the older boys. In reading novels like *Riders of the Purple Sage* and *The Rainbow Trail* he could indulge his romantic fantasies. He wanted to emulate these lone-wolf heroes who rescued women from danger. The perfect heroine was loyal and resourceful, able to care for an injured man or run lightly up the side of a canyon, but helpless to save herself from the situations in which she became entrapped. The role of protector belonged to the male. Gerald modeled himself after these heroes. He wanted to be stoic about pain, walk long distances, survive in the wilderness, and rescue damsels in distress.

With both boys away at boarding school, it seemed an excellent opportunity for Mr. and Mrs. Brace to take the two older girls on an extended trip to Europe. They were still away at the Christmas season when Gerald broke his arm in a sledding accident. It had been arranged for him to spend the holidays with relatives. This was his opportunity to emulate his Zane Grey heroes by acting brave. His arm was still in a sling when he travelled to Philadelphia to visit the Donaldsons. Norman was home from Yale and John from Johns Hopkins Medical School. They had always gone out of their way to give their young cousin a good time, but this time everyone was especially sympathetic knowing that he was in pain and without family.

Gerald also visited the Hendricksons in New Haven. Young Gerald, whose romantic dreams did not include sweet little girls, was always terrified that Aunt Marion, his mother's best friend, was conspiring for him to marry her only daughter, "Little Marion" as soon as they were of age. He would repeat over and over to himself "I will *Not Marry* Marion," and worried how he could escape his fate without upsetting the two families.

In August 1914 war broke out in Europe. The older Braces had already returned home, but Dorothy and Eleanor, joined by John Donaldson, had stayed on with the Croswells. Now they were all trapped in Switzerland. Staying at the elegant Suvretta House in Saint Moritz they were suffering no hardships. Although neither John nor Dorothy were athletic, one day they climbed Piz Nair, a small nearby mountain. At the top he proposed marriage and she accepted. He was stepson to Aunt Emma so not really a cousin, but it made one more link in the close family chain. Soon after, they all managed to travel to Genoa where they were lucky to get passage home on the *Adriatic*.

In spite of worry about his sisters' safety, the war seemed remote to Gerald. His father, whose main passion was trout fishing, took his wife and children Charlie, Betty, and Gerald to Lake Kennebago in the Maine wilderness. Their guide showed them where the best fish were supposed to lurk, but it was Gerald, alone in a canoe except for his mother (to hold the boat in position), who managed to catch a three-pound trout, the largest fish caught on that expedition. His father was immensely proud, and for once Gerald found himself the center of attention even after the return home.

His second year at the Gunnery was even more enjoyable than the first. Charlie transferred to the school and Gerald admiringly hung about his big brother impressed by his athletic abilities and his sophisticated knowledge of women. Sometimes when Charlie would arrive late for supper, Gerald and all the rest of the boys would know he had been out with a girl they called Buzzy—because the boys would all audibly buzz when Charlie came walking into the dining room. She lived on a country estate and had her own riding horse. To Gerald she seemed just like a Zane Grey heroine.

Gerald joined a secret fraternity, Beta Theta, and though they seemed to do little other than conduct torturous initiations and make up secret pass-words, it made him feel part of a group. He basked in the reflected glory of his brother who was a campus leader. Once Charlie rented a car and allowed his young brother to join the older boys on a trip to New Haven to see the first Harvard-Yale game played in the Yale Bowl. The Braces were so loyal to Yale that Betty always trained her dogs to roll over and play dead when they heard the word "Harvard" and then jump up joyously at the name Yale. Although Yale was defeated in this game, the boys sat on the Yale side where they were given blue silk handkerchiefs to form a background for those holding the white cards that spelled out Yale. It was a thrill Gerald would never forget and he kept the blue handkerchief all his life. On the way home from the game the boys went to a vaudeville show in Waterbury. It was all very innocent, but made more exciting by their belief that the family would have disapproved. Gerald had passed another milestone.

Although he was enjoying the Gunnery, Gerald was not being challenged academically as even he recognized. Charlie was going off to Yale, and the family decided that Gerald should also be sent to another school. His mother took him to visit Loomis School in Windsor, Connecticut. Although it was only three miles north of Hartford, it was set in rural surroundings at the junction of the Farmington and Connecticut Rivers. In 1874, Mr. and Mrs. Loomis, who had no children of their own, turned their large family home-stead into a school free of religious or political bias. A similar school for girls, called the Chaffee School for Mrs. Loomis' side of the family, had been estab-lished on the far side of the Farmington River. Though now merged, boys and girls were then kept very much separated. The Loomis students seemed much less sophisticated than the Gunnery boys. It seemed impossible to Gerald that they were still whistling "When You Wore a Tulip" when any self-respecting school boy knew it was already out of date. Nevertheless, he was impressed with the modern buildings and the enthusiasm of everyone he met. He suc-cessfully passed his placement exams and entered the school as a sophomore.

The family reunited that summer at the Stanley House on Mount Desert Island. Charlie arranged for their knockabout *Bettina* and a dinghy to be brought down from the shipyards where they had been stored for the winter. Having boats was a sure way of being invited to be part of the summer activities. They were soon racing, going to picnics on the islands, and mountain climbing. One of the young ladies in their group was Ellen Warburton, a rather unhappily married attractive matron. It became evident that she and Charlie had fallen in love. To young Gerald it was all immensely romantic and sad. She was the daughter of Christian missionaries to China, and much too moral to be unfaithful to her husband even though he was rather crude and inclined to drink too much. Gerald at fourteen wanted desperately to rescue her. He thought he was in love with her himself, but he would be noble and let his brother have her. Having spent his life in all-male schools, he was immature for his age where women were concerned. The fact that both boys knew that nothing could come of the relationship only made it more like the plot for a novel. The two brothers became closer. They began taking cruises, enjoying pushing *Bettina* to her utmost limits. Together they sailed to Deer Isle to visit their relatives.

Gerald was very happy back at Loomis. He discovered for the first time that he liked to write. At sixteen he wrote a sensitive, descriptive essay of the cruise he and Charlie had made on *Bettina* from Southwest Harbor at Mount Desert to Deer Isle. They had anchored in Sylvester's Cove, then an "unfrequented little haven for fishing boats" and sat up late watching the moon reflected in the water. They sailed down past Owl's Head to Yarmouth near Portland and then back up the coast to North Haven. Gerald believed then, as he would throughout his years, that life had nothing greater to offer. "What more can be desired than the deep bays, the many islands, the beautiful scenery, and ever-changing color."

He became co-editor of the weekly newspaper, *The Log*, reporting the school news and writing articles exhorting the boys to have more school spirit and, since they had been reading *Walden* in English class, to be more aware of the beauty and transcendental harmonies of nature. With war in Europe, the boys were required to participate in semi-professional military training, learning to march in formation and to present arms with their wooden rifles. None of them doubted that America was making the world safe for a democracy which would be in the hands of White Anglo-Saxon Protestant leaders like themselves.

Although later Loomis would become more like other major prep schools, "the original founders had had a vision of a plain and useful life style and the virtues of old-fashioned work on the farm and in the house" (*DTW*, p. 155) The headmaster, Nathaniel Horton Batchelder, was trying to keep the school as close as possible to their wishes. The students all had tasks such as cleaning dorms, waiting on table, and working on the school farm. In addition, they could earn extra money doing special chores. Gerald spent hours with bucksaw and hand mower at fifteen cents an hour to enable him to buy sodas and *Adventure Magazine* which was publishing the latest Zane Grey serial. This was all a new experience for him. He even volunteered to walk to the post office to pick up the school mail each day. It meant starting off at 6:30 every morning in all kinds of weather. He was not paid for the job, but he was excused from morning chapel and given a late breakfast which included any cream left over from the headmaster's coffee. It gave him a new sense of importance.

Athleticism was much admired and while Gerald never was good at competition, he became known for his long distance running. He was something of a loner, but he enjoyed having his feats recognized. He always remembered that one day when he ran fifteen miles to Simsbury to attend the Loomis-Westminster game and then back in time for supper he received the only formal cheer of his life. Skating too was a joy—not only on the Farmington and Connecticut Rivers, but once when spring floods overran the school grounds and froze, he was able to glide on his skates over the fields and lanes.

At Loomis, Gerald became friendly with Carl Dennett who would remain one of his closest friends as long as he lived. Since both boys lived in New York they were able to be together during vacation time as well as at school. Together they went on long walks, attended concerts, and visited museums. Carl's mother and father were divorced, which in those days was uncommon. At the Dennett house he heard many subjects never discussed in the Brace household. Mary Ware Dennett was much involved in the struggle for women's rights and was even tried for "obscenity" after publishing a pamphlet on sex. She also defended well-known radicals. Gerald had previously believed that only foreign anarchists were involved in political revolt. He found her charm disarming, but his mother warned that this only made her more dangerous. Although Carl was always loyal to his mother, he did not seriously espouse her causes. He later became a successful teacher of mathematics, but in their Loomis days, it was Gerald who helped him with homework problems in algebra and geometry.

Gerald took manual training in the hopes that he would learn to make fine model boats. He soon discovered that he couldn't even make a cutting board that met his teacher's exacting demands. Though frustrated, it gave him an increasing respect for the skill needed for good craftsmanship. He also began to enjoy academic studies. It had always been taken for granted that he would apply to Yale, and now it seemed certain that his grades and preparation would make him acceptable.

While in later years Gerald sometimes expressed doubts about the elitism of private academies and sent his own children to public schools, he was aware that Loomis had given him good academic training for the future. Whether an all-male school is good preparation for life is open to debate. Although the boys were given a good deal of personal freedom, they were not taught anything about sex and knew little about women. When a young nurse who worked in the school infirmary during an outbreak of German measles invited Gerald to her apartment in Hartford, he had no idea what she had in mind until after he arrived. Although he secretly longed to have a sexual relationship, at sixteen he was too scared to take advantage of the opportunity. In spite of listening to the boys boast about their experiences with women, Gerald graduated from Loomis almost as innocent as when he arrived.

The Brace family took over the house at Dunham's Point in 1916, the year after Uncle Jim Croswell died, but Gerald's father still wanted to go deep into the wilderness to fish for trout. Between Gerald's junior and senior year at Loomis, the family hired two guides and camped at Salmon Lake in the Adirondacks along with Uncle Rob and Aunt Bessie. There they enjoyed six weeks of camping and fishing, though they did not catch many trout. Betty was in love with Huntington Gilchrist, a captain attached to the general staff in Washington. Remote as the Brace camp was, the young suitor found his way there to spend his short leave with them.

In spite of the scarcity of trout, Gerald's father spent much of the next winter planning a return expedition to the Oswegatchie. In that final year of the war, Charlie had leave from the Army Air Force while he was waiting for his commission as a second lieutenant and pilot. Gerald graduated from Loomis and for a brief time worked at the Children's Aid Society Farm School in Valhalla. It was hard physical work; just what was needed to build muscles for a summer of paddling and portaging. He joined his parents, Betty, Charlie, and two guides to paddle down the river to Cranberry Lake in upstate New York, where they set up camp. This summer the fishing proved excellent and Gerald was taught by the guides how to be a good camp cook.

When Betty and her mother returned home, the three men continued their fishing by paddling across the lake to a village from which they could catch a train to Raquette Falls where Uncle Rob and Aunt Bessie owned a camp. If anything, Uncle Rob enjoyed trout fishing even more than his brother. His wife, like Gerald's own mother, was a New York socialite who was not used to the woods. Aunt Bessie had been middle aged when she married, but like her sister-in-law, she believed that if your husband is happiest canoeing, fishing, and travelling by packhorse, you learn to do the same. Naturally timid, she even learned to drive a Model T Ford, something neither of the men ever accomplished. It is not surprising that Gerald would take it for granted that it is a wife's duty to follow wherever her husband might lead.

Gerald's father eventually had to return to work in the city and Charlie and Gerald continued alone down the Raquette River to the Lower Saranac. It was a difficult trip for they missed the first carry and had to portage around a number of beaver dams. They camped on an island, climbed Ampersand

Mountain, and finally paddled back to Raquette Falls to Uncle Rob's where they abandoned their canoes. The boys had become very close, and returned home strong and healthy from their rugged summer. Both took pride in their physical dexterity. Gerald had learned how to handle Charlie's impetuousness and quick temper, and admired his daring and adventurous spirit. Young and seemingly invincible, the two brothers shared a romantic view of nature and of life.

Charles Loring Brace III —
"Charlie"

3

Amherst

Gerald was in a quandary. He knew that everyone was expecting him to go to Yale and he had always assumed that he would follow in the family tradition, but the nearer the time came, the less the thought of going to a big university in a large city like New Haven appealed to him. Then the senior boys from Loomis were invited to attend a sub-Freshman weekend at Amherst College where they stayed overnight in the Alpha Delta fraternity house. As soon as Gerald saw the campus, set in the rural hill country of western Massachusetts, he knew that this was where he wanted to go to college.

His family raised no objection. In fact, one Sunday at morning service in Grace Church in New York, his Aunt Leta introduced him to a pleasant white haired Amherst alumnus who invited the boy to his office to talk about the school. When he arrived at the man's old-fashioned office, Gerald was a little surprised to be greeted with affectionate warmth, but since the man was a friend of his aunt, he suspected nothing. Although he had been well trained at Loomis in Caesar, Cicero, and Virgil and had read his Shakespeare, Milton, and Dickens, he was still as sexually innocent as any fourth grader today. He had heard at school about homosexuals, of course, but he thought of them as disreputable perverts lurking in public restrooms. Now, when this distinguished businessman with shining eyes and moist lips asked to inspect his genitals, he was embarrassed, but allowed the man to unbutton his trousers. It was not until he actually began to touch him, that Gerald realized that something was wrong and pulled away, though even at the time he felt a certain sympathy for the yearning loneliness in the man. The following year Gerald met another student at Amherst who spoke with such warm feeling for the old gentleman, he suspected that this boy had not been repelled by the man's overtures the way Gerald himself had. The psychologist Erik Erikson has suggested that the bisexual confusion of adolescents is a natural part of developing identity consciousness, but this early encounter left Gerald uneasy whenever in the future he felt any sort of attraction for a male acquaintance.

The episode did not deter him from going to Amherst and he was too embarrassed to tell anyone what had happened. Arriving at his dormitory room in South College the first day of school, he immediately dropped his bags and headed for the hill, four miles away, that he could see from his window. It would establish the pattern for his undergraduate years there, as he explored the countryside in ever widening circles.

He had an unusual amount of freedom his freshman year. In October of 1918, all classes were cancelled because of the "Spanish" influenza. It had been brought to this country by returning sailors and spread rapidly, killing more people worldwide than had died in the war. By mid-September it had been contracted by a quarter of all Americans and over 500,000 died. Gerald was one of those lucky to escape it. He spent much of the unexpected free time playing tennis. He wrote to Carl Dennett that he had recently played over forty sets.

The college had hardly settled back into its routine when the army took over the campus, including his dormitory, to train officers for the war. Gerald could have joined a unit of the Student Army Training Corp for boys under eighteen years of age, but a dislike for regimentation and group activity, rather than any strong feelings of pacifism, deterred him. He had joined Delta Tau Delta fraternity, but since it did not have a large house like Alpha Delta, he was forced to seek lodgings in the town. He and one of his fraternity brothers found rooms in the home of Arthur and Carrie Johnson.

As soon as Gerald entered the brick house on South Prospect Street, he felt at home. There was instant rapport between the shy young student and the warm-hearted, outspoken middle-aged woman. In later years he tried to describe the moment in an article he wrote for the *Amherst Alumni News*:

> I felt adopted, taken in, absorbed, I had a family, a home—and so it remained for years. I carried up buckets of coal, split wood in the back yard, painted floors, brewed coffee, played the phonograph, talked beside the kitchen stove—my landlady, older than my mother, bossed me and scolded me and loved me and I responded in kind. I came back to her, then and later, as to a refuge, as a place where I would be taken in no matter what, a place for food and drink and warmth—many of my all-day hill-country tours ended beside her stove, with hot cocoa and pie and the stories of my discoveries. She too came from that eastern hinterland, a country farm girl, and she never tired of talking of the old times and places. She was a natural adventurer—like me she loved to explore, especially the world of her own past; she loved to 'go'—I can still hear her say that eager little verb: 'Ah I just like to *go*.' She was, of course, the talkative, positive, active force in the house; her husband said almost nothing, kept out of sight, and for a long time I thought he didn't

live there—perhaps he was what we usually think of as a typical Yankee; it took me two years to make friends and to find out that he was at heart a more romantic adventurer that his wife. ("I Travelled a Good Deal in Amherst," *Amherst Alumni News*, Winter 1963, pp. 5, 6)

The kitchen had never been the heart of the Brace household—that was the domain of the cook. Then he had lived in boys' boarding schools. Now at the Johnsons he was living the kind of life he had previously only glimpsed from outside. Later when he wrote his novels of New England, the Johnsons, especially Carrie, would be among the folks he would remember and try to recreate.

> Not that I could reproduce her nor did I ever try, but I can still hear the voice, her accent and idiom, and her trick of pushing her spectacles up on her forehead, and her wide-apart blue eyes shining with pleasure at the prospect of being alive and able to eat and talk and listen to music and go out in a Model T and see the world. And, of course her husband too—I've heard his voice, seen his gaunt sad face, felt his almost agonizing shyness, his alienation in a modern, mechanized world—together the two of them have been an essential part of my consciousness as a writer." (*Amherst Alumni News*, p. 8)

Certainly the Johnsons were in his mind when he created the Gaunts in *Light on a Mountain* and Mr. Shattuck in *Wayward Pilgrims*, but Carrie Johnson is most lovingly recreated as Mrs. Kingsley in *The Garretson Chronicle*. The narrator Ralph Garretson remembers the moment when he first met her. "I felt a spread of warmth in my cold body and I grinned idiotically. Those wide-set eyes had looked at me with love. I didn't really know it, and it didn't make sense—I have thought about it many times since and all I can say is that it was simply and truly love at first sight." (*GC*, p. 166) Gerald would later meet other such New England women, in actual experiences as well as fictionally in the pages of Sarah Orne Jewett, but Carrie Johnson would always remain for him the perfect prototype.

With the campus in turmoil and the war soon reaching its climax, little attention was paid to a freshman who was a natural loner. He was free to roam at will. At first, he ventured toward the Pelham Hills and Petersham, seeking out places that Carrie Johnson had known as a child. Much of the country region was in decline, with dilapidated farms struggling for existence, but he found a harsh beauty in its bleakness. His classmates sometimes thought he was exaggerating when he said he had walked over thirty miles, but he always knew he would find an accepting listener in the Johnson kitchen.

During his early college years, the Brace family spent their summers at Southwest Harbor, Maine, where they stayed in the Stanley House on Mount Desert. Betty came from Bryn Mawr where she was studying, and Gerald from Amherst. Charlie joined them in 1918, but the following year he had a job in Mexico working for the Phelps Dodge Mining Company. There was no real future in it, but the pay was good and most of all he enjoyed the feeling of adventure.

Gerald was dreaming of women, though not the ones that his Aunt Emma picked out for him. He wrote to his friend Carl on July 23, 1919, "There's one that lives on an island in the middle of the bay—but it's the dickens & all to get to her. She goes to Bryn Mawr, by the way. I wish she'd come over to see me. She has numerous speedboats & yachts etc. etc." Two weeks later his wish was partially granted. Mr. and Mrs. Porter, her parents, came to visit the Braces at Dunham's Point. Gerald's relatives bragged about his superior handling of sailboats and shortly after the Porters had returned to their yacht, a speedboat brought a note asking if he would like to spend two weeks at Great Spruce Head Island teaching the young people to sail the new boat that Mr. Porter had just purchased for them. It was the golden opportunity he had dreamed about. He would see their daughter, Nancy, every day.

The Porter boys were athletic and highly competitive. They immediately challenged him to play tennis and ping pong, to race them in swimming, target shoot, and even play chess. To his delight Gerald won at them all. He almost forgot his purpose for coming. Besides, while Nancy was good at picking up moorings, she did not always instinctively know what to do in a stiff breeze. In spite of the nautical skills of his sisters Eleanor and Betty, Gerald was scornful of the ability of most women in a boat. He wrote to Carl that though Nancy was learning, "she has a girl's customary slowness at grasping ideas. It's the dickens of a job to teach a girl anything." Of course, many of his disparaging remarks about women are simply the accepted posturing of a young undergraduate of the time.

Gerald did not even stay into the second week. Nancy had not reciprocated with any special warmth to his attentions and his ardor had somewhat cooled. His father was coming to Maine and Gerald wanted to do things with him. Besides he did not like being tied to anyone else's schedule during the free days of summer. He had not lost hope that Nancy might become more interested in him and wrote to Carl a week later that he was looking for an excuse to get out of going to a party, though he would "go in a hurry if Nancy were here, you bet." During the rest of the summers of his college years, he and Nancy enjoyed many sails together, and his feeling for her grew. He wrote to Carl, his one confidant, "You should see her hanging on to *Bettina* with the wind in her hair and the spray flying." He was too shy to make any romantic advances toward her and she continued to treat him like one of her brothers.

With the ending of the war, the Amherst campus returned to a semblance of normality. Gerald moved into the fraternity house where he shared a study with two friends, popular Clermont Cartwright and Walbridge Buffum whose family had known the Braces ever since they had both lived in Dobbs Ferry. The college took no responsibility for students' meals. Mrs. Johnson found a place in a village house for him to board at six dollars a week, though she frequently invited him for meals, especially Sunday dinner. Later, he joined local townsmen at various of the town's many boarding houses, where he heard more authentic Yankee dialogue than ever experienced by Oliver Wendell Holmes at the breakfast table.

The second semester of his sophomore year, Gerald had a fortunate encounter. When Alexander Meiklejohn, the president of Amherst, had read the poem "The Road Not Taken" by Robert Frost, it seemed to him just the message he wanted Amherst boys to hear. He invited the poet to speak at chapel and then made an offer for him to join the faculty in spite of his lack of a degree. It was a daring step for those days and many of the other professors resented it. Frost too was rather reluctant to come, afraid that academia would harm his poetic talent, but he could not afford to turn down a salary of $2,000 a year, with a proviso that he could give readings at other colleges whenever he wished. He was currently living in Franconia, New Hampshire, and the winters were physically difficult for his growing family, especially his son Carol who was in frail health. Since he desperately needed the money, he agreed to give it a try. He moved his family to West Pelham, a few miles outside of Amherst. As the only non-academic on the faculty he was rather wary of his colleagues, but he and Professor of English George Whicher became good friends. The two men would walk back and forth between West Pelham and Amherst talking briskly all the way, though one suspects that it was Frost who did most of the talking.

Gerald had not signed up to study with Frost, but in his sophomore year, when he elected a course in American Literature taught by Professor Whicher, he discovered that the poet would meet the class for an hour each week for part of the semester. A devotee of Romantic poetry, Gerald was at first unimpressed by Frost's poems, finding them harsh and unpoetic. The grim pictures of country life clashed with Gerald's own happy explorations of country roads and mountain farms. Then one day he heard Frost read his poem "The Hill Wife." Listening to the New England cadence, he suddenly felt the loneliness of the young bride on that bleak farm in the Shutesbury hills. He would be a Frost disciple from that time forth.

That June he decided to extend his walking expeditions all the way to Vermont. He was enthralled with the beauty of the Green Mountains which awakened all his romanticism. "Near Shelburne I met a girl with green-gold eyes under a big maple tree, and I fell in love with her—and promised myself I would come back and find her again, which I eventually did on her wedding day (the romance was all on my side.)" (*DTW* p. 183) In later years he could not even remember her name—it really didn't matter—for she was more a fantasy than flesh and blood. Like the mountains themselves, women were distant beckoning beacons. One of his favorite authors, Thomas Hardy, who understood this penchant for idealizing briefly glimpsed women, had a character in *The Woodlanders* explain it: "Human love is a subjective thing. . . . It is a joy accomplished by an idea which we project against any suitable object in the line of our vision."

The back country roads that Gerald followed in his search for adventure passed by old farms, some abandoned and derelict; others still inhabited by their elderly residents. Always he was searching for early ways of life. The tiny villages clustered around white steepled churches seemed to him the loveliest sight he had ever seen. One May day in southern Vermont, he walked until dark. He had covered over thirty-five miles and stopped in a farmhouse to ask for a drink of water and to inquire about a place to sleep for the night. There he met Mrs. Hancock and had the same feeling of instant rapport that he had felt for Carrie Johnson.

The Hancocks welcomed him so warmly, giving him dinner and a bed, that in the morning he decided it would be insulting to offer to pay for his lodging, and, indeed, they didn't seem to expect it. Gerald had found another home. Whatever he may have lacked in knowledge about girls his own age, he had no problems with older countryfolk. These women offered the warm homeyness that his childhood had lacked. Mrs. Hancock was happiest when preparing food or caring for a man. Everything about the farm fitted his dream of the perfect idyll: this Vermont homestead "with barns and cattle behind, the immaculate housewife of infinite kindliness of spirit, the snug kitchen with wood-burning stove, the rill of icy water always flowing, the quietness and warmth of a long settled way of life." (*DTW*, p. 186)

For many years he continued to search out different back roads and trails in all kinds of weather. He became friendly with the Hancocks' neighbors and once he even earned several gallons of maple syrup by painting a watercolor of their friend's sugar house which was reproduced for the farmer to use as a label. But it was not enough to try to capture the beauty of the countryside in paint; he longed to put his feelings for the landscape and its people into words.

At Amherst, Gerald had developed a strong admiration for Professor Whicher and took almost every course he taught. Although the professor was a cool, reserved man, he reached out to the shy student. The two took long

walks together and played tennis frequently, which Gerald to his delight usually won. In his course in creative writing, which had several highly talented
writers including Dickie Richard (who later became the friend and protege of
Robert Frost), students were encouraged to read their works aloud to the class
for critique. Whicher would also read them passages from great writers of the
type Gerald enjoyed: sea fiction of Conrad, melodramatic poems by
Chesterton, travel books by Belloc, and especially for the edification of
Gerald, an essay on the process of writing by Dorothy Canfield Fisher, who
described so successfully the New England landscape and its people. Gerald
was impressed by Hilaire Belloc's *The Path to Rome,* and later used it as a sort
of guide for his own walking trip through the Alps. Some of the descriptions
in his autobiography of first encountering the majesty of the mountains are
amazingly close to the writing of Belloc in vocabulary and technique as well
as in spirit. What he learned from Whicher's class became an ingrained part
of his own style.

Perhaps one of the most important things that Whicher did for Gerald
was to urge him to read *Ethan Frome* and *Desire Under the Elms.* Publishers
and critics were at this time hailing the new realism which exposed the darker side of human nature. Edith Wharton's highly acclaimed *Ethan Frome* and
its companion novel, *Summer*, were models of craftsmanship, but she really
didn't understand the country people of New England as well as Mary Wilkins
Freeman, Sarah Orne Jewett, or even Harriet Beecher Stowe. Bernard DeVoto
later described her bleak descriptions as the forerunner of a "literary conven-
tion that was hardening into cliché when she wrote and has since ossified."
Eugene O'Neill and Van Wyck Brooks strengthened this credo. Their picture
of New England life was the antithesis of Gerald's nostalgic view, but it did
force him to see that beyond the romance of the deserted farms and dying villages were the harsh realities of those who had been defeated by the barren
soil, hostile climate, and changing times. Under Professor Whicher's guidance
and encouragement, Gerald began to think seriously about becoming a
writer. He would create his own visions of New England life.

Gerald was completely in accord with Robert Frost's theory that a potential writer gets his best education outside of the classroom, and Gerald would
have a wide variety of experiences off the campus. Although he did not like
city living, he enjoyed going to theatres, concerts, and operas when he went
back to New York to see his family. He wrote regularly to Carl Dennett giving
his reactions to the performances he attended. At Christmas time, Eleanor and
her friend Telo, an Italian girl who worked with her at the settlement house in
Boston, took him to see Ethel Barrymore in "Declassé," which he thought was
a terrible play: "Bum acting—bum everything." At the spring break he was
thrilled to attend a performance of "Parsifal" with his father. In May he saw

Walter Hampden in "Romeo and Juliet." He enjoyed the performance, but not Hampden "hopping around in pea green tights and emitting sighs and groans the entire evening." He felt that the middle-aged actor was much too old for the part and made a complete fool of himself. Gerald could lose himself completely at a concert, but he was a harsh critic of stage performances.

Gerald's walking expeditions grew ever longer and he finally decided that he should be able to walk the hundred miles to Walbridge Buffum's home in Shushan, New York, if he made a stop overnight at the Hancocks. Ondawa Farm was not far from the Vermont border, but tired as he was, he was conscious of the strong line of demarcation between the two areas. Unlike the wooded hills and neat villages of northern New England, rural New York consisted of broad cleared fields around sturdy brick Dutch Colonial houses.

The large exuberant family of Buffums always welcomed him as one of them. They had little money, but the three girls all attended Mount Holyoke and the boys went to Amherst and Middlebury. While Gerald and Mr. Buffum were not very compatible, Mrs. Buffum, a Smith College graduate who took great pride in her New England heritage, immediately bonded with her son's friend. Keeping a neat house with only primitive equipment was difficult for her, and dirty dishes often filled sink and sideboard, but she provided good meals, and more importantly, there was always intelligent conversation and laughter. She was a great reader of classic literature and well informed on almost every topic. When Gerald created Mrs. Kyle in his novel *Winter Solstice*, he made her grimmer and sadder, but he must have had Mrs. Buffum partly in mind.

Walbridge's sister Anne treated Gerald like a brother and once when he had walked the whole distance over the mountains to join them at Thanksgiving dinner, she scolded him for his appearance and made him borrow a jacket and tie from one of the Buffum boys so he would at least look respectable from the waist up sitting at the dining room table. She used to tease him that he only played at country life. She considered his vanity and pride in being able to walk so far, and his sentimentality and pleasure in using a scythe and axe in the old-fashioned ways, as the mere posing of a gentleman's son, but she knew that his love for the country people and places was genuine. When he wrote his autobiography in later years, he dedicated it not only to such male mentors as Uncle Jim Croswell, Uncle Harry Donaldson, Uncle Lincoln Hendrickson, and Dean Briggs of Harvard, but also to "the good women who took me in as though I belonged to them—like Carrie Johnson of Amherst and Mary Hancock of Vermont." He included Ellen Coolidge of Boston and the Buffum family of Ondawa Farm as well.

Much as he loved the mountains, summers always meant the coast. During one of the college vacations the Braces stayed at Woods Hole, which still seemed to Gerald a poor substitute for Maine, though he did learn to play golf there. In spite of his Aunt Emma's endeavors to introduce him to young eligible girls from proper families, Gerald was able to write to Carl that "except for one or two stray sirens on the golf course, I have been entirely free from the pernicious influence of the female species." He longed to be at Deer Isle. The one person that he could confess his inner feelings to was Carl Dennett.

He had tried to interest Carl in coming to Amherst to study when he graduated from Loomis, but Carl had neither the money nor the academic interests. Instead he took a variety of jobs, often living in his car while on the road as a salesman seeing a side of life that Gerald would never really know. Gerald attempted to get him to read novels, especially Thomas Hardy, but he preferred lighter works. He was never financially or socially able to keep up with the lifestyle that the Brace family took for granted.

Although he missed the companionship of Carl, Gerald had an active social life. He had a fine tenor voice and sang in the glee club, even dressing up in evening suit to sing in the concerts. He took pride in his endurance and, when the snow came, he joined friends for long cross-country walks on snow-shoes. He longed to own a pair of skis, or at least know someone from whom he could borrow, but skiing was a comparatively new sport on college cam-puses at that time. He played a lot of squash and was chosen to represent his fraternity in the annual tournament. He took up boxing and, while he lacked the competitive nature that made his brother Charlie such a good fighter, he learned to compensate for his lack of blood lust with skill, though not before he had received some severe poundings. Even a serious bout with the flu that put him in the infirmary slowed him down only temporarily. He was a fine swimmer, and after taking a few of the required gym tests, he was excused from the rest because of his superb physical shape. What he excelled in most was cross-country running. He won three races. Newspaper headlines for one said, "Brace wins on three mile course, time 14 minutes," Actually it had been 18 minutes, but Gerald hoped that the error would strike terror in the hearts of his opponents and give him an advantage. Still he knew he would never be a first class runner because he always over-trained and became too tense and nervous. Competitive running seemed to sap his strength and enjoyment. He preferred sports where he either tested his own physical agility or pitted his skill against a single opponent.

He loved tennis and in his junior year met Lincoln Fairley, a sophomore with whom he seemed about evenly matched. The two soon became close companions. Not only did they see each other at college, but they could also get together during vacations, for their summer homes were only about six miles apart across the water. The Fairley home at Weir Cove on Cape Rosier was an easy sail from Deer Isle. Lincoln's father, the Reverend James Fairley, was a minister in Jamaica Plain, Massachusetts. During the years of the war, his pacifist ideas had displeased his former congregation. He was a gentle man who had bowed to their wishes and quietly left to take another parish, but it upset his son so much that he had become an ardent Socialist.

The newly formed League of Nations was considered radical by most of their friends, but both Lincoln and Gerald supported it. In 1920 Gerald's sister Betty, the beauty of the family, married Huntington Gilchrist in a big society wedding at Grace Church, New York. Huntington, who was deeply involved in the League, seemed the ideal husband for Betty, a Bryn Mawr graduate. The only one of the Brace girls to have gone to college, she was interested in aiding her husband in a diplomatic career. He had the best of educations—an A.B. from Williams in 1913, an A.M. from Harvard in 1916, and a Ph.D from Columbia in 1918. Before going to Harvard for his Masters he had taught at the Anglo-Chinese College in Foo-Chow and at Peking University. He had entered the service after graduation and been made a captain in the American Air Force where he caught the attention of R. B. Fosdick, Under-Secretary General of the League of Nations, who asked him to serve as his personal assistant. There he had helped administer the Saar Valley and Danzig and had recently been promoted to the International Secretariat, a position he held until 1924. He was obviously a man with a great future ahead of him and Betty looked forward to being a diplomat's wife, even though it meant leaving family and friends to live in Switzerland.

In spite of his romantic nature, Gerald did not date seriously during his undergraduate years. Anne Buffum attended most of the fraternity dances with him, but she was almost like a sister. In fact, she was always more than willing to fix him up with her Mount Holyoke classmates. Dances were full dress affairs, and Gerald was constantly having to borrow articles of clothes from his fraternity brothers. Since he was both handsome and courteous, he had no difficulty dating girls, but he did not really learn much about what women were like. Dates in those days consisted mainly of decorous walks on the campuses of Mount Holyoke or Smith or, if the weather was too cold or stormy, they sat in the chaperoned, large dormitory parlors. It was a ritual known as "fussing." Some of the fraternity brothers bragged of more daring activities, but Gerald was always unsure how much was truth. Everyone accepted the idea of a double standard, and girls were expected to be innocent and virginal. As for Gerald he never even went so far as to kiss one of them. Just to hold a girl in his arms while dancing a waltz or fox trot fulfilled his dreams. He had been taught that a man should practice moral restraint, and since his sex drive had always been sublimated, he had little sympathy for the young men in love suffering from the strict moral standards of society. The Roaring Twenties only gently murmured in most of New England.

Sex and marriage still went firmly together, and he wasn't seriously ready for either.

Gerald would always consider himself fortunate that he attended Amherst during the time that Meiklejohn was president. As a student, Gerald had been unaware of the depth of animosity surrounding the president whose Socratic approach to education he himself so admired. "He made all other academic leaders seem stodgy and dull. He imbued us with a spirit of eager adventure in learning and living. He faced us always with quick-minded charm and wit, and set us to laughing at him and ourselves, but always with an affectionate and somewhat rueful awareness of his hopes for a better and brighter life for all of us." (*DTW*, p. 216) Though many called him a dangerous radical, Gerald felt that Meiklejohn was really just too idealistic for this imperfect world.

President Meiklejohn had hoped that by bringing Robert Frost to the campus he could create a more open, intellectual atmosphere in the college. However, by giving him full rank, he had alienated many of the regular faculty, and Frost's own unconventional, undisciplined temperament didn't help. Although the poet liked to appear a renegade, he was basically conservative. When Meiklejohn brought Stark Young, a brilliant homosexual writer and critic from Texas, to teach at the college, Frost was outraged. No doubt it was partly jealousy at having another writer, especially one accepted by the academic community, as a rival, but he also distrusted his courtly Southern manners and charm. Frost demanded that Young be fired because he considered him a moral threat to the students. Meiklejohn countered that since the boys were bound to learn about homosexuals out in the world, Amherst would be a good place to start. Frost, he added, could serve as a counteraction. This angered the poet still more and on May 20, 1920, he handed in his resignation. Moving to South Shaftsbury, Vermont, he spent his time writing poetry and planting trees, unmoved by the fact that it had been Meiklejohn's tolerance that had led to his own appointment.

Graduation passed peacefully in spite of the growing faculty rebellion. Jerry, as his friends now called him, was on the staff of the 1922 yearbook, *The Olio*. The classmate chosen to write his mini-biography seems to have known him well, for the man Jerry was to become is already clear.

> Ecce! the primitive man! In the spring this young man's fancy turns to the great out-of-doors. Benighted Shutesbury—and heathen Belchertown bear the imprints of his basketball shoes. Jerry thinks nothing of reeling off twenty-five miles between luncheon and dinner, and his preference in the fairer sex runs to those of amazing physique. It is only fitting that such a man should have no vices— though he did once admit in a moment of garrulity that he had

been tempted to taste coffee. But, he added, it had happened when he was really too young to know right from wrong. But, ah, his many virtues! Were cleanliness near to godliness, Jerry would occupy half the throne of Olympian Zeus. The Delt house matutinal hot water supply can scarce efface the imaginary dirt acquired since the previous night's shower. . . . And then the calm dignity which has never deserted him since his sojourn among us! We tremble to think what might happen should the peaceful water awake some day and the thunder of the mighty deep be heard. Or is it possible that the owl-like complacency could be likened unto that of a frog.

Shortly after Gerald's graduation, Meiklejohn was dismissed as president of Amherst College, which divided into two acrimonious camps. Fourteen faculty members resigned and some of the students transferred to other schools. The following year at commencement some of the seniors refused to accept their diplomas. Gerald would probably have joined with the rebels, though he was glad he hadn't been put in that position. His biggest decision had been only what choice of career he should consider. He had become interested in architecture when he wrote a paper on the Palladian period for a course on the Renaissance. His professor "Crock" Thompson had singled it out for

Gerald's Graduation Picture, 1922

praise. Later he had taken a course in Greek Civilization taught by Henry DeForest Smith, a close boyhood friend of the Maine poet Edward Arlington Robinson and also a friend of Uncle Lincoln Hendrickson. The class had awakened an interest in Gerald for both Classical and Colonial architectural styles. Ornate Victorian architecture was now scorned and a house like Ches-Knoll was totally out of fashion. Gerald admired the pure lines of the white houses in the New England villages clustered around the churches with their pointed spires. This romantic vision led him to dream of becoming an architect.

Although he had been only an average student at Loomis, at Amherst his only stumbling block had been public speaking. His junior year he had a straight B average, and by his senior year, he had four A's. Only a C in Economics narrowly prevented him from being elected to Phi Beta Kappa.

Since he had no plans for becoming an academic, this seemed unimportant. He did graduate *cum laude*, however, so he felt fairly certain that he would be accepted into any graduate school that he chose. He first considered Columbia, where he had been awarded a fellowship to study history and would have been able to commute from the family's New York apartment. However, he changed his mind when Lincoln Fairley decided to transfer to Harvard in his junior year and Gerald learned that he could room with him in the Yard. He made up his mind to attend Harvard School of Architecture.

A rural Vermont scene painted by Brace

4

Epiphany

In 1922 when his father offered him a trip to Europe as a graduation present, Gerald booked a second class passage on the *Rotterdam* to sail to Boulogne, France. He left as soon as his final exams were over without waiting for commencement. His sisters Betty and Eleanor were already abroad. Betty was living in Switzerland with her husband and year old son Johnny, and Eleanor was in France. On the trip over, Gerald met a young man named Graves to whom he was instantly attracted. The two seemed to find many topics of mutual interest and Gerald was flattered to be befriended by such a sophisticated man of the world. They talked so easily and intensely that Gerald, usually reserved with new acquaintances, later wondered uneasily if possibly there might have been undertones of sexuality in their relationship. Certainly there had been no indications that this was true, but Gerald's earlier experience with the Amherst alumnus had made him suspicious of any overtures of friendship even though Graves was an acquaintance of proper Aunt Emma. At any rate, after the ship docked they went their separate ways, and Gerald never saw him again.

While on board he also met George Howe, a Harvard architectural student from Bristol, Rhode Island, and the two explored the cathedrals at Amiens and Rouen together. Howe was very knowledgeable and pointed out architectural details which Gerald might otherwise have missed. He was awed by the grandeur of the great Gothic structures. Inside Notre Dame in Amiens, the largest cathedral in France, with its soaring 370-foot spire, fourteenth-century transept, and sixteenth-century rose window, even an agnostic like Gerald could believe that something greater than man must have inspired such magnificence. After that, the cathedral at Rouen was something of a disappointment to them, but they were more than compensated when they visited the church of Saint Ouen in the heart of the city. Here Gothic architecture had been brought to technical perfection. Elaborate flying buttresses supported a soaring fabric achieving an almost unbelievable sense of lightness. There was little decorative detail in the interior, but the east windows set in tiers added to the sense of loftiness, and the great rose window suffused the nave with a warm glow. Once again Gerald was overwhelmed by the romance of the past.

Continuing on to Paris to join Eleanor, Gerald was surprised to see how little war damage there was. Eleanor, who was staying at the Saint Pères Hotel, spoke fluent French so was able to travel freely around the city and show him all the sights. Though Gerald knew some school boy French and read it fairly well, he found—like so many tourists—that the natives seemed to speak too fast, running their words together "like the babbling of a brook." The two of them spent time at the Louvre and visited Chartres where he climbed one of the towers. He never had a good head for heights and later wrote to Carl Dennett "I never was so giddy in my life—just from the thought that the thing was nothing but balanced stone." He enjoyed a day at Versailles. Prices were low and the French were still grateful for the help they had received from America during the war. But the Paris he and Eleanor experienced was that of Henry James, not the city described by Hemingway and Fitzgerald. Gerald did not care for wine or beer and neither of them enjoyed night life. The society they witnessed still observed pre-war proprieties and manners. It was all very cultured and old-world.

Soon it was time to take a train to Geneva, from which they proceeded by local train to Creux de Genthod where the Gilchrists lived in a house called Chalet de l'Aile. Huntington was doing important work at the League of Nations in Geneva. They were part of a sophisticated international circle of friends who firmly believed that the new league was the only hope of bringing lasting peace to the world. Already it had settled a debate between Sweden and Finland over the Åland Islands and had assured the safety of Albania. Now it was attempting to stabilize the economic situation in Austria.

Gerald and Eleanor stayed with the Gilchrists slightly over a week while equipping themselves with maps, rucksacks, mountain boots, and alpenstocks to prepare for a long hike through the Alps. Crossing the head of the lake by steamer gave them a chance to see the Castle of Chillon; they caught a train at Montreux then to take them up into the mountains. It all exceeded Gerald's dreams. For almost a month they followed foot-trails, admiring the shining peaks of Bernese Oberland and the Tyrol. There were very few tourists and even fewer skiers. The weather was perfect, cool and sunny. Signs along the way gave the time it would take to hike to the next destination, but the times posted seemed absurdly slow to these two eager travelers.

Just beyond Gstaad, they climbed up a trail to a notch in the wall where the path abruptly turned downward to a hidden valley below. Suddenly they found themselves looking across empty space to the Wildhorn, part of a range extending to the Jungfrau. The mountain loomed directly in front of them.

For the first time Gerald fully understood Hilaire Belloc's assertion that the most stunning view of a mountain is from an elevation halfway up; so that you are able to look both up and down its slopes.

William James has asserted that, "A man's character is discernible in the mental or moral attitude, in which when it came upon him, he felt himself most deeply and intensely active and alive. At such moments there is a voice inside which speaks and says this is the real me." Such was Gerald's stunning moment of self-discovery. He wrote in his autobiography how the sudden view of the snowpeak remained forever after in his dreams.

> It looms there as a sort of ultimate goal, and again and again I have approached it—though I rarely get to its actual summit. The dream of it is a genuine sleep-time dream, and I am exalted by the possibility of achieving such a climb as I have longed for, and I am at the same time saddened by the knowledge that I am alone and probably incompetent to cope with the technical difficulties of a major climb. I wake up in a state of triumph and frustration. I see the way ahead of me up the icy steeps, I am almost there, I feel brave and competent, I have a sense that the wondrous adventure is at last being brought off—and then almost invariably the vision recedes and seems to crumble away and I am left with the poignant awareness that the adventure has once more eluded me and I am back in my own limited life again. But I can never forget the mountain as it looms up silently and whitely in my dream. (*DTW*, p. 243)

It seemed part of a sublime beauty which was a manifestation of heavenly grace. No height seemed beyond the reach of his youth. The reality of the mundane—getting and spending, family and job—would eventually frustrate his lofty goals, but the light of common day never succeeded in extinguishing the vision.

Eleanor and Gerald continued south and east through the Grimsel Pass, the Furka Pass, and the Julier Pass to Silvaplana just below Saint Moritz where Eleanor had been detained during the opening days of World War I. At Saint Moritz they searched for the grave of their grandfather Charles Loring Brace, buried there in 1893. They located it in a Protestant churchyard, neglected, but with the printing on the stone still legible.

They had kept in touch by phone with the Gilchrists from various villages along the way, and at Silvaplana they were joined by Huntington's younger brother Douglas. Gerald had been eager to climb one of the mountains, so the two men decided to tackle the 11,300 foot Piz Corvatsch. On their way up they met a line of descending climbers, roped together, placing their Alpine sticks cautiously as they made their slow way down the mountain.

Gerald and Douglas had to move carefully on the slippery crest, but once they began their descent they joyfully glided and slid down the slippery slope. They arrived back with a great sense of accomplishment. Their pride, however, was soon deflated by veteran climbers who said, "Oh yes, easy climb, isn't it."

The three continued by mountain train over the high Stelvio Pass to an area recently annexed by Italy. It was lonely and picturesque, with a genuine medieval castle strategically overlooking the valley which was the main north-south route between Italy and Austria. In the shadow of the Dolomites, farmers were haying the sloping fields. As the three travellers watched the haymakers sing their way home to the music of a baritone horn, the scene before them appeared idyllic, but the marks of the war five years before were still obvious. For the first time, too, they began to hear rumors of a man named Mussolini, who was organizing a Fascist party, and there were Italian police in all the towns.

They stopped in Cortina for over a week to walk and climb in the surrounding hills. Gerald was attracted by a beautiful blue-eyed Danish girl and the two climbed a small mountain together. She was a governess who spoke good English and seemed to him very learned and wise, but he was too naive and shy to develop any kind of relationship and he never saw her again.

Douglas had left Eleanor and Gerald for a while, but now he rejoined them in Venice. They visited palaces, churches, and art galleries. Their luxurious hotel was a converted palace with a Tiepolo painting on the dining room ceiling. Below their windows, they could hear the gondoliers singing and see the city spread below them like a Canaletto painting. They would never have imagined that in just two months, Mussolini, who seemed to them rather ridiculous, would be sending his Fascist troops into Rome and that King Emmanuel would invite him to form a cabinet. To be sure, they sometimes heard Fascist hymns being sung, and at night they could hear the heavy sound of marching feet, but it was difficult for them to take it seriously. Gerald was far more concerned with having the opportunity to pole a gondola than he was with politics.

Gondolas are difficult to handle and it took a lot of persuasion and a good tip to convince a gondolier to let Gerald try his hand at propelling one. It required more skill than he had imagined, but, to the gondolier's surprise, Gerald finally succeeded in propelling it successfully down the Grand Canal. Pleased with his achievement, he would later recreate the event in his first novel, *The Islands*. In the novel, Brace has Edgar, his young hero, convince the gondolier to let him try his skill, and the scene is described exactly as Gerald remembered his own experience.

Edgar worked carefully, feeling out the oar and the boat, studying the oar-rest. Then deliberately he began throwing his shoulders forward and down, keeping the tension on the oar-rest. The gondolier bobbed up with wreathed smiles, cheering aloud: "Buono, Buono!" . . . . They proceeded stately down the Grand Canal, threading traffic, shooting under bridges with the oar dropped aft. "That's where you'd bust it if you had regular oar-locks or pins," Edgar pointed out, swinging the nose six inches one way to slide past a pile. "It's easy enough out here, but I wouldn't tackle one of those little alleys."
(*TI*, p. 172, 173)

To successfully handle a gondola in Venice is an opportunity few Maine sailors ever have, and Edgar is expressing his author's quiet pride in the accomplishment.

Before leaving for home, Gerald wanted to visit the cathedral at Lake Como that had been the subject of a paper he had written for his course in Renaissance architecture at Amherst. In *The Path to Rome*, Hilaire Belloc had extravagantly praised its polished marble facade "so exquisite in proportion, so delicate in sculpture and so triumphant in attitude." The church failed to live up to Gerald's expectations, but the countryside around Lakes Como and Maggiore were bathed in a magic light more beautiful than he had ever envisioned. Like Belloc he discovered that the total experience is not just what is seen by the eyes, but more like the feeling one has when music is played.

Autumn was rapidly approaching and it was time for him to return to his studies once again. He and Eleanor took a train through the Simplon Tunnel for a last reunion with the Gilchrists and then returned to Le Havre to embark on the *Mauritania*. They arrived in New York on September 23, 1922, Gerald's twenty-first birthday. He was now officially an adult, expected to settle down to the serious business of life. He wrote Carl Dennett a mournful letter which he ended with the words: "The thoughts of youth are long, long, thoughts." These lines from Henry Wadsworth Longfellow's poem "My Lost Youth" would echo in Brace's memory down through the years. Like the poet, he too would later remember the magical summers spent in Maine.

> And with joy that is almost pain
> My heart goes back to wander there,
> And among the dreams of the days that were,
> I find my lost youth again.
>   And the strange and beautiful song,
>   The groves are repeating it still:
>   "A boy's will is the wind's will,
> And the thoughts of youth are long, long thoughts."

A half-century after Robert Frost published his first collection of poems in 1913 under the title *A Boy's Will*, Brace would choose the remaining half of the line *The Wind's Will* for his novel of a young boy coming of age in a small Maine town. In 1976 he returned to the poem again, entitling his autobiography *Days That Were*. But even as a young man preparing to enter graduate school, he empathized with the poet, for young Gerald's thoughts were indeed "long."

5

Studying Architecture

Gerald had vague dreams of becoming a novelist, but it was not the kind of burning passion that would have made him willing to starve in a garret or struggle with a menial job. He was by nature a dilettante who wanted to write poetry as well as prose, build model boats, paint pictures, and design both graceful sailboats and New England style houses. While his father had never tried to influence him to carry on the family tradition at Children's Aid—no doubt he realized that his son did not have the temperament for it—he did expect him to prepare for a practical profession. Since Charles Loring II had grown up in a household where the Olmsteds and Vaux had been frequent visitors, and he himself had become a designer of bridges before rather reluctantly returning to take over his father's work, he was pleased to learn that his son wanted to become an architect.

Gerald had little idea of what training in architecture would be like. He had no visions for buildings of the future—only a romantic appreciation for the colonial houses and the white churches with pointed spires he had seen on New England commons. While his trip to Europe had given him some feeling for Gothic cathedrals, he had paid little attention in Paris to such details as the Grecian outline of the Madeleine or the Roman Arc de Triomphe. Now, Mr. Haffner, the head of the program at Harvard, immediately set the beginning students to work copying classic forms, and showing how these designs had been adapted for use on French monuments. Training was primarily technical—drawing projections and learning

Gerald loved New England architecture, as shown by his watercolors

to use the T-square. Because he had a natural artistic ability, Gerald was able to do well in his classes, but he found the work stultifying. His one attempt at creating an original design for a house convinced him that he had no talent. He also realized that he lacked true commitment.

He attempted to release his frustrations by running, or by taking long hikes through the Green Mountains often to visit the Buffums. Cooped up in Cambridge, he frequently suffered severe colds and twice he had to spend time in the infirmary, once for measles and later to have his tonsils removed. Throughout his life he must have often felt betrayed by the body he trained and tended so religiously. He would have been thoroughly miserable if his life outside of the classroom had not been so satisfactory. Because his roommate, Lincoln Fairley, was still an undergraduate, they could share a room at Thayer Hall right in the middle of Harvard Yard. Gerald never asked for more than the companionship of one close friend. He and Lincoln enjoyed playing hard games of squash together and both loved tennis. Gerald also did a good deal of skating. He wrote to Carl Dennett that he could "now proceed with one foot suspended aloft and arms waving to and fro in most approved fashion." On the weekends when Lincoln went home to Jamaica Plain, Gerald usually walked the five miles to attend the Unitarian church there. He felt that its minister, Lincoln's father, was undoubtedly one of the wisest and best men he had ever met.

By spring, Gerald had another reason for going to Mr. Fairley's church. One day on the street car, Lincoln had introduced him to one of his father's parishioners, a small, red-haired girl named Huldah Laird. She was a science major at Boston University. Born in 1902, she was only a year younger than Gerald, but she seemed to him immensely young and innocent. She was very different from the sophisticated, athletic girls with whom he played tennis, swam, and sailed. They were types that his family considered suitable, and certainly some of the girls had secretly hoped that their casual dates would lead to a serious relationship.

He had conventional ideas of settling down to a career and family. Even before he met Huldah he had already expressed to Carl his intentions to marry in the spring of 1929 or 1931 though he had no particular woman in mind. He was depressed because he feared that all his lady loves were abandoning him. Nancy Porter had agreed to marry Mike Strauss. Although he was a man with excellent prospects, Gerald was sure she was making the wrong choice. Gerald tried to tell himself that she was just "an ordinary little girl that he happened to know better than any other," but when he heard of her wedding plans, he wrote Carl that "the world immediately took on such an atmosphere of melancholy that I hastened off to Vermont and buried myself in the solitary mountains. Even now I gaze wistfully across the bay to where she used to live—and indeed it goes heavily with my disposition." He added romantically, "I fear I shall have to wait for the princess golden eyed to come down from her hilltop in the sun." He was ready to cast Huldah into this role as soon as he saw her red hair.

It didn't take him long to discover how different she actually was from the other girls he had known. First of all, she showed little interest in him. She was enterprising and self-sufficient, though uneasy in social situations. She spoke freely—sometimes even sharply—and she prided herself on her practicality. He didn't quite know what to make of her, but he found her fascinating. He sat in back of her in church just to watch her. Soon he was weaving fantasies about her similar to those of his prep school days when he had begun reading the novels of Zane Grey.

It was always easier for Jerry to put his feelings into written words than to speak them. In spite of his shyness, he wrote to her in March that he had deliberately plotted to get to know her better, perhaps attracted by some superficial quality such as "the color of your hair." He explained that if he acted diffident while in a group it was because he had little use for idle chatter with mere acquaintances. "I avoid people almost as much as you do—but I don't think I'm afraid of them. I avoid the people I don't know or don't like because conversations with them consists mostly in telling lies." He ended his letter to her with an explanation of why he would be unable to attend church on Easter morning, adding that perhaps it was just as well for "Easter is April and April is Folly—and where is that in a church? So goodby. I wish you joy and a robin." She treated him like the irresponsible young romantic that he was. He wrote to Carl in mock seriousness: "May I offer a very profound sentiment? Thus: Beware the females; if you avoid them you are pursued; and if you pursue them you are avoided. I speak only after long acquaintance with the matter. Of course, my life is not blighted by them—but I expect that will come in time."

In May he invited Huldah to a dance, writing in the half-playful, half-romantic tone he usually adopted with her. "I'll make you a present—a bribe it is—of very great value. Valuable things are easier to give (aren't they). So mark this:

> I give you one beat of a bird's wing,
> And the twilight wail of a drowsy loon.
> Tie them together with a turkey feather
> and climb up the stairs on the back of the moon.

You'll have to hurry because the moon is nearly gone. You need a fairly big one to climb up the back of it—and if you think this one isn't big enough wait for the next one."

He enjoyed her seriousness of purpose, but he hoped she realized that he was very different. He didn't want to be ambitious and practical. "I want to be on my back on the slope of a meadow—a gold-green meadow where a bob-o-link lives—and watch the floating clouds. And I want a dryad with red hair and a Maxfield Parrish dress to be there too and talk to me." He chided her for being too concerned with common sense. "I tell you, Miss Dryad, that as long as you believe the moon is real you will be unhappy and puzzled and some part of you will eventually die and your life will no longer be useful to you." It is a poet addressing a scientist. To Huldah the moon was very real. She was flattered to be receiving the attentions of a handsome Harvard graduate student, but she did wish that he wouldn't talk such nonsense.

That spring, the Braces bought their first car, a new Model T Ford, and Gerald was summoned to Yonkers, New York, to teach Eleanor how to drive it. Driving together to Deer Isle gave them a chance to see all the places that they had missed when travelling by boat and train. It took five days from Yonkers. That first season they stayed with friends along the way. They stopped for a night with the Johnsons in Amherst, on to Boston to stay with Ellen Coolidge, the friend with whom Eleanor had lived the two years that she had worked at the South End House, then to Kennebunkport, home to Eleanor's two best friends, the Burrage sisters. They had been her classmates at Miss Wheeler's Boarding School in Connecticut and had often stayed with the Brace family in both Dobbs Ferry and New York City; so Gerald had known them since he was seven years old. After a night in a rooming house in Belfast, Gerald and his sister crossed on the Bucksport ferry and eventually arrived at Deer Isle.

There was a great gathering of family in the Dunham's Point house that summer. Aunt Leta, the Donaldsons, and the Gilchrists were there. Gerald and Charlie slept in a tent. Mrs. Pickering, the cook, and her daughter Beatrice, who helped with the housework, stayed in a separate little house that later became the garage. It was Gerald's job to split the cordwood and keep the woodbox full. Each morning he went before breakfast to pick up twelve quarts of milk from the Sylvester's farm. On sunny days he often helped Freddie Sylvester with the haying and learned to stack the load like a professional. Still his siblings continued to treat him like a kid brother. They criticized him for daydreaming and ordered him about. He wrote to Huldah in June that he wished he were with her. "You don't say 'Why not do it some other way—like— this.' Besides I can call you a bloomin' idiot. If I called anyone here a bloomin' idiot (as I'd like to seven times a day) (No, twenty-seven times a day—some days) I'd be in for terrible trouble. And everybody calls *me* an idiot."

He confessed to her feelings of insecurity that he would never have admitted to his family. "Huldah—I do get troubled about myself some-times—in spite of what I say—I'm such a discordant, meandering, useless sort of person." He had learned that he was not cut out to be an architect, though he wasn't quite sure what he ought to do. He was in love with Huldah, but when he thought about Nancy Porter or visited Millicent Lewis at North Haven, he was in love with them, too. Sea and woods seemed to be apparelled in a Wordsworthian "celestial light" and his whole being responded. He vacillated between bliss and melancholy. He wrote to Huldah one day after taking a solitary walk: "There was a cliff there that dropped a hundred feet into the sea—and I stood on the edge a long time and considered jumping off it. I thought I would never again be so happy or be in so beautiful a place again." The words are those of a youth, but it was probably true that there would never be a time when he would feel such pure rapture again.

The summer of 1923 was a time of great activity. He spent four days at North Haven, Maine, enjoying the company of Millicent Lewis and family in their lovely old restored farmhouse near Webster Head, although he spent much of that time working on *Bettina*, which had been wintered at Ozzie Brown's boatyard. Carl Dennett joined him there and the two cruised home by way of Mount Desert and Swans Island before finally mooring at Dunham Point. Gerald and Millicent became lifelong devoted friends even though they had first been brought together at Mount Desert by Aunt Emma Donaldson, usually reason enough for Gerald to be wary. As he wrote to Carl, "You see Aunty Emma is a great factor in my affairs. I spend my time dodging around corners from her—and watching her closely through a crack where she can't see me. I have, as you know, most profound admiration for her—yet I fear her more than anyone in the world—and furthermore I am fascinated by her policies and methods." For a while she tried to manage Carl's life for him too, but she soon gave up on him as hopeless. Undoubtedly if her wish to see Gerald married to a young socialite like Millicent had succeeded it would have forced him into the type of life he wanted to avoid. But he and Millicent immediately hit it off, especially when he discovered that she too was a good friend of the Porters. According to her son Norman Pettit, Millicent for a while had harbored a secret wish that Gerald might propose to her, but in 1924 she married Horace Pettit.

Earlier in the spring of 1923 John Donaldson called Gerald to come to Falmouth, Massachusetts to look at a thirty-five foot sloop that he had a chance to buy for $300. He had decided to give up his research at Wood's Hole so that he and his family could spend their summers at Deer Isle, which meant they would need a boat of their own. Gerald, who was enamoured with the sleek lines of Maine boats, was shocked by the sloop's ugly appearance and huge centerboard, but he pronounced it seaworthy. John, with his usual wit, promptly named her *Bufo Aqua*, for he said that from the front she looked exactly like a water toad.

In July John had her ready and called Jerry and Charlie to help sail her to Deer Isle. Since neither John nor Charlie knew anything about cooking, Gerald was put in charge of provisions. The boat was not designed for cruising. She had only a primus stove, no plumbing, and uncomfortable bunks, but she proved fast and able. They reached Martha's Vineyard the first afternoon where they surprised Lincoln Fairley who was working there for the summer. There was time for a few sets of tennis and then they entertained him on board with a canned bean supper. They reached Nantucket in three hours the next morning, but the following day they ran aground off Cape Cod and had to wait for the tide to lift them afloat. There was no damage and they had good sailing until Bailey's Island, Maine. Here a storm came up which almost blew them onto the rocks. They made the harbor safely and Gerald went ashore for provisions. It was an expedition he always remembered nostalgically:

> The whole adventure of our little voyage around the Cape and down east and the safe anchorage after the stormy seas and the close call on the rocky shore of Bailey's Island and then the rain and fog closing in and the long sleep in our quiet cabin and the walk up over the wet fields to the old fashioned country store and the storekeeper's query about the yacht, and the accent and look and feel of the Maine coast again.

So powerful was the memory of those halcyon days of his "lost youth" that many years later he dedicated *Between Wind and Water*, his nonfiction evocation of the Maine coast, "to my cruising companions of long ago particularly to the memory of my brother Charlie and to John Donaldson and to Lincoln Fairley." The cruise had enabled him to postpone all thoughts for the future.

Summer days in those early years seemed endless and full of promise. Eleanor felt constricted by all the guests in the house and she determined to build a private place of her own. She had long been eyeing some weathered silvery gray wood which had once been an old pier and float belonging to the Croswells before it was destroyed by ten-foot tides and the northwest exposure. She cleared away the underbrush from a sixteen by thirty foot area just north of the main house and cut the wood up into manageable lengths. When Gerald arrived she challenged him to demonstrate what he had been learning in his architectural studies by drawing up plans. He designed a small cabin with living room, bedroom, small kitchen, and space for a bathroom to be added later. He undertook the job of building the fireplace himself. Lugging stones from the shore proved too difficult so he made the chimney of brick. Mortar was made by carrying sand by rowboat from a beach a mile away. His little niece Julia Donaldson had a lonely time as the only small child in the

Brace household much of the time. She delighted in this new activity and got under everyone's feet trying to help. Watching Gerald hard at work adding slaked lime, Julia observed knowingly, "You make cement and then you make more ment." (*DTW* II, p. 13)

John energetically pitched in to help. None of them really knew what they were doing but they had immense enthusiasm and good will. Gerald and Eleanor shingled the roof together. It was a bit crooked, but watertight. John refused to get up on the roof, but Gerald remembered him happily bustling around, his contribution being "a bit like Brer Rabbit's in Uncle Remus—he went around measuring and marking with a pencil behind his ear and seemed very busy with essential technical problems, but he didn't do much actual sawing and hammering." (*DTW* II, p. l4)

By the end of summer the exterior of the house was finished. The measurements might not have been quite plumb, but the three were very proud of their achievement. Gerald later wrote to Carl Dennett that they had nailed over 10,000 shingles onto the roof and that the fireplace and chimney drew well. Eleanor found an old trivet for the fireplace in an antique shop. It seemed the finishing touch—so the house was christened "The Trivet."

All this gave Gerald little time for daydreaming. Having a car was still a novelty; so it was an adventure to meet the Stonington boat when guests were arriving, or even drive into Ellsworth to collect them. This gave him an opportunity to become familiar with the little inland farms along the way. Thrifty Mainers only survived by "making do." They never disposed of old machinery and broken down equipment because they never knew when the parts might prove useful. Eleanor always referred to these messy yards as "Maine nests," not because they were cozy, but because they reminded her of the "treasures" collected by pack rats.

"The Trivet" is still in use today

Good days meant sailing. Gerald visited the Fairleys at Cape Rosier. He sailed to Eagle Island and to Duck Harbor on Isle au Haut. It was all becoming background for future novels, but at the moment he was mainly concerned with trying to explain to Huldah the feeling of almost religious ecstasy that filled him whenever Isle au Haut came into view.

> It is blue—and always a long way off—and very lovely. It is a mighty place. . . . It has white granite cliffs that stand up against the deep blue sky, and the sea piles up and gurgles in the canyons—and sometimes it thunders and bursts—we saw six blue herons and the sea and the sky and granite cliffs all on an opalescent day. . . . It is very far away and alone, with tangled forest and a steady cold wind. I heard one white-throat of the year he was alone too—and very far away.

He wanted her to understand his yearnings and feeling of isolation. He rarely showed any curiosity as to how she was spending her time, but he did try in every way possible to show her his own Wordsworthian approach to nature.

But even the timeless days of summer must end. He wrote to Huldah of the joy he felt when he had found himself aboard *Bettina* one day completely enclosed in a thick fog that closed him off from the rest of the world. It was impossible to hide forever though. Even the knowledge that he would see Huldah again could not compensate for the unhappiness of returning to his architectural studies at Harvard. He returned to Cambridge in a mood of deep melancholy.

Gerald had entered architectural study with romantic visions of designing simple lovely facades. He had little interest in practical problems of drainage, plumbing, or urban planning. In his Loomis days he had learned that creating with words was easier for him than trying to achieve the technical perfection demanded by his manual training instructor. Later at Amherst College, his pleasure in writing had been reinforced by Professor Whicher. He had thought even then that he wanted to be a writer, but unless he became an educator, it seemed an impractical way to earn a living. Architecture offered both a respectable and remunerative career as well as creative scope. Perhaps if he had studied at Harvard in the days when the designs of Bauhaus, Gropius, and Wright were in the ascendency, he might have been more inspired, but the Harvard School of Architecture in the early twenties was old fashioned and conventional. He found that the classes only deadened his spirit.

Entering his classroom in Robinson Hall on opening day of the new semester, he spread his drawing instruments out on the table in front of him. Suddenly he was overwhelmed by the certainty that he had neither the talent nor the commitment to be an architect. Although it came as a revelation, it had been taking form in his subconscious throughout the summer. Leaving his things behind, he fled into Harvard Yard. For a long while he walked aimlessly. Finally he summoned the courage to go see Harold Edgell, dean of the Harvard School of Architecture. The dean was understanding and when Gerald confessed to him that what he really wanted to be was a writer, he immediately picked up the phone and made an appointment for him to talk with LeBaron Russell Briggs, dean of the Harvard Graduate School and professor of a highly regarded course in writing. As soon as Dean Briggs discovered that Gerald was the nephew of his old friend and classmate James Croswell who had died a few years previously, he immediately made room in his already over-enrolled class. He had no idea whether Gerald even had any talent. As for Gerald, he was giving up the profession of architecture for the uncertainties of becoming a writer.

He wrote to Huldah the following week: "Did you know that I have become a person of dubious prospects? I decided that the study of architecture was useless and unintelligent and merely led to the building of more horrid buildings—and that therefore I would immediately quit. Which I did forthwith. I shortly became a serious minded student of English literature— including Elementary German—which I still am as you doubtless observe. As to my future it does not exist." Although he knew he wanted to write a good novel some day, he still felt he should be preparing for a more practical profession. He wrote to Carl Dennett in October to say that he was considering going into a Vermont lumbering business.

With his change of direction came an immediate lifting of his spirits. His brother Charlie was planning to marry a girl named Helen Storie in Houghton, Michigan, and Gerald wrote Carl that he was contemplating going to the wedding even though it would mean wearing "high hat and cutaway coat with white carnation." Charlie did everything with a panache that Gerald admired; however, he had no desire to emulate his brother's adventurous life style. He was content at the moment to become a candidate for a Harvard Master of Arts degree in English.

Huldah

6
Harvard English Department

Gerald was still not sure if he had made the right decision. Though he wanted to be a writer, he had no desire to be a college professor which seemed to be the only professional path open to an English major. He wrote to Carl, hiding his insecurity behind a tone of humor, "So again my future is plunged into uncertainty (hear it splash!)—I stagger through a wilderness of doubt with slack rein and eased sheet—hitching my wagon to a fountain pen (You see I'm taking an advanced course in Composition.)"

As a graduate student, Gerald was able to enroll in courses taught by Harvard's most prestigious English professors, a fact which failed to impress him, though it gave him a thorough grounding in English literature. He considered highly admired Charles Lyman Kittredge, his professor in Shakespeare, to be dogmatic and assertive. He felt that his emphasis on research and historical facts minimized the aesthetic beauty of the dramatist's words. Doctorates were not as important as a good classical background in those days, and Kittredge had studied in Germany after graduating from Harvard as both Valedictorian and Ivy Orator. He could read in almost every language of western and central Europe. Although he was a member of Gerald's final oral examination committee, the two never got to know one another personally.

Gerald elected to take Chaucer under Fred N. Robinson mainly as a means of postponing the Gothic, Old English, and Old French required for a graduate degree in English. Professor Robinson had a doctorate in English Philology from Harvard and was the first to introduce the Celtic language as a regular college offering. Later he would publish the edition of Chaucer which after 1933 became required reading for graduate students in medieval studies across the country. Though Gerald had no special linguistic interests, he enjoyed Robinson's ability to bring the poet's words alive for the class.

The course Gerald took in drama had become famous in the days of George Pierce Baker, but John Tucker Murray brought a new dimension to it, having researched drama performances in towns across England. He saw the plays as living performances. Born in Brazil, he had studied in Wales and

Canada, as well as at Harvard, so he had a more worldly outlook than some of the professors. The semester thesis Gerald wrote for him on "The English Comedy of Manners from Ben Jonson to Shirley" earned him an A and reassured him that he would be able to do graduate work.

Most universities in those days used graduate assistants to read and criticize papers and exams in the large classes. At Harvard, students often saw more of them than they did their professors. Gerald recalled with astonishment how forty-five years later he met Professor Murray's assistant, Theodore Baird, who not only remembered his name, but apologized for having unjustly criticized as dramatically unsound the final scene of a short play Gerald had written as a class assignment. He had chosen Nathaniel Hawthorne's fable "The Snow Image" and had represented the spritely girl, fashioned by the children out of snow, by a dancer dressed in white. The dancer sinks slowly to the floor to simulate melting after the prosaic father insisted that she be brought into the house and warmed before the fire. Gerald may have been ahead of his time with his modern choreography, but his choice of story to dramatize is subconsciously revealing. Any lingering doubts in his mind about not continuing the family work at the Children's Aid Society must have been eased by Hawthorne's warning "that it behooves men, and especially men of benevolence, to consider well what they are about, and before acting on their philanthropic purposes to be quite sure that they comprehend the nature and all the relations of the business in hand." He failed to grasp the second moral that any female image created out of the imagination of mortals is bound to melt away amid the realities of household life. He continued to weave his fantasies about women—especially about Huldah—even while he was being taught to approach literature and new ideas analytically.

Gerald also was studying the English novel with Howard Maynadier, but the course that he looked forward to each Tuesday and Thursday afternoon was his writing course with Dean Briggs. At that time the professor was close to retirement. He had begun teaching at Harvard in 1875 and he too had never bothered to earn a doctorate, though he had a number of honorary degrees. He had originally been a teacher of Greek and had never done any creative writing, but he had the knack of bringing out the best in his students. They responded to his warmth of spirit, and found that he shared many of their non-academic interests from baseball to charades. When in later years Gerald wondered in despair if creative writing could be taught, he would take comfort in Dean Briggs' words, "Perhaps you cannot teach men how to write, but you can teach them how not to write." He also recognized that student writers needed encouragement. Shortly after Gerald had turned in his first short story, Dean Edgell showed him a note he had received from Dean Briggs. It said simply, "Thank you for sending me Mr. Brace."

The short story was entitled "Mr. Sandgate and the Mountain." The name Sandgate was adopted by Brace from a remote Vermont village not far from Shushan, New York. Professor Whicher had instilled in his Amherst students the belief that they should write about places they knew well; so Gerald based this story on one of his own Vermont walking excursions. The narrator, a hiker very like Gerald himself, convinces Mr. Sandgate, the farmer with whom he is staying, that he should climb the mountain on the edge of his property to gain a new perspective on his land. The farmer has never seen the high mountains to the northwest or how the rivers run down into the valley. Snow and cold wind impede their progress, but they make it to the summit. Mr. Sandgate is rather pleased at his accomplishment, but all he will say the next day is "We was fools." Later, Brace would use a similar character in his novel *The Wayward Pilgrims*. The name is changed from Sandgate to Shattuck, but while the character is more imaginative, hoping to find the shape of life itself around each bend of the mountain road, he too walks with a farmer's gait and makes the sound "whish" as he climbs.

Professor Briggs always read student papers aloud in class, identifying the writer and making gentle comments. The students in the class were not always as kind, but the professor's commonsense approach to writing and his encouragement made the course the pleasantest and most satisfying that Gerald ever took.

Because Lincoln Fairley was no longer an undergraduate, he and Gerald could no longer live in Harvard Yard. Together they found rooms in a big Victorian house on Quincy Street, owned by the sisters Anne and Jane Dodd. In order to maintain their old home, the women took in four or five boys each term. There was only one bathroom for all the lodgers and the shower was simply a sprinkler hose. Gerald was fastidious about bathing but since he and Lincoln played squash regularly, they could use the showers connected with the courts.

Gerald still went to Vermont whenever he could spare the time. In March he walked for sixty-five miles and had the joy of stopping by a sugar house where he ate maple syrup on snow with a fork. He had to stop his hike when the glare of the sun seriously snow-blinded him. He soon recovered, but then had a serious bout of flu. At least this gave him the time to read *The Rover*, Joseph Conrad's newest novel about a pirate-patriot in Napoleonic days. He was too busy to go to any New York plays, though he did attend plays at the Boston Copley theatre where he especially enjoyed a performance of Galsworthy's "Justice." However, nothing was as important to him as his weekends with the Fairleys when there was always the chance that he might get a glimpse of Huldah at church.

She still kept Gerald at a distance. She was more aware than he of the social differences between them. The Braces had been brought up in a world of private schools, country clubs, summer homes, sailboats, and travel. Their name and family connections opened doors to almost any social circle. Though high-minded and moral, they were unintentional snobs. Huldah's family had to struggle for everything they achieved. Raymond Laird had the harsh inflexibility of a self-made man. As an Indiana farmboy he had struggled to get a good education and had worked his way up to become Master of Roxbury Girls School in Jamaica Plain. He had met his wife, Huldah Blanche Potter, a native of Rutland, Vermont, when he was teaching Palmer method penmanship at a Schenectady Business School. She was a Universalist who sometimes found his strict Methodist principles difficult, but she handled him diplomatically and effectively. Mr. Laird had very old-fashioned ideas about proper behavior for young ladies. He was very proud of Huldah, who in many ways resembled him more than either her sister Jane or brothers Noel and Glover did, but she always felt that Noel was given far more freedom than she. Huldah wished desperately that she had been born a boy. Still, her father was willing to pay tuition for her to study science at Boston University and made no strong objections when she decided to leave the Methodist church to become a Unitarian.

Huldah was reluctant to let Jerry visit her at her home. Although her father was an educator with a natural talent for mechanical matters, he had few genuine intellectual interests. He sometimes made errors in grammar and vocabulary and lacked polish. She knew too that he would disagree with Jerry's liberal ideas, especially about theology. Though Jerry was not very serious about religion, he considered Mr. Fairley the best man who ever lived, so he disagreed with her father's comments about her new faith being heathenish. Jerry assured her that in spite of her father's doubts, she had "all the qualifications for a perfectly good halo—everything quite regular (except perhaps your hair)."

It was the hair that was to lead to trouble. Jerry considered Huldah one of the most attractive women he had met. He liked her fair skin which flushed so easily and her small compact figure. His greater height made him feel protective of her. But most of all he admired her long wavy red hair. He mentioned it in every letter. He gave as his reason for missing her that she had "red hair." Huldah began to wonder if he really knew her at all or whether he was just infatuated with her hair.

In 1923 Huldah had moved to Maryville, Tennessee, where she was teaching physical education. Her long thick hair required to be washed frequently after her gym classes and was difficult to dry. She determined that the only practical solution was to cut it short. The flapper with bobbed hair and short skirts had emerged in novels and films as the new woman. A flapper wore lipstick on a mouth shaped like a bow and plucked her eyebrows. If she were daring, she drank cocktails and smoked cigarettes. To read the literature of the twenties suggests that women had finally been emancipated, but if Hollywood, Paris, and New York might accept them, the conservative families of Boston and the hinterlands still viewed them with disapproval.

Huldah undoubtedly was aware that her father would be displeased; so she wrote to her mother to prepare him for the shock of seeing her. He waited two weeks to answer her letter and then responded with deliberate cruelty. It was so devastating that though she and her father eventually reconciled, she could never forget. He wrote that he did not wish to see her again, adding, "If I am foolish enough to believe you have sacrificed your principal claim to beauty, there is no reason that you should agree. I am very fond of remembering you with those lovely red curls, and I want to go on with that memory unmarred." Then he twisted the knife even more by evoking the memory of her little brother Glover, whose final words before he died were "Kiss me Papa." He told her that still, whenever

Huldah Laird bobs her hair — 1923

he went to the barber for a shave and the hot towels were placed over his face, he was reminded of the wet sheets in which his dying child was wrapped. He was afraid that if he saw her with cropped hair it would replace his memory of her lovely curls with a mental image that he would detest, and this latter might be the permanent one. He was aware that she had a job for the summer, and would arrange to be away from home so that she could visit her mother, but he did not wish to see her. He begged her not to tell her sister Jane because "so many have told me how pretty she is this year, and the mention is always coupled with her hair. She has been a good girl." He did not want Huldah to be a bad influence on her.

Distressed by her husband's anger and daughter's hurt feelings, Mrs. Laird ultimately did the one thing that she knew would convince her husband that bobbed hair did not mean immorality. She bobbed her hair, too. She must have felt trepidation—and, perhaps, regret—but her action worked. Huldah was welcomed back into the family circle again, though the relationship with her father was never quite the same. As for Gerald, while he expressed mild disappointment that her short hair didn't "catch the glint of sunlight as it once did," he took the matter lightly. Women's styles and foolish fads mattered little to him. Perhaps at the time she did not show him her father's letter. At any rate, he made no mention of it in his response. Instead he wrote a playful ditty.

> Go wash your hair in three tin pails
> And rinse it off with rusty nails;
> Dip it once in a sunset pool
> And hang it on the wind to cool;
> Sprinkle it with pale red wine
> And wrap it tight in columbine;
> Melt it over a dying fire
> And stir it up in copper wire,
> Take it out when the moon is full
> And polish it off with steel wool.
> Then you'll have red hair.

If she had been worried about Jerry's reaction, the humorous lines must have reassured her. He invited her to take a seventy-mile walking tour with him in Vermont. No doubt he did not expect her to accept. Even if her short legs could have kept up with his long strides, she had enough of her father's puritanical attitudes not to go off on a vacation with a man to whom she was not married.

During the spring term in Dean Briggs' class, Jerry had begun to structure a novel. When he told Huldah, she worried that he might make her one of the characters, but he assured her that he had no such thought. "My book isn't very good—and you wouldn't feel at all comfortable in it," but he added mischievously, there is "an Important Character who says 'please go away' when spoken to." Huldah was still wary of becoming too committed. Her handsome suitor's romantic impetuosity and playfulness were attractive, but she wasn't sure that she would be at ease in his world of creativity and culture.

Back at Deer Isle, Jerry wrote to Huldah again. "I love wild things such as cold and wet and Huldah." By then he and Lincoln had each received their diplomas, making them "Magister in Artibus—all in Latin by consent of the president and Fellows etc." As his letter shows, he didn't take the degree very seriously—a Harvard Master's was only seen as a step toward a doctorate. He hung the new diploma on a nail on the wall of the Trivet and there it remained through the decades. Although he made light of his achievement, he wrote about it to Anne Buffum who promptly responded: "Jerry, Geraldus, (Magnificent in Artful boats) I sigh to think of you stepping out into the cold world, for it is not at all happy like a boat race." She had enjoyed his accounts of island life, but reminded him "You mustn't forget, with all the splendor of your life on the ocean wave, the little friendly roads that go round corners and over the hills." These roads would become the inspiration for his novel *The*

Wayward Pilgrims, for like the sea, they too were part of the glorious freedom of his life.

By now he knew he wanted to be a novelist. His mind was so full of Huldah that his heroine began to resemble her more and more. He wrote to her in Chocorua, New Hampshire, where she was working for the summer for Norton Kent, Boston University professor of physics, to complain that as his heroine, she had "done absolutely nothing all summer." He didn't add that one reason the book was progressing so slowly was that he was so busy with other activities.

The most exciting—and almost unbelievable—thing that had happened was that a new boat was being built from one of his designs. Aunt Emma Donaldson's friend Mrs. Lewis, who had bought a farm on the north shore of North Haven island, decided that instead of continuing to hire a Friendship sloop for her use each summer, she would like a boat of her own. Neither her husband, nor her son was much interested, but her daughter, Millicent, thought it a wonderful idea. Mrs. Lewis loved fishing and sailing, although she felt she needed a man to bait her hooks and handle the ropes and sails. When none of the boats she saw in the showrooms pleased her, she asked Roy Coombs, a local boat builder on nearby Vinalhaven, to draw up some plans for her. When she showed these to Gerald, he agreed that they were sensible and seaworthy, but lacked graceful lines. She immediately challenged him to do better. It was something he and Charlie had done for fun many times, but now he had to consider all the practical needs as well as appearance. He sent the finished plans to Roy Coombs who built a scale model from them. Mrs. Lewis declared it was exactly what she wanted. Mr. Lewis wanted to hire a professional architect and have the boat built in one of the larger shipyards, but the boat was to belong to Mrs. Lewis and she commissioned Roy Coombs to build it.

Gerald was filled with eagerness and anticipation. When he and Lincoln arrived the following summer, he expected to see a half-finished boat, but he should have known the ways of independent Maine workers better. Typically, Maine builders take on all kinds of assignments, working on them according to weather and mood. Fully cognizant of the importance of time and tide, they live by a different timetable than the summer folk. A Maine native's year is twelve months long, not the three months of vacationers. True to form, Coombs had barely begun working on the boat, but at least the late start gave Gerald the joy of watching its progress. Then, when it was half-finished, all work came to a halt because Mr. Lewis decided it needed an engine. Gerald was appalled. He could not understand why any sailor would want to mechanize something meant for wind and water. Just when it seemed that there could be no agreement, Gerald's father suggested as a compromise that the motor be placed in the tender. It was an impractical solution for it made the tender too heavy to be used for anything except a motor launch, but it saved face for everyone. As a result of the delay, the boat could not be finished that summer, but a name was chosen for her. She was called *Charmian* from Shakespeare's "Antony and Cleopatra." She would always be special to Gerald as the first boat he ever designed.

Gerald had been kept busy finishing the interior of the Trivet and making shutters for the windows so the cabin could be secured in winter. Eleanor scoured second-hand shops for furnishings and she, Gerald, and John created boat models to give it a nautical decor. Still, Gerald found time to do a lot of sailing. Lincoln had become interested in a girl at Boothbay, so Gerald and he went there on a cruise. There were good games of tennis with the Porters at Great Spruce Head, and, of course, regular family picnics on favorite islands. Gerald made no serious effort to find an academic position, luxuriating in the freedom to remain in Maine later into the season than usual.

At last he knew he must return to look for a job. He sailed *Bettina* to be left at North Haven for the winter, and took a final look at *Charmian*, now almost ready for her first coat of paint. The dismal day, with the wind blowing northwest and autumn clouds hanging heavy and low, seemed to mirror Gerald's feelings. The next day, he reluctantly caught the *J. T. Morse* for Rockland, from there to board the boat for Boston and to begin the serious business of earning a living.

7
Williams College

Gerald had no idea how to go about searching for a job; so, in late September of 1924, he stopped at Dean Briggs' office for advice. To his surprise, he discovered that the dean had been trying to locate him for the past several days: by telegram to Deer Isle, by telephone to his Cambridge lodging house, and even to his family's New York apartment. Williams College had an unexpected opening for an instructor in English, and had called Harvard to see if anyone there could suggest a suitable candidate. At this point Gerald would have been ready to accept any reasonable offer, but the idea of returning to western Massachusetts, especially to the college from which his great-grandfather John Pierce Brace had graduated in 1814, delighted him. The administrators wanted an immediate interview; so he returned to New York just long enough to pack a bag and then took a train to Williamstown.

He had a rather perfunctory interview with President Harry A. Garfield in the beautiful eighteenth-century house that had served as home to the presidents of Williams since the days of Mark Hopkins. President Garfield came from a distinguished family. His father had been a faithful Williams alumnus. When in 1871, at a fund-raising dinner at Delmonico's in New York, alumni were asked for money for new buildings and equipment, it was then Representative James A. Garfield coined the oft quoted line that "the ideal college is Mark Hopkins at one end of a log and a student on the other." On September 19, 1881, shortly after becoming the twentieth president of the United States, James Garfield had been about to board a train in Washington D.C. to attend a Williams trustee meeting and his twenty-fifth class reunion when he was assassinated by Charles Guiteau, a disappointed office-seeker. Garfield's son Harry was just sixteen at the time. He too went to Williams, graduating in 1885. In 1908 he was made president of the college. Like his father, he was active in public service. During World War I he went to Washington D.C. to become Fuel Administrator at the request of President Woodrow Wilson, a former colleague at Princeton, but he returned to Williams after the armistice. Always dressed in dark suits and starched collars and cuffs, he had little awareness of the ideas and needs of the students; however, he brought dignity and prestige to the college. Meeting with prospective faculty was primarily a formality. Gerald must have seemed satisfactory for he was immediately hired.

Dean Briggs had told Gerald that he could probably expect to get a salary of $2,000 a year, but the reality was somewhat less. On October 19, 1924, Gerald wrote to his friend Carl Dennett, "I have the job—Instructor in English @ $1,700 (not per month)—and my duty is to instruct 100 raving Freshmen how to write. . . . Teaching, you may not know—is no easy job. After four hours of freshmen, I feel as though I have been through a prize fight. Fortunately, I have only twelve hours a week of it. Correcting themes is a long and weary business."

Actually it was traditional in those days for new teachers to be given four sections of Freshman English with twenty-five students in each class. Gerald had had no training in teaching and the department gave new instructors no guidelines to follow. Everything had to be learned by trial and error. He had always been nervous speaking in public. He wrote Carl that he was trying to be dignified and learned. "Gentlemen—er—we will now take up the—er— consideration of the—er—abstract prepositional copulas beginning in—er —oh, ow, and blah." He claimed to have corrected 799 themes in the last ten days and while that was probably an exaggeration, he undoubtedly did find it easier to give his classes writing assignments than for him to lecture. It worried him that he must be boring his students, but since they were even more lost and bewildered than he, they treated him with respect. Still, he wrote to Huldah, he felt very humbled by the thought that he was responsible for the literary future of a hundred young men.

On his interview visit to the president's house Mrs. Garfield had promised to find Gerald a place to live and arranged for him to have a room at a boarding house run by a Mrs. McCormick. Professor Licklider, who had been assigned to introduce the insecure young man to the campus, took an immediate interest in him. They were soon calling each other Lick and Jerry, and Lick eventually managed to get him a room at the Faculty Club where he himself lived. They attended concerts and went on long walks together, for Lick had been a founding member of the Dartmouth Outing Club and was proud of his mountain climbing ability. He was something of an esthete, perhaps even homosexual, but he had cultural interests and knew how to live well. He introduced Jerry to his interesting circle of friends. In fact, it was at a dinner they attended at the home of Professor and Mrs. Pratt where Lick used his histrionic abilities to lead the game of charade. Jerry, as he was now called by almost everyone except his family, would later use the incident for a scene in his novel *The Spire*.

Jerry fitted in well at Williams. He was accustomed to all-male surroundings, and their conservative tastes matched his own. Professor Maxcy, the chairman of the department, had been trained as a student of oratory. He favored Victorian morality and Romantic sentimentality over the new realism and experimentations of the post-war writers. As Brace later explained:

> The mid-Twenties has been considered a time of ferment and revolt, and is still labeled with the word "roaring" but in comparison with the Sixties and Seventies it was a mild and modest period: the revolt was carried on by a small minority who were more conspicuous than influential, and their aim was more personally hedonistic than political or philosophical. (*DTW* II, p. 36).

Private institutions like Amherst and Williams considered it a responsibility to be bulwarks of civilization teaching taste and discrimination to the future gentlemen of a world that they believed was increasingly becoming controlled by Babbitts.

But at Williams, as at Amherst, Jerry was most captivated by the countryside surrounding the campus. Williamstown was close to two mountain ranges—the Taconic to the west and the Hoosic, with its towering Mount Greylock, four miles to the east. The school color was royal purple, the color of the distant mountains. It had been adopted in 1865 when Jennie Jerome (later Lady Churchill, mother of Winston) had purchased some purple ribbons that she and a friend made into rosettes to pin on the baseball players the day of a Harvard game, saying, "Let the royal purple be the Williams color and may it bring you victory over Harvard." The belief persisted, however, that the color had been chosen because of the purple hills surrounding the campus.

These hills constantly beckoned Jerry to leave his papers and explore. They inspired him to write a poem to Huldah when he returned one day from a long hike over a forgotten mountain road.

> I've seen the purple land, Huldah,
> Under the edge of the sky,
> I've seen November cloud shadows
> Swiftly sliding by.
>
> I've heard the sound of the wind, Huldah,
> November wind from the west,
> Beyond the wildest hill meadows
> Alone on a wild hill crest.

Gerald now found himself taken more seriously than ever before, though he still did not think of himself as a scholar. He wrote to Huldah: "I just love—if that's the right word. I give myself away to the beautiful things—and let them keep me." He wanted to be a novelist, a poet, an artist, a Transcendentalist; he did not want a life of research and critical thinking.

He spent a great deal of time preparing a book to give to Huldah for Christmas. He carefully wrote it by hand in a journal with simulated leather covers. In writing two fables for the woman he loved, he dared reveal more of his inner self than if he had been writing for publication. In his *Two Cloudy Stories*, "The City of Snum" and "Belinda," he parodies the pedantry of academia. Subconsciously, he also reveals his attitudes toward women. The tone is both playful and romantic. After the title page he wrote "Published by Jerry, Williamstown, Massachusetts (The Purple Land) 1924." Under "Books by the Same Author" he has written "Not yet" and the Preface warns "Not very many people ought to read this book. The stories in it are queer." Academic pretentions are satirized by an excessive number of foolish footnotes and annotations. Some of these are written just for Huldah's amusement:

> Footnote 39. Red-gold hair of Swinburne
> "Whose hair was a gold raiment on a king"
> and "Thy red hair's color burns me."
> Dr. Blink remarks in this connection: "One fails
> to see the purpose of red hair."
> Dr. Wink remarks: "The skill with which
> the author introduces color as the
> crowning feature of this vivid picture is
> little short of amazing."
> H. sticks out her tongue.

Throughout her life, Huldah would often stick out her tongue in place of an impertinent retort. Perhaps because it was a mannerism one could not imagine any of the Brace family using, Jerry always seemed to find this habit especially childlike and endearing.

Pages of footnotes are followed by a page blank except for the heading Appendix. Next comes a page stating simply "Appendix removed (P.S. What is an appendix?)" The whole spoof is dedicated to Huldah in the form of a poem written by the author.

> A little book of fairy things
> Misty clouds and airy swings,
> Close to a star;
> A little book of lollypops
> Bluebells and mountaintops,
>   Reaching afar,
> All for the solemn child,
> Red-haired and sun-beguiled,

Dryad or devil mild,
Infant or spirit mild!

A little book of summer skies
Saffron winged butterflies
   Floating in the blue:
A little book of moon flowers,
Castle roofs and grey towers
   —Written all for you.

Huldah did not seem to mind that he persisted in calling her an infant and treating her like a child because in many ways she felt infinitely more adult than he. Still one wonders what she thought of this latest offering. Both stories are foreign to her practical, no-nonsense nature. "The City of Snum" expresses Jerry's disfavor at the way civilization and politics destroy the freedom of men to walk strong and free. Giants (which he calls Wimble Men) are inveigled into giving up their life in the mountains to build a great city which is ultimately destroyed by war. The magnificent buildings crumble to ruins and the drab inhabitants who survive are dirty and ugly. But high on the mountaintops, the descendants of Miffle, the sage who had tried to warn them, still can be heard singing as they stride in the lofty Alpine meadows. Women had no role in the building of the city, which Jerry considers the business of men, but they too become victims of urban life.

The second story "Belinda," which he had originally written for Huldah's birthday while he was still a student at Harvard and she was working in Maryville, Tennessee, is more revealing of Jerry's penchant to see women as the stuff of dreams. He is still an almost unbelievable romantic. Inspired by the purple hills beyond Williamstown and perhaps by the color of Huldah's hair, he added a poem to the original account of Princess Belinda.

Sing a song of amethyst,
   Amethyst
Drifting on the breeze
Sing a song of mountain mist,
   Mountain mist,
Brushing through the trees;
   Brushing mist,
   Drifting mist,
Twisting, floating amethyst.

Sing a song of columbine,
   Columbine
Nodding one by one

Sing a song of amber wine,
    Amber wine,
Underneath the sun;
    Gleaming wine.
    Shining wine,
Winking, sunny columbine.

Belinda, "a little girl with red-gold hair" is transported to a pink cloud by a witch-like woman with a crooked nose. She sees a castle in the clouds, but when she tries to reach it, it slowly fades away. Making a last desperate leap for it, she falls to earth, landing near a maple tree next to her house just in time for supper. Jerry realizes that Huldah is too aware of the need for practicality to spend her life in a castle in the clouds, but he continues to try to make her aware of what she is missing.

He had hoped to buy her a copy of *Alice in Wonderland*, but now he had created his own version especially for her. Huldah may have been prosaic, but she could not help being moved by his final wish for her:

I wish you now the silver flakes
    Of softly falling snow
When winter wind the silence wakes
    And clouds come drifting low.
For Christmas time is fairy time
    And wishes may—perhaps—come true.

I wish you too the riding moon
    The radiant frozen light,
To give your heart the endless time
    Of every Christmas night.
For Christmas time is fairy time
And wishes may—perhaps—come true.

I wish you all your heart may hold
    Of gifts that beauty gives.
She's older now than stars are old
    —And in your heart she lives.
For Christmas time is fairy time
And wishes may—perhaps—come true.

As long as Jerry continued to return to his family at the holiday season and remembered the magical days of his youth, Christmas remained for him a magical time. As for Huldah, she was young and susceptible. Whatever her common sense told her, she couldn't help being flattered by his attentions.

In February he poured out his feelings about Huldah to Carl Dennett. He recognized their unsuitability for one another, but he was hopelessly smitten. "I love the lady very much—just as I love any beautiful and unconscious thing: the flight of a sea gull, a mountain, an orchid, the song of a thrush. Only I love her more than that: there is a magic in her; she is a sort of elf-child come to earth and she has come and taken hold of me, and she won't let go . . . . I can't imagine us living together: it wouldn't quite do to marry an elf-child would it? Sometimes I think she is just an animal: and yet she is too Christian to live in this brutal world." Love blinded him to Huldah's true character, both strengths and weaknesses, though to give her credit she didn't try to hide her faults from him. Even though he portrayed her as "fragile and pathetic" he was amused that she seemed to be "always raising Cain." Instead of sensing that the fact that she looked and behaved like a twelve-year-old might be a problem, he felt instead that it proved that like a child "she has never lost her cloud of glory." On the other hand he failed to credit her courage, competence, and strong determination.

Throughout the spring he continued to write volumes of letters to her in Boston. He felt that he was in no position financially to marry and wasn't sure that he wanted to give up his freedom, but as he wrote to Carl, "I have a fatal feeling that I am enmeshed! But then—I had the same feeling once before and I am still divinely free (or think I am). What can you do when you hold in your hand (theoretically) the power of life and death (figuratively) over a rare and red-haired maiden (literally)?" At the same time that he was thinking of marriage, he was determining that he would never be a traditional husband and father:

> I have made a General Resolve. When the day comes that I am a Family Man, I shall not be like other family men. No, I shall not bear upon my shoulders a load of coal bills and preferred stock and dinner parties. I shall not take Sunday walks with babies and cameras. I shall not wear a hat and muffler, neither shall I be respectable and afraid to look the sun in the face. I shall not be middle aged or well preserved. For all these and others destroy Life and Freedom, and bring about 100% citizenship.

He could not stop age and coal bills, but, as much as it was possible, he always remained true to this resolve.

Though Jerry professed to feel like an imposter in the academic world, his colleagues considered him competent, and his students took his teaching seriously. A small coterie of the school's most outstanding students began to gather around him as someone who represented a freedom from prejudice and a liberality not found in the older faculty. Mostly members of Kappa

Alpha fraternity, they treated Jerry as one of the brothers, and he would count them as friends for many years: Gordon Bailey Washburn, Dwight Little, John and Richard Sewall, Richard and Wentworth Brown, Lane Faison, and Ted Banks. They were only slightly younger than he, and in their company he found the intellectual stimulation and physical challenges he needed. They shared his idealism.

> We lived at that time in a state of considerable hope—hope for a life of usefulness and discovery and even adventure. We believed in the possibility of peace and freedom. We were still in the old-fashioned sense romantic idealists without much inkling of the world's drift toward catastrophe. The war, we thought, was over and done with, and all we had to do was follow our conscience and our heart's desire. We had a sense of things unfolding for the better, an illusion of constant and infinite progress on and on without end—an attitude that may have always persisted among men, but was specially characteristic of the American nation in the first half of the Twentieth Century, particularly during the decade of the Twenties when we were filled with a sort of confidence that amounted to hubris. 'Progress' was a daily fact, and we took it for granted that it was our national destiny. (*DTW* II, p. 40)

But the self-confidence of these young men was not hubris; they all went on to successful careers. Washburn and Faison both made names for themselves in the art world and were eventually made Chevaliers of the French Legion of Honor. Gordon Washburn was art director at both the Albright Art Gallery in Buffalo and at Rhode Island School of Design before becoming director of the Department of Fine Arts at Carnegie Institute in Pittsburgh. Lane Faison would spend most of his life teaching art at Williams, though during World War II, he took time out to serve in the art looting investigations under the OSS and the United States Navy. In 1950–51, the State Department made him director of the Central Collecting Point for Art in Munich. Dwight Little became an artist and for many years headmaster of Pine Cobble School in Williamstown. Richard Sewall would gain recognition as a distinguished biographer and critic of Emily Dickinson.

They talked about art and literature. Jerry enjoyed Jane Austen and Henry James. When they read Sinclair Lewis it confirmed their belief that it was their responsibility to save civilization from the Babbitts of the world. While against censorship, Jerry found James Branch Cabell's *Jurgen* unnecessarily explicit. They knew little of James Joyce or D. H. Lawrence, though the more sophisticated friends of Jerry's colleague Licklider spoke appreciatively of these new writers who were threatening to change the direction of modern literature.

Gerald had always lived his life largely in terms of books. Even the girls he went out with he saw as if they were fictional characters. "That's the way I see people—in terms of a page or two of description." This is useful for a budding author, but not the best way to choose a girlfriend or wife. He himself was aware that he often couldn't tell the difference between reality and his imagination.

He still fell easily in love. He met a young lady of "lyric splendor" at Smith and for a brief while he thought that perhaps she instead of Huldah was "the essence of the celestial glory of immortal human beauty." He had enough self knowledge to realize that he was fantasizing, for the same thing had happened to him "once or twice before." Perhaps because he suppressed his sexual urges, his flights of fancy made him prey to any pretty girl.

He was designing a boat that he was eager to have built, though he realized that he really couldn't afford it. Carl was selling stock for a company called Phonofilm and, convinced that there was a great future in "talkies," he was sure it would eventually provide Gerald with all the money he would ever need. Gerald agreed to buy some, both to help his friend out and in the hopes of a good financial return, though he wrote "I do hesitate at the thought of any more movies in the world—especially movies with a noise."

Dwight Little and Wentworth Brown were both members of the Williams Ski Team and they invited Jerry to train with them. He knew nothing about the sport, but he was immediately converted to the pleasures of both cross-country and downhill skiing. His equipment was primitive: unwaxed hickory flat skis with flimsy bindings, poles made from broom handles, and hiking shoes with heels altered by a cobbler. There were no ski-lifts or groomed slopes with man-made snow. The sport was still new enough that few people used trails. From the first time that Jerry found himself gliding down hill, he began to live in a dream of snow with "the yearning for greater and greater speed, the compulsive quest for perfect snow and endless downhill trails and slopes." (*DTW* II, p. 41) For once Jerry was with friends more athletic than he. Dwight Little could not only out ski him, but he was also a pole vaulter and runner. Jerry had great endurance, however. He took pride in the fact that he could run from Williamstown to the top of Mount Greylock and back to town in under three hours, and he still enjoyed walking thirty or forty miles a day in Vermont. He wrote Carl Dennett in March that he had recently climbed Mount Greylock in deep snow three times. The first time he had been accompanied by two athletic sophomores. The first one quit half way up; the other made it to the top, but nearly passed out. The second time he went with Lincoln Fairley, but the last time he went on skis alone. He was constantly having to physically prove himself.

His second year at Williams, Jerry brought back from Deer Isle the family Model T, though it proved rather useless in snowy weather. It lacked the power to buck through the snowbanks on the unploughed country roads. Finally he stored it in the Buffum's barn for the remainder of the winter. Jerry had always had a sense of invulnerability, walking alone over remote trails in all kinds of weather, with no fear of broken bones or hypothermia. That autumn, however, he became aware how death can strike when least expected. The family received word that his brother Charlie had died in a mining accident in Peru. He was only thirty-two and had a young pregnant wife. He would never get to see the daughter born in Lima, Peru, and named Helen Warner Brace, though called Elenita to distinguish her from her mother whose name was also Helen. Naturally impetuous, the fearless young man had been first to enter a shaft filled with deadly carbon monoxide. His grief-stricken parents were driven to Williamstown so they could be with their younger son who found lodgings for them in an old farmhouse on the edge of the village. Although it was only the fourteenth of October, that night it snowed. It seemed to Jerry that even nature was reflecting "a poignant end-of-the-world grief" obscuring the brilliant red and gold leaves under a heavy blanket of wet snow.

Gerald, at twenty-five years of age, now became the remaining hope in this male-oriented family. It was clear that if he was going to remain in academia, he needed to study for a Ph.D. His father was willing to provide the finances needed, but Jerry dreaded the thought of returning to the rigors of study and research. He wanted to be creative and free. However, proper credentials were becoming increasingly important for those with hope of advancement. His friend Licklider insisted that graduate work was essential. While the older professors were less certain, Professor Maxcy promised that there would always be a job waiting for him at Williams if he wished to return. Jerry was enjoying life in Williamstown; so it was with some reluctance that he decided to enroll in the doctoral program at Harvard. His only comfort was that there would be a long summer at Deer Isle before he had to return to Cambridge.

8
Marriage

Back at Deer Isle, Gerald was able to postpone all thoughts of academia. He and Eleanor continued perfecting their boat models to decorate the "Trivet." He worked on a novel in a desultory way, but it could always be put aside for a visit to the Lewises or Porters, or to go cruising with Lincoln Fairley or John Donaldson, or to spend time with Gordon Washburn who was staying for the summer at the Sylvesters' farm. Gordon, nicknamed "the Poet" by John because of his pose as an artiste, thought he too would like to try his hand at writing a novel. Each sunny morning, the two would-be writers took their chairs and lapboards outside to write. When their stint was over, the whole group of Braces, Donaldsons, and Gilchrists would sail in *Charmian*, *Bufo*, and Eleanor's dinghy in search of a deserted island on which to picnic. John and Gerald would carve little four- or five-inch boats with paper sails to launch into the waves to the delight of the children, for Betty's three little ones, as well as Dorothy's Julia, now spent part of each summer at Deer Isle. Usually the small boats would swamp, but when one did manage to sail to windward until it disappeared from view, there was a great sense of achievement. Vacation time was never long enough.

It was always hard to settle down after the carefree days of summer to a life of duty and discipline. The return to Harvard Graduate School was especially difficult. Jerry had never been a strong linguist and in those days a Harvard Ph.D. in English meant studying Anglo-Saxon, Gothic, Old French, and Middle English. Courses were bearable only because they met in the Germanic Museum where there was a ten-foot Viking ship model. Jerry could pretend that he was studying the language of the crew, though he was fully aware that they would have spoken Old Norse. If it had not been for his friend Cyrus Day who drilled him in grammar and Grimm's Law, he might never have succeeded in passing his courses.

Fortunately he was also taking a small seminar in Edmund Spenser taught by Douglas Bush who had received his Ph.D. from Harvard in 1923. He was just four years older than Jerry and had been equally dismayed when he learned that of the sixteen courses he was required to take, fourteen were in medieval languages and philology. Although he passed all his courses with high honors and had written an important thesis on *Mythology and the Renaissance Tradition*, he had determined that some day he would bring the Harvard English department into the modern age. It was not until 1936, after five years at the University of Minnesota, that he returned with enough prestige to renew his battle for a more humanistic approach. Meanwhile in his seminar, he indoctrinated his students into the beauty of Spenser's lines. He had a prodigious memory and could recite long passages. Still he insisted on sound scholarship and after writing one paper, more enthusiastic than scholarly, Jerry learned that he must carefully research every available source before turning in his work. He learned his lesson well and on his final paper "The Evidence for Spenser's View on Religion," he earned an A, though even on that Bush pointed out that while he admired Brace's writing style, he wished he had gone more deeply into the importance of Platonism.

Life outside of the classroom was enjoyable. Once again he and Lincoln Fairley roomed together with the Miss Dodds on Quincy Street and Jerry was allowed to park his Model T in their yard. He played a great deal of tennis with Cyrus Day. They became close friends who sailed and skied together, though Cyrus never let him forget that when they first met in Widener Library and Cyrus had invited him for a game of tennis, Jerry had responded stiffly, "I don't believe I know who you are." Day lived with his somewhat unstable mother who had once been a mental patient at McLean Hospital in Belmont, but it was his father from whom she had separated who entertained the boys. It interested Jerry that he was a cousin of Clarence Day whose *Life with Father* seemed to mirror the lives of many of Jerry's relatives. The stage set for the play almost replicated the drawing room, with its ornate Victorian furnishings smothered in drapes and tassels, where as a boy Jerry had visited the parents of his Aunt Bessie in their old-fashioned brownstone house in New York.

Jerry had a great fondness and respect for Ellen Coolidge, a friend of Aunt Leta and Uncle Jim Croswell. The year that Eleanor had worked for the South End Settlement House she had lived with Miss Coolidge in her house on the corner of Marlborough and Clarendon in Boston's Back Bay. Now in spring and fall, Jerry would drive Miss Coolidge and her companion Lillie Peck to the Coolidge summer place in Cotuit. The Italian girl, Telo di Benardi, still shared their apartment, and one day he drove them all to a big house on the foggy shores of Manchester-by-the-Sea. Perhaps he recalled this day years later when he was writing *Bell's Landing*. At the time, he was currently working on the novel that would be published as *The Islands* in which Miss Coolidge became a major character. No doubt Telo inspired the character of

Rose Fucci, the Italian fisherman's daughter, with whom the protagonist Edgar fantasized that he was in love.

One weekend while he was supposed to be studying for an Anglo-Saxon examination, he and Eleanor escaped by bus to Maine. They stopped at Camden where he climbed Mount Megunticook before supper and Mount Battie after supper. They reached Deer Isle that night. The unexpected freedom from the city and the passionate joy he found back in his own private world gave him a lift in spirits that he could only suggest in a letter to Anne Buffum.

> I woke—at first I didn't know where I was—And then I breathed and felt the air go flooding into my lungs—spruce and sea; and then I came to a little—and I heard: rustle of waters, breathing of big sea, one white-thrush far away: and then I looked out where the sunlight was, and the quiet trees shining up to the sky, and the flickers of silver light across the blue of the bay; and then I knew everything. That was the Biggest Moment—and if I were only a child, I could lie down and cry.

He could still be as passionate about Maine as for any woman.

Huldah had graduated from Boston University in 1925 and was now teaching science and mathematics at Lasell Seminary in Auburndale, six miles from Cambridge. She lived in Woodland Park Dormitory, a large Queen Anne former hotel once frequented by President Taft, and also by the Yale football teams whenever they played Harvard. Jerry had become firmly convinced that she was the only girl he loved in spite of her sharp tongue. When he couldn't manage to see her, he wrote letters. She warned him that he had created a picture of her that was false and that she certainly didn't understand half the nonsense he wrote to her. His reply was unworried. "Your fireworks belong to you as closely as my mountains belong to me." If her life was a constant series of highs and lows, he was afraid that she would find his more even temperament boring. He was not in the least alarmed by her warning that many people found her difficult, even fearsome. He answered: "I can perfectly well retort that your notion of me is also perverted—that I am selfish and hard and jealous of my freedom, that my life has all sorts of departments to it that you have only guessed at—and it would be perfectly true. . . . Of course if you handle me right you can do almost anything with me—as you have discovered."

Though Jerry was willing to admit that he was pliable, he felt she was wrong in calling him lazy, even if he did drift with whims "full of the echoes of the glories of life." He had been seduced while reading George Borrow's *Romany Rye* into believing that "Youth is the only season for enjoyment, and the first twenty-five years of one's life are worth all the rest of the longest life of man." Whatever disappointments or struggles he had, he was convinced of his own invulnerability, though he sometimes felt trapped between the world of his elders and his desire to liberate himself. He tried to explain that he was driven by a fierce independence; while she worried that she didn't belong in his world, she failed to understand that in many ways he didn't either.

Spring awakened his romantic fancies. In April he wrote expressing a wish that she could share the depth of his love for art and music and understand the emotions that flooded him whenever he listened to Tchaikovsky's "Symphonie Pathetique," "the most hopelessly beautiful of all human things." He begged her to try listening to it with her whole heart and soul. "There's a song in the Symphonie as remote as the sea—as strange and quiet and lonely—and there's another song that floats and dances like a swallow." He felt certain that she understood him better than anyone else, but he complained that his love for her was affecting his ability to write. His own emotions had become more important to him than those of his fictional characters; so he was not too surprised when the publishers sent back to him, with kindly regrets, the manuscript he had submitted.

Huldah still did not allow Jerry to show his feelings for her in any physical way. No doubt he was a bit awkward and self-conscious for he confessed that he had not kissed a girl since a birthday party when he was ten years old. It is difficult to know whether Huldah was prudish, certainly she had much of her father's rectitude, or was just afraid where it all might lead. Jerry apologized for revealing to her his "animal" needs, but assured her that she need not fear him. "I do admit that now and then the ordinary sex instincts get hold of me—but I can also say that in the last three months I have been more sure of my control over them than in any time over the last five years. Not that they have ever been very dangerous." Freud was just academic reading for these two proper young people brought up to believe in restraint and abstention.

For the first time Jerry was not looking forward to the summer if it meant their separation. He wrote to Huldah suggesting that she consider applying for a job at Deer Isle with the Olmsteds who were looking for summer help. The Olmsteds and Braces had been friendly for so many years that he was sure he would be welcome to see Huldah there regularly. He thought they would be pleasant to work for, though at that time he did not really know their tall, vivacious daughter Margaret well. Carol Olmsted was "like a little shadow—silent and very shy. People think she's queer, but I like her. They aren't personal, they aren't fussy, or selfish or critical or bossy." Huldah still had doubts about the wisdom of their becoming too closely involved. She felt that his romantic fantasies were blinding him to more practical considerations. She wrote suggesting that they break off their relationship, or at least that they try a three-month separation to sort out their feelings.

Perhaps it was well that Huldah chose not to live with the Olmsted family and have Jerry court her there, for later she would become jealous of Margaret. Shortly after Jerry and Huldah were married, Margaret had taken Huldah aside and warned her, "I'm going to take him away from you, you know." Undoubtedly it was only her dry Yankee sense of humor, but Huldah took it seriously. Son Loring, too, believes that the interest was more than casual, and recounts how once when Margaret visited them at Deer Isle, he "had the distinct feeling that she could easily have been the lady of the house instead of Mummy if events had taken a different course." Huldah wisely never tried to drive a permanent wedge between her husband and his lady admirers. Jerry was sometimes invited to bring his family for tea to the Olmsted home in Brookline where the two sisters lived in rather faded elegance. Loring remembers one occasion when his mother got the upper hand. The biscuits were tough, and Margaret complained that she couldn't understand why, since she had not left them to a servant, but had kneaded them with her own hands. Huldah remarked, with some self-satisfaction, "Everyone knows you handle biscuit dough as little as possible." If she could not match Margaret in social conversation, she felt secure when it came to knowledge about baking.

Instead of coming to Deer Isle that summer of 1927, Huldah went off to Brattleboro, Vermont, to work for the L. M. Bradley family of Milton. Jerry wrote to her with great regularity always entertaining and friendly, but not amorous. He described in detail visits with friends, especially a dinner with the Olmsteds, no doubt hoping that she would wish that she had been there. He amusingly described Frederick Law Olmsted's youngest son Rick who was there mending a fence. Like his famous father he preferred to be comfortable rather than stylish. Jerry thought he himself wore shabby clothes on the island, but, he wrote to Huldah:

> Uncle Rick had on older clothes than mine—trousers tied up with a rope—little spectacles on the end of his nose (so he could look out over them). . . . At supper he was explaining how he had been to a distinguished luncheon in New York—he's fixing up Central Park for them—and found when he got home that he had forgotten his necktie. Aunt Sarah didn't seem to mind. Aunt Sarah is Bostonian and strong-minded—and rather funny. Happy too. A bit impersonal both of them—one could like them for years and never make friends.

For the moment he had given up novel writing, but he was storing up images that would later resurface. He wrote of a sail to Isle au Haut. As he entered Duck Harbor he seemed to have reached the end of the world. "One small grey house, one lobsterman (who smiled), one boat—and the hills and the forest and the roar of the sea on the high shore. Nothing else for miles." It would later appear as *The World of Carrick's Cove.*

Jerry still had a long way to go before finishing his Ph.D., but the three months away from Huldah had made him decide that he couldn't live without her. If this meant marriage, then marriage it would have to be. He wrote to his family that he wanted to settle down even though he realized the financial problems. He was only earning a one-third salary at Radcliffe College as a part-time instructor and tutor. Huldah had given up her position at Lasell and had gone back to Boston University to pursue a Master of Science degree in biology. His father was willing to help financially, but he had other reservations. He wrote to his son: "I am sure that you and Huldah are wrong in believing that you can live together with less emotional strain than when apart. On the contrary, you will both of you be under an emotional sex urge that plays the devil with us and you will not be able to concentrate on your work." Jerry, however, could not believe that a man as old as his father could possibly understand his emotions. He, himself, felt certain that it would be much easier for him to return to his books once his longings for Huldah had been satisfied.

He had still not introduced Huldah to his family. At Thanksgiving he brought her to their New York Park Avenue apartment. Huldah was self-conscious, and perhaps a bit defiant. The Braces were courteous, but cool. It was not just that she was unsophisticated and from a different social class. Marriage would be an obstacle to their son's career. He still had his doctorate to finish and was partially dependent on his father for financial help. In addition, Huldah did not seem to share any of his interests. She knew nothing of sailing, had no aptitude for mountain climbing or skiing, was not artistic nor a lover of literature, and had little interest in society. Certainly, they must have felt that this was just another of their son's romantic fantasies.

It came as a shock to them to hear a week later that Jerry and Huldah planned to be married on December 6. There had been no engagement nor announcement. Mr. Fairley, who had left Jamaica Plain for a more liberal community church in White Plains, New York, would perform the small private ceremony. They would stay at his parsonage the night before. It was practically an elopement. They got the marriage license after they arrived in White Plains and Jerry bought Huldah a ring in Woolworth's Five and Ten Cent store. Not having a large wedding appealed to both of them. Jerry disliked all formal ceremonies and thought a near elopement much more romantic. Besides he always tried to avoid controversy, and the speed of their wedding forestalled any possible arguments with their families. Huldah took pride in being thrifty. It would be a very simple affair. There would be no trousseau, no attendants, and perhaps, they thought, no guests. Both families proved loyal, however. Gerald's father had suffered a slight stroke the summer before so was unable to go out in the bitter cold weather, but Mrs. Brace came accompanied by Eleanor, Muriel Postlethwaite, and Charlie's widow Helen. Mr. and Mrs. Laird and Huldah's sister Jane arrived by night boat from Boston. Most surprising of all was the arrival from Boston of Ellen Coolidge; so it turned into a festive occasion.

Gerald and Huldah marry

Except for Gerald's beloved Ellen Coolidge, it really was a family affair, for Muriel Postlethwaite was by now an important part of the Brace household, helping to care for Gerald's father and making life easier for Mrs. Brace. Muriel had been born in England, the daughter of an actress who left the baby in the charge of a nursemaid. Muriel always blamed her twisted, humped back on the fact that she, like the Dame of Sark, had been dropped down the stairs through the maid's carelessness. This explanation has been used so often it has entered the realm of myth and leaves one with an impression of careless nursemaids dropping their charges down long flights of stairs all over Britain. Whatever the truth, her mother had no place in her life for a crippled child and had sent her to Miss Wheeler's Boarding School in Providence, Rhode Island. Here she had been befriended by Eleanor who brought her home during school holidays. The two girls became constant companions. The kindnesses of the Brace family to Muriel were more than repaid as she took on the task of keeping their lives running smoothly.

As soon as the wedding ceremony was over, Jerry and Huldah had to leave. School was still in session so the honeymoon had to wait. After a night in a tourist home in Washington, Connecticut, and lunch in Amherst with Carrie Johnson, they arrived back in Boston. Lillie Peck, Ellen Coolidge's companion, had offered them the use of her apartment at the South End Settlement House and had a supper which included artichokes and drawn butter prepared for them, a dish which ever after Jerry remembered with nostalgia. She then left them alone to enjoy the apartment until school closed for the holidays.

Their first Christmas together, they stayed in Jamaica Plain with Huldah's parents who gave them the practical things they would need to start house-keeping. Aunt Leta Croswell gave them a silver tea service that had been presented to the family by Aunt Mary Greenleaf, sister of the poet Henry Wadsworth Longfellow. It was a symbol of her faith that someday they would have the kind of house and position to enable them to formally entertain.

Finally, the day after Christmas, they were able to leave on their honeymoon. Jerry had long wanted to show Deer Isle to Huldah. He had romantically dreamed of her first seeing its sparkling blue water edged by a coastline white with snow. It was a difficult trip in winter, by train to Rockland, then steamer to Vinalhaven, and then to Stonington, where they were met by Fred Sylvester in his Buick. In addition to their luggage, Jerry awkwardly carried his skis, determined to do some cross-country skiing. The reality proved nothing like his dream. Everything was bleak and grey with a raw, bone-chilling wind off the choppy, lead-colored water. Fred greeted Huldah with amusement. "You'd better watch out . . . he'll expect you to go off boating in the wet and cold—it's what he seems to like to do best." (*DTW* II, p. 66)

They were welcomed by Lillian Sylvester and her young daughters in the snug kitchen of Edgewood Farm. Normally the Sylvesters took boarders only in summer. Since there was no heat upstairs, the newlyweds were given a south facing room to catch any warmth available from the wintry sun, and supplied with handmade quilts on the bed and a hand braided rug to cushion the shock of stepping out of bed into the cold. Outside the window in the grey morning light of the next day they could see the sheep pasture and the wood lot, but they did not stop to admire the view. The pipes in the upstairs bathroom were drained in winter to prevent freezing; so Jerry and Huldah had to dash shivering to the heated kitchen to wash. Huldah must have appreciated a letter from Jerry's father commenting on their courage in going to Deer Isle in winter. "You must be brave to follow that wild boy about the world."

Huldah had often visited her grandmother's home in Vermont and enjoyed country living. Deer Isle still followed the old ways of life with most of its inhabitants earning their livelihood by farming, lobstering, or quarrying granite. It was a hard life. On days when the ground was frozen solid, Fred Sylvester spent his time chopping and sawing spruce into four foot lengths, burning the brush, and hauling the logs out of the woods on carts or sleds pulled by his two gentle oxen, Star and Bright. Fred quoted the old maxim "It'll warm you three times—cutting it, splitting it, burning it—and maybe lugging it makes a fourth." Jerry enjoyed working with him and proudly noted the calluses he was developing on his hands. It gave him great satisfaction to come back to the farmhouse after a hard day's work to find Huldah waiting for him in the warm kitchen redolent with the smell of newly made brownbread and slow-baking beans.

As a new bride, Huldah may have felt a little neglected, but she enjoyed the domesticity of the Sylvester household. Even though a sudden thaw turned all the roads to mud, Jerry insisted that she tour the island. He walked her to both Dunham's Point and Mill Island to see the boarded up old fam-

Fred Sylvester with Star and Bright

ily home of his childhood. She was less pleased another day when he took her on a long walk down muddy Dow Road to meet a plump, amusing girl who had worked for his parents the summer before. His new bride was tired, cold, miserable, and, perhaps, a bit jealous. Jerry never did get to use his skis. Though the damp cold could penetrate even the warmest clothing, the island rarely had the kind of deep powdery snow found in the hills of Vermont and western Massachusetts.

Huldah must have been ready to return to Cambridge and their new living quarters. Jerry's former landlady had found an apartment for them on the third floor of an Irving Street house for $35 a month. It was in a very genteel neighborhood, and the owner was really willing to rent it only because she knew Uncle Lincoln Hendrickson. Once again Jerry's relationship to that much admired gentleman had proved useful. Huldah was happy to settle into a place of their own even if the rooms were often cold and the supply of hot water erratic. Big Victorian houses were expensive to heat and Mrs. Warren, the owner, carefully monitored the fuel. There was no refrigerator; the wooden box they set outside the window kept their food cold enough in winter, but it was often invaded by squirrels. Huldah, however, was efficient and thrifty.

She abandoned both her graduate studies and plans for a career. Both she and Jerry accepted this as proper. Few women prior to World War II considered the possibility of having both a profession and family. To be a good wife and mother was deemed a full-time occupation. Huldah's married friends had all made the same decision, and felt vaguely sorry for single women pursuing a career either by choice or default. Though Huldah's Boston University classmates recall her as always in a white lab coat, busy with experiments, there is no suggestion that she ever regretted abandoning science for a family. Women rarely rose higher than being poorly paid laboratory assistants, especially if they were married, since it was rightly assumed that they would leave their jobs whenever their husbands found employment in another part of the country. Huldah was naturally domestic, and shared society's belief that a good marriage was the ultimate goal of a woman's life.

The couple had a busy social life. Mildred Norton, a college classmate of Huldah's, and her husband William Norton, a history professor at Boston University, saw them frequently. Then there were all of Jerry's friends: Cyrus Day, Lincoln Fairley and his wife Margaret, and his old roommates from Miss Dodd's, Leslie Janncey and Brodie Taylor. Sometimes it seemed to Huldah as if he had too many friends.

One day Jerry and Huldah returned from a concert at Symphony Hall to find a letter from his friend Dwight Little. He was planning to meet Terry Moore to ski Mount Washington. Even though the upcoming semester break was the first time that he and Huldah would have free time together in their new home, Jerry decided to join the men. In those days there was no weather station on the summit, and it seemed a very remote and dangerous place in winter. The three friends took their skis and caught a train from Boston's North Station to Intervale, New Hampshire. Somehow, Dwight and Terry's skis got left behind; so while they stayed to await the arrival of the next train, Jerry set off alone to ski the sixteen miles to Pinkham Notch. It was a dark, cold, solitary trip, but he arrived safely at the warm hut run by Joe Dodge. There were already two young men settled in. At nine o'clock that evening, they were finally joined by Dwight and Terry who had hired a car to take them to the end of the plowed section of road and then followed Jerry's tracks.

> It was actually, I believe, the last year the Pinkham Notch road was to remain unplowed, but at the time the place seemed forever locked in its wintry fastness. Its future as a resort for hundreds of cars and thousands of skiers was still undreamed of. In 1928 it was part of the vanishing Eden of wildness and beauty that we are forever seeking and losing. (*DTW* II, p. 72)

In the morning the three men, fortified with a hearty breakfast, took off along a trail that led to a carriage road. It was 10 or 15 degrees below zero with a northwest wind, but the snow conditions were good, dry powder on a four or five foot base. The Halfway House was shut for the season. It was only eight miles to the top, but on their primitive skis, they were unprepared for the force of the wind which threatened to blow them over into the ravine. They managed to reach the freezing cold cabin on the summit, which had a good supply of firewood; so they soon were able to get a warming fire started in its cast-iron stove.

As they started down the treacherous slope the next morning, they had to cross a brook on a couple of frozen logs, and then herring bone up the steep bank on the other side. Dwight became caught in a snow slide and fell head downward into an airhole directly above the running water, his skis caught crosswise between two spruce. It seemed hilariously funny, but they realized that if he had been alone he would have perished because there were no automatic releases on the bindings. No doubt it was this expedition that later suggested to Jerry the fatal accident atop Mount Washington in his novel, *The Garretson Chronicle.*

It was obvious by summer that Huldah would have to work to augment their meager income. She took a job at Camp Kekonka in Wolfeboro, New Hampshire, in May of that year. She was unhappy there, but Jerry urged her to try to stick it out. She did her duty, but it did not help her mood that he seemed quite content to study and spend time with his friends. To be sure he promised that if he got too lonesome he would drive up to see her, but said he was finding the time alone a good opportunity to get work done. Teaching, studying, and old friends were putting more strains on the marriage than either had anticipated. When Jerry was courting Huldah, he had never considered that marriage would mean changing his way of life. Nurtured on romances that ended with the lovers riding off into the sunset to live happily ever after, he had visualized married life as a continuation of his youthful days, minus the sexual frustrations, and with Huldah as a pliant partner. She had warned him that she could be sharp-tongued and possessive, but he had never considered that her blunt remarks might alienate his friends. He couldn't understand why she should feel hurt and neglected when he chose to spend his rare leisure with male companions. He answered her complaints that he seemed to enjoy their company more than hers with an underlying irritation of his own. He began his letter to her pleasantly enough with an account of going to visit the Nortons only to find their house in darkness. Soon his true feelings emerge, however.

> You talk about being "yourself"—but I don't know what that is . . . what is the "yourself" you must be: is it the part of you that boasts and scolds and criticizes and antagonizes? The part that insists on being the center of attention, that contradicts and lays down the law? Why should that be the 'real you'—any more than the part of you that is kinder and more thoughtful than anyone in the world? Why should you expect people to like the bad part of you as well as the good? . . . . You say your friends do: but your friends are always making allowances—and your friends are unnaturally kind. Is it fair to ask anyone to make allowances all the time?
>
> If I speak of these things you are desperately hurt: you say I do nothing but criticize you. If I loved you I wouldn't notice them. But when

the world I have lived in most of my life is suddenly estranged for no other reason than that you need self-discipline—should I keep silent?

He realized that his words would be hurtful, and he did try to mitigate them. He confessed that it took him a long time in school and college to realize that other people didn't consider him as important as he considered himself. He assured her that he depended on her "body and soul." Part of his pleasures with his friends had always been telling her all about them, but he realized now that this only made her more jealous of them. He promised to see less of them; he would even "try to give up Lincoln." Though he admitted that he could be moody and touchy, he found her demands difficult. He added plaintively: "I never thought you would demand constant affection—especially when you knew I wasn't specially affectionate."

Marriage had not turned out as Jerry had imagined it and the tensions didn't lessen when he took her back to the family home at Deer Isle for a visit. They all meant to be kind, but conversations were all about ropes and sails and weather. Huldah didn't even know how to row the small pram. She was not interested in any of the people they discussed; they might as well have been talking a foreign language. It was all polite, but distinctly strained. Knowing that she was being judged and found wanting played on all Huldah's insecurities and made her act even more prickly and difficult.

Huldah knew that, in spite of his lack of consideration, Jerry truly loved her and was trying to help her adjust to a new way of life. Fortunately they now had a second-hand Packard touring car with a canvas roof that could be folded back so they could make their visits to the island for just brief intervals at a time. They both enjoyed the breaks in their routine and the drive through some of the most scenic parts of Maine.

During the summer months, their third floor apartment became unbearably hot. At Boston University, Huldah had known Professor Samuel Waxman, head of the Romance Language department. She heard that he was looking for a house-sitter for his Cambridge house while he and his wife travelled to Mexico for the summer months of 1929. When she inquired about the possibility of their living there, he welcomed them to move in for ten weeks.

Jerry was working on his doctoral thesis and enjoyed having Waxman's comfortable study to read such eighteenth-century writers as Dryden, Walpole, Pope, and Addison who had written on landscape gardening. He was fascinated to discover that these writers whom he had previously scorned had been the arbiters of good taste for the emerging middle class in England as well as the aristocrats. Jerry's own interest in both art and literature combined as he saw how the landscape paintings by Claude and Poussin and Salvator Rosa had inspired the gentry to hire men like William Kent and Capability

Brown to reconfigure their estates—adding artificial lakes, grottoes, and fake ruins. He began to experience something of the pleasures of scholarship.

Jerry could never entirely live the sedentary life of a student. He and Huldah found time to play a lot of tennis: he often with Cyrus Day while she played a more leisurely game with Martha Sharp, who lived in an apartment on the second floor of the Waxman house. Huldah was not really a strong enough player for her competitive husband, though on occasion they played doubles. Cyrus Day's father invited Jerry and Huldah to join him and his son on a schooner he had chartered to sail from New Bedford, around Cape Cod to Marblehead. Jerry would crew and Huldah would serve as cook. Unfortunately she was so seasick all the way she could not go near the galley. It worked out fine because Mr. Day really liked to go ashore for meals, but it seemed incredible to Jerry that his wife was no sailor. Still they had fun. At the Cotuit Inn they lunched with Ellen Coolidge and Lillie Peck. At Nantucket they dined at another inn where they added Henry Stebbins, a famous yachtsman, to their crew. Huldah was relieved, however, when they reached Marblehead and turned the boat over to Cyrus' brother to continue on to Maine.

Back in Cambridge, she immediately turned her energies to painting and papering their hot third floor apartment to ready it for their return when the Waxmans came back on the 29th of September. Jerry's thesis had to be finished by the following March. Then he would have to face his Orals. He was still earning only $666.66 for his part-time teaching at Radcliffe; so Huldah took various part-time jobs assisting students with their research. The stock market crash and ensuing Depression meant little to them. Jerry did worry a great deal about his teaching, however. He disliked the pedantry of many of his fellow tutors, but he feared that he himself was inadequate. Under the old-fashioned, paternalistic presidency of LeBaron Briggs, education at Radcliffe had been mainly to create cultured young ladies, not place them in competition with men. When the formidable Ada Louise Comstock became president, women began to be taken seriously as scholars. Jerry had never taught girls before coming to Radcliffe. If they got poor grades he was afraid that it might be the fault of his teaching. He recognized also that he was susceptible to their charms and attentions and was concerned that this might affect his judgment. This happened at least once when an attractive, intelligent girl failed her comprehensive written examination. He wrote her a sympathetic letter suggesting that her readers must have been biased or stupid. President Comstock heard about it and promptly called him into her office where she soundly reprimanded him.

Although colleges were not yet feeling the full force of the Depression, they were becoming more cautious about hiring new faculty. Jerry spent the whole spring searching for a teaching position for fall. He had almost resigned himself to accepting an offer from Texas when he heard of an opening at Dartmouth College. He approached the interview with trepidation. Dartmouth was not only a fine ivy league college, but the country around Hanover, New Hampshire, fulfilled his dreams of mountains and woods. As Jerry later wrote in his autobiography, "I looked to the country of northern New England as my own promised land, and the prospect of cold winters and deep snow seemed wonderful to me." To his delight he was offered an instructorship in English for the coming academic year.

Meanwhile, his dissertation went quickly and well. The difficult economic times meant that good typists were willing to take any job available at very low fees; so he was able to afford a Boston Clerical School graduate to type his manuscript. When it was completed under the title "A Study of Literature in Relation to the Fine Arts in England 1650–1750," his readers accepted it without change. The three-hour Oral was a far greater challenge, for he was never very articulate, especially when all attention was centered on him. He worried about the first hour on linguistics, though his friend Cyrus Day had tutored him well and Professor Grandgent, who conducted that part of the examination, was kindly. Professor Kittredge was dubious about Jerry's knowledge of Shakespeare, but in spite of a few blanks he was passed unanimously by the committee.

Jerry was so exhausted and limp from the ordeal that Lincoln Fairley had to take over the job of moving the Braces' possessions in a hired truck to Jamaica Plain to be stored for the summer. Jerry knew he was fortunate in those difficult economic times. In addition to being granted his Ph.D. from Harvard, he had been awarded the Charles Dexter Travel Fellowship to finance a European summer trip, he had a job at Dartmouth for the fall, a new baby was on the way, and a house was being built for them just across the river from Hanover, in Norwich, Vermont. The future looked bright.

9
Travel With Huldah

When Jerry had toured Europe with Eleanor it had awakened in him an interest in the art and culture of the places they visited. Now he hoped it would do the same for Huldah. She was in the early days of pregnancy, but the obstetrician they had visited in Hanover, New Hampshire, had pronounced her health excellent. While the Harvard fellowship he had been awarded was not large, the severe economic depression in Great Britain and the comparative strength of the dollar made it a good time to travel.

The night prior to their departure they stayed in the New York apartment of Uncle Rob and Aunt Bessie. On June 5, 1930, they boarded the small, one-class, American steamship on which they would cross the Atlantic. Knowing her tendency to seasickness, Huldah must have had some qualms, which were quickly realized as soon as they were at sea. However, their send-off was exciting with both of Jerry's parents, his sister Eleanor, Muriel Postlethwaite, and Aunt Emma all at the dock to wish them bon voyage.

Although the weather remained calm for the seven-day crossing, Huldah was sick until they reached the calmer waters of the English Channel. The ship stopped at Plymouth before continuing all the way up the Thames estuary to London's Royal Albert Dock. Huldah revived at the sight of St. Paul's dome and all the Wren church towers against the skyline, while Jerry gloried in the activity of the river barges and a full-rigged ship which was under tow.

Betty and her husband were there to meet them at the dock. When Huntington was made European representative of the American Cyanamid Company in London, the Gilchrists moved into a large house in Edwards Square across from a semi-private park which had lawn tennis courts and plenty of room for the nursemaid to take their children, Johnnie, Charles, and Brenda, for walks and play.

As soon as Huldah had regained her equilibrium, the Gilchrists took them to see the British countryside. They drove across the South Downs, dotted with sheep, to the towering white cliffs of Beachy Head. They visited Battle Abbey and Hastings, to see where Harold had been slain during the Norman

Conquest, and then enjoyed the romantic ruins of Bodiam Castle with its moat filled with waterlilies.

Huldah dutifully began a travel journal, more factual than descriptive, but like so many sightseers, she abandoned writing in it before the trip was over. When Huntington's mother arrived on the 17th of June, the Gilchrists arranged for Jerry and Huldah to stay at Lloyds on 48 Claringdon Road. The next week they all drove to see the cathedrals at Canterbury and Rochester. In London, Jerry tried to see the Wren churches that he had described in his dissertation. In those days he believed that the excesses of Baroque and Victorian architecture bordered on the sinful, and even the neo-classical churches of England seemed over-decorated. He considered them ostentatious and less functionally beautiful than their American counterparts. Although he admired St. Paul's, it too appeared pretentious and less genuinely Christian than the austere purity found in New England churches.

Careful as they were of finances, they did do some major shopping, for the currency exchange made it possible to get some excellent bargains. Huldah bought a raincoat in Burberry's, and Jerry bought a tweed suit. Then they bought a small Morris-Cowley coupe just big enough for the two of them and their luggage. There were no locks on the doors, but they were assured that this was because there was no traffic in stolen cars in England. They had chosen the car because of its buy-back agreement. Later, when he was charged an additional sixty dollars for misuse, Jerry felt that he had been mistakenly identified as a wealthy American and cheated. He failed to consider that when the car had had engine trouble, he had inexpertly tinkered with the motor himself instead of getting professional repairs.

Driving on the left was difficult at first, especially in London traffic, but he soon grew used to it. They successfully made it to Winchester, a city that interested him more for its Jane Austen connections than for the architecture of its cathedral. Entering Salisbury, he was thrilled to see the pointed steeple of its cathedral rising up against the clouds just as it appeared in the paintings by Constable. This was the gateway to Thomas Hardy's Wessex where, in one day, they visited Cerne Abbas, Puddletown, and Dorchester.

On the earlier walking tour of Switzerland, Jerry and Eleanor had had time to absorb the landscape around them. Driving rapidly through Britain he and Huldah could not fully appreciate the English countryside. Tense from driving, with Huldah too carsick to want to alight, they missed the very things that Jerry would have most enjoyed. Huldah seems to have taken little real pleasure in the literary and historical sites. Jerry did not feel he should leave her in the car while he took long walks. A Hardy enthusiast, he would have rejoiced in striding across Egdon Heath, perhaps even stopping to stand like Eustacia Vye on top of Rainbarrow, or to follow the path through the watermeadows along the Frome to Stinsford Church. He would have thrilled to the sound of larks over Bulbarrow, and to circle the high embankments of Maiden Castle. One suspects that they even failed to notice the Cerne Abbas giant, for Huldah makes no mention of it in her journal and certainly she would have been shocked by that great chalk fertility figure. Although Jerry's fellowship entailed no requirements, he felt a certain responsibility to visit the grounds and great houses of the seventeenth and eighteenth centuries in which he had specialized, but when they did stop at a church or garden, he had just time for a quick survey of architectural features or the layout of the landscape knowing that Huldah was waiting impatiently in the car. He had never before had to travel with another person in the cramped confines of a tiny car with only limited opportunity to explore the places that interested him. Travelling with a wife, especially one in the first trimester of pregnancy, was not at all what he had anticipated.

The fact that Huldah could not find any food that she could stomach did not help the situation. As non-drinkers they avoided the country pubs where they might have found plain, wholesome fare. They didn't want to spend money for expensive restaurants, so they ate in cheap eating places in the centers of the towns along the way which meant that they were served a steady diet of tinned peas, fried fish and chips, boiled broad beans, cold toast, and greasy bacon.

They were both momentarily revived by the sea air when they reached the west coast. They climbed down to the sea at Clovelly, visited Boscastle, and scrambled across the rocks at King Arthur's castle at Tintagel. Their difficulties returned as soon as they turned inland across Dartmoor where they had to spend scarce money on a new tire to get them to Exeter. Jerry's frustration was mounting as they drove through Glastonbury, Bath and Cirencester. At the latter, he was able to relieve some of his tensions by running up the long avenues of Lord Bathurst's park. Huldah recorded in her journal that he "ran for miles & miles thru endless avenues of trees."

Jerry considered Gloucester Cathedral, its nave flooded with light from the great fourteenth century East window, the most beautiful of all the churches he had seen. He was eager to reach Tintern Abbey where he looked forward not only to seeing the ruins, but to experience Wordsworth's "sounding cataract . . . the tall rock, the mountain and the gloomy wood." Instead, he drove the car into a hole and had to walk to the castle at Penbridge to find someone to help extricate it.

The food proved no better when they reached Wales, but while Huldah waited in the car, Jerry had the pleasure of climbing to the summit of Mt. Snowden, cutting a half hour from the time suggested in the guidebook. Although not much higher than Mt. Greylock, the trail was much steeper, especially near the bare and rocky top. Always proud of his climbing speed, Jerry carefully recorded his time in the old 1911 Baedeker which he had borrowed from the Gilchrists and which is still treasured by his nephew John. But here, as so often, he spent little time enjoying the magnificent panorama of sea, lakes, and valleys.

It was not until they reached the English Lake Country that they both felt that all their expectations were fulfilled. There were few tourists and the weather was fine. With only sheep for company, Jerry finally found the pristine beauty he was seeking, as he followed the grassy trail where Coleridge and Wordsworth once had walked. The poetry of Wordsworth had filled his soul with exultation and taught him the pleasure of solitary contemplation. At Grasmere he came close to the England of his youthful dreams, and even Huldah took pleasure in the picturesque surroundings.

Scotland with its mountains, lakes, and spruce reminded him of northern New England. He left Huldah long enough to climb Ben Nevis, a feat he accomplished in two hours and forty minutes, far faster than the guidebook estimate, and once again he carefully recorded his time in the margins of the guidebook. He spent little time at the top. He had a poor head for sheer heights. It was not the view, but the climb itself that challenged him.

They continued on to Edinburgh where they picked up mail for the first time and Jerry finally received official notice of his Dexter Fellowship. They found that in Scotland, the addition of salt to the porridge made it slightly more palatable, but otherwise the diet was unvaried. Jerry enjoyed the hills surrounding the city; however, he was appalled by the Victorian memorial to Sir Walter Scott. Although he had read little Scott at that time, they visited Abbotsford, his baronial home, and Dryburgh where he was buried. Later, when he read the novels, Jerry was amazed at how Scott had managed to encompass the whole range of people from monarchs to gypsies during all periods of Scottish history. He felt more than ever that Scott was worthy of a monument that accurately suggested his "spiritual presence" rather than the ornate monstrosity that dwarfed the statue inside.

The car continued to be a source of frustration. While on the streets of Edinburgh, Jerry misunderstood a traffic policeman's signal. He was mortified to have him yell at him "Hae ye no been in the ceety beforr!" When the car developed a gas leak, Jerry fixed it himself, but it was always difficult to get the engine started. The tires constantly needed repairs. Nevertheless, they set out through the highlands to Oban where they were delighted to find a room in an inexpensive Temperance Hotel until they discovered it was just across a narrow alley from a dance hall where bagpipes skirled all night. After managing about two hours of sleep they took the ferry to the Isle of Mull. They returned to Edinburgh by way of Glasgow and then turned south to

Housesteads. Here they walked on Hadrian's Roman Wall and admired the green fields with grazing sheep far below.

Though Huldah always recorded in her journal how Jerry felt about the places they visited, she never commented on her own reactions. She considered it his trip. At Lincoln Cathedral, he quickly visited what was left of the shrine to little Saint Hugh, whose story he knew from Chaucer's Prioress' Tale, but once again Huldah did not go inside. At Cambridge, too, she sat on a bench in the sunshine while he visited the University Library and Fitzwilliam Museum.

It was Jerry who was feeling ill by the time they reached Oxford. He recovered enough to go to the Bodleian Library where he found it incredible that nobody questioned his right to handle an original edition by Christopher Wren. At Blenheim Palace, Jerry had the opportunity to see a lake and park designed by Capability Brown. He had received his grant partly for the purpose of seeing the gardens he had written about in his dissertation, but in this he was not very successful. Although many of the owners of stately homes were in financial difficulties, they still had not reached the point where they were forced to open their gardens to the public. If Jerry had written ahead, he undoubtedly could have arranged to see some of the important ones, but he had not bothered to do that. Neither aggressive nor enterprising, he usually just assumed that things would work out.

Jerry was worried that Huldah might be becoming seriously malnourished. It was with relief that they returned to the Gilchrists where for a week the cook prepared fresh fruit and vegetables for her. By the time they left for France, they were both much more cheerful. Huntington had to be in Paris for a business meeting. Though they had a room in humbler quarters than the Hotel Crillon where he stayed, he took them to his private club for dinner. It was a memorable experience. Not only was the food delicious, but they were able to observe "the full ritual of the French cuisine, with long preliminary discussion of a menu and the solemn selection of wines and soups and entrees and the miraculous operation of chafing dishes and the succession of courses with profound and anxious obeisances." (*DTW* II, p. 93) Huldah began to take great pleasure in the sidewalk cafes with their brioches and omelets and casseroles. By the time they left for Switzerland she was once more energetic.

They stayed in a chalet inn surrounded by the Alps. Huldah even climbed trails at the foot of the mountains while Jerry ran on ahead. After five days they left for Italy, going by train to Milan, from which they visited Lake Maggiore, and then on to Rome, Florence, and Venice. Their hotel was far different from the palazzo on the Grand Canal where Eleanor and Jerry had stayed. Huldah was always afraid that Jerry was being cheated, which on one occasion led to an altercation with a gondolier who pursued them, cursing, up to St. Mark's Square. No one paid them much attention, but Jerry was thoroughly embarrassed.

Huldah abandoned writing in her journal after they travelled through the Tyrol to Innsbruck, though they continued on to Munich and then west to take a steamer down the Rhine to Holland, a country which they thought self-consciously quaint and over-commercialized. In Hamburg, where they stayed for several nights, Jerry bought himself new skis, bindings and boots to replace the rather primitive equipment he had always had to use. It was a slow nine-day voyage home, for the ship made stops at Boulogne, Galway, (where they picked up a group of loudly drunken priests), and Halifax before arriving in Boston. Here they were met by Huldah's parents.

They were glad to be home. The trip had been too long and covered too much, especially since they had felt a need to be economical and Huldah had been ill so much of the time. It had failed to fulfill Jerry's expectations. He had been fully cognizant when he married Huldah that she did not share the cultural interests of the Brace family. Recognizing her intelligence, he had looked forward to educating her. In his innocence about women he had not only seen her as his Princess Belinda, but had thought he would be Pygmalion with her as Galatea. He learned on the trip that she had no desire to be transformed. If she had used her feminine wiles to cajole him, he would have done anything she wanted, but she scorned pretense and would not evince an interest in art and foreign culture that she did not feel. She intended to be a good wife and mother, but she had no intention of changing her ways for any man.

10
Dartmouth College and a Growing Family

In spite of the Depression, Jerry was secure in his knowledge that he was returning to a good position in the fall and, at least the promise of a new house. The Trustees of Dartmouth College had voted on April 28, 1930, to make him instructor in English with a salary of $2,600 a year. They would have arranged housing in the town, but he and Huldah wanted to be out in the country.

They had gone to Hanover, New Hampshire, in June, before leaving on their trip, to look for a place to live and to visit the campus. Everything about the place seemed perfect! The college was located in the heart of ski country with mountains and woods and trails all around. The medical facilities were excellent. Even though the medical school had at that time lost its right to offer an M.D. degree, the hospital had wisely set up the Hitchcock clinic in 1927 with a multidisciplinary group practice which encouraged top physicians to come to Hanover, including the obstetrician who would care for Huldah. For the first time they would have a real home.

As soon as they saw the village of Norwich, Vermont, just across the Connecticut River from Hanover, they were charmed by its rural surroundings and gracious brick houses. They soon realized that such big homes would be too expensive to heat. By good fortune, they met a part-time real estate man by the name of C. C. Hills. He informed them that he owned a piece of land that would be perfect for them. It had a brook, a stand of maple trees and a good spring. Furthermore, electric lines were all in place. He could easily build them

The new house in Norwich, VT

87

Jerry proudly shows off sons Gerald and Loring — 1934

a small Cape Cod type house with two bedrooms before they returned in the fall. Rent would be $35 a month. Some of the people at Dartmouth who knew Mr. Hills thought they were being too trusting, but they closed the deal before they left.

It all worked out exactly as they had hoped. The house was receiving its final coat of paint when they arrived. The white had been faintly tinged with pink so that it glowed warmly in the autumn sunlight. The maple trees were a riot of brilliant colors against the dark green of the firs. With the gift of an electric range from Mr. Laird, and some new furniture to augment the little they already had, they were ready to settle in. The house was near enough to the campus so that Jerry could walk across the meadow, down the dirt road and across the wooden covered bridge to the college.

It was an exciting time to be at Dartmouth. It had just gone through a major period of expansion under the leadership of its eleventh president, Ernest Martin Hopkins. Several imposing brick Georgian buildings had been built at right angles to the old wooden buildings on Dartmouth Row. The centerpiece was the Baker Library surmounted by a white spire and weathervane which depicted Dartmouth's founder Eleazer Wheelock teaching an Indian under a pine tree. Although the library had been dedicated two years before Jerry arrived, it was still in the process of growth. George Fisher Baker had given a million dollars for its construction just before the 1929 stock market crash. While Jerry was teaching there, Jose Orozco, the Mexican muralist, came to paint his famous frescos for $300. Later he was made a member of the Art faculty to get financing which would permit him to finish them after the college had to cut back on its expenses.

Sanborn House, which sheltered the English department, had been newly added next to the library. It too was a handsome brick building. The poetry room was a replica of the study of its donor Professor Edwin Sanborn. There was also a room patterned after one designed by Christopher Wren. Tea was served every afternoon to both students and faculty.

The Humanities Division had a distinguished faculty. Professor Stearns Morse, author of several books on the White Mountains, was a noted raconteur.

Sidney Cox was a close friend of Robert Frost. When he discovered that Jerry had studied under Frost and admired his poetry, he immediately sought him out as a friend. Ramon Guthrie, a war hero who had been in Paris with Ernest Hemingway and F. Scott Fitzgerald, was also a close friend of Sinclair Lewis. He had come to teach French at Dartmouth the same time as Jerry, and the two became frequent skiing companions.

The Dartmouth Outing Club sponsored skiing and snowshoeing activities. Jerry was in his element, but it must have been lonely for Huldah, pregnant and isolated from the other campus wives. She had only her Irish setter puppy, Terence O'Shay, for company much of the time. Not that she would have wanted to be part of their circle, for as on any rural campus where the wives had nothing to do but promote their husbands, there was a lot of rivalry and gossip. Sidney Cox's wife resented her husband's adulation of Robert Frost. He had first met the poet in 1911 when they were both teaching at the New Hampshire State Teachers College in Plymouth. They continued to correspond all the while that Frost was in England and remained good friends for most of their lives, though many decades later, Frost rejected Cox as too fond and embarrassing. Now, Cox was happy to be at Dartmouth which had given a scholarship to Frost at the time of his graduation from Lawrence High School. To be sure Frost, who decided that academic studies were interfering with his poetic creativity, did not complete his freshman year, but he frequently gave poetry readings at the college once he became known.

Jerry had plenty of opportunities to indulge his love for outdoor activities, for at Dartmouth most of the professors, as well as students, were athletic. Stearns Morse, a veteran mountain climber, and Sidney Cox kindly invited their new colleagues, Jerry and Harold Blodgett, to climb Mount Washington. Starting at Willey's House in Crawford Notch they reached as far as the Cloud's hut where they spent the first night. The next day they reached the summit. Jerry sprained his ankle so had to whittle a crutch from a scrub spruce to enable him to make the descent. Once again he saw how quickly accidents can happen. Carl Dennett and Lincoln Fairley also often joined Jerry in expeditions to Killington, Moosilauke, and Tuckerman's Ravine.

All this athletic activity did little to promote Jerry's creative writing or scholarly research. He did try writing one article called "The Age of Taste" based on his Harvard studies of the eighteenth century, but no one seemed interested in publishing it. He also wrote an academic paper entitled "Reflections on Looking Backward." Though it remains unpublished it is a good source for learning about Brace's admiration for the past. He felt that the golden days of colonial architecture and the pure lines of the clipper ships like the *Flying Cloud* had given way to a more ephemeral type of art and architecture. Even though he disliked Gothic reproductions, he suggested that Keats in "The Eve of St. Agnes" and Beckford in building Fonthill Abbey had some of the right feeling no matter how absurd the details. By the 1930s he feared that art had reached the end of its momentum. Throughout his life he would express the belief that "the tenderest of our few illusions is that of the idyllic past."

On December 19, 1930, Huldah gave birth at Mary Hitchcock Hospital to a son who inherited the family name of Charles Loring Brace IV. She had been inconsolable when her Irish setter had contracted distemper and had to be put to sleep, but now the new baby filled her time. At Lasell she had taught child care as well as biology and mathematics, so she felt competent to assume motherhood.

In April the trustees renewed Jerry's contract with a modest raise of $100. As the baby made traveling complicated, they spent most of the summer in Norwich. Jerry tried to do some writing in the college library, but it went slowly. They briefly visited the Buffums in New York and made a short trip to Rutland, Vermont. Finally near the end of the summer they felt the baby was old enough for them to attempt the long ride to Deer Isle. They arrived back in Norwich the day before school was to open. Jerry was feeling ill, but he felt it his duty to meet the new students. He came home that afternoon feeling so miserable that Huldah sent for the doctor. By the time he arrived Jerry had already become semi-conscious and delirious. He was transported to Dick's House, the college infirmary, where he was soon diagnosed as having polio.

Before Dr. Salk discovered a vaccine, polio was the scourge of summer. The aftermath, iron lungs and heavy braces, was all too common among those who survived. Jerry was one of the lucky ones for he was not permanently paralyzed, but he never had quite the same indefatigable endurance again. He was fortunate that he was able to spend his month in quarantine on the third floor of Dick's House. The new Georgian brick building had been given in memory of a Dartmouth sophomore who had died of polio in November of 1924. It had been built to look as much like a private home as possible. The rooms were modern and comfortable, and the lounge—furnished by the Class of 1927, the year Richard "Dick" Hall would have graduated—had in it the flag brought back from the first trip to the South Pole. The flag was given by Richard E. Byrd, a friend of the Hall family. Best of all, the building was attached to the main hospital so Jerry was assured the best of medical care.

His illness was catastrophic for Huldah who had never learned to drive and knew nothing about finances. With the bank account in Jerry's name only, she could not even cash a check. Her parents drove up from Massachusetts to bring her some money, but mainly she was dependent on Ed and Jean Booth for transportation and succor. They were the only members of the faculty to realize how much she needed aid, though a number of Jerry's colleagues, especially Sidney Cox, took on the burden of teaching all his courses on top of their own loads. Even when Jerry was allowed to come home, things were not much improved. He could not tolerate bright light and his muscles were weak and painful. Of course, there was always the fear that he might never totally regain his strength. To add to their worries, Huldah was pregnant again. In one short stretch of time, the idealistic, hedonistic young man had become an enervated mature man uncertain about the future.

Huldah was a good nurse, and Jerry gradually regained his health. By Christmas they were able to drive to Jamaica Plain. Here, Mr. Laird, who always seemed to know someone who could make a deal, found an auto dealer willing to sell them a small heated Studebaker in exchange for $700 and their old temperamental Packard. The new car was not only more comfortable, but it was much safer on icy roads. While the two men might not have had much in common, Jerry appreciated his father-in-law's instinctual knowledge of machines and mechanical devices. Like the Maine islanders, Mr. Laird could repair almost any clock or motor; Jerry always seemed to end up with either an extra piece or one missing.

By the opening of the new term, Jerry was able to return to teaching and even walk or ski the distance to Hanover. A month later, on February 26, 1932, a second son was born and named for his father, Gerald Warner Brace. In time of need Margaret Buffum, Anne's older sister, was always willing to help. She came from Shushan, New York, to look after the household while Huldah was in Mary Hitchcock hospital. Women stayed in the hospital for two whole weeks in those days, but after Huldah returned home Jerry took Margaret to a gentle slope in Norwich where he taught her to ski. It was his first attempt at downhill skiing since his polio. The first time he succeeded in making a complete turn he had a great sense of accomplishment. He realized that he was slowly gaining back his strength and control.

Margaret, with a high school girl to help during the day, came again to look after both babies when Huldah's sister Jane was married in Jamaica Plain. Huldah served as matron of honor. Jerry and Huldah managed to smuggle the newlyweds off to Boston's South Station to begin their honeymoon, but they both had a sense of foreboding that the marriage wouldn't last—which, indeed, it didn't. Within a couple of years Jane returned to Boston alone. When her father died, she moved in with her mother and resumed her maiden name. After the wedding, Jerry and Huldah returned home tired and disturbed. Unfortunately, young Gerald picked that time to be ill. As Margaret Buffum recalls he "heaved Jonah" all over himself and his crib "and his parents came home before I got all cleaned up. Huldah, looking very grim, did a great scrub job almost as soon as she arrived. Anne and her husband offered to drive up from Shushan to drive me home, but Jerry wouldn't hear of it—

he'd take me himself. So he did—singing quite a bit of the way." No doubt he was much relieved to be with an old friend on the open road instead of home with a sick child and an unhappy wife.

The Depression was finally seriously affecting the college. When Jerry received his contract in the spring, he was rehired for the following year, but without a raise in salary. For the first time, he wore his new doctoral robe to the Dartmouth commencement. Meanwhile his parents decided to sell their New York apartment and spend their time alternating between Santa Barbara, California, and Deer Isle. They said they would need a place to stay in the spring and autumn and offered to pay for Jerry and Huldah to move into a bigger house large enough to accommodate them. It was a fiction that the older Braces devised to aid their younger son and his growing family. They even arranged for them to hire a cook and a maid to help with the housework and the children.

Jerry and Huldah found the perfect place to rent. It was a brick house on the edge of Norwich village. There was a room and bath off the kitchen for the cook and four bedrooms and two baths upstairs so that the elder Braces would have a private room and bath when they stayed there. The two car garage was heated. Best of all there was a pretty little waterfall which had powered the gristmill when the miller had lived there. The house was partially furnished, but there was ample room for their things. Its owner, Professor Stacy Mays, a Dartmouth economist, had been called to Washington to help Franklin D. Roosevelt set up his plan for the New Deal. The Mays wanted to return to Norwich in the summer which was when the Braces would be at Deer Isle; so it was an ideal arrangement for both families.

That summer the Gerald Braces, accompanied by their cook, rented a small cottage near the main Brace house at Dunham's Point. John Donaldson promptly dubbed it the Pepper Box, playing on the word "salt box." With his new seriousness of purpose, Jerry set aside three hours every morning to work on the novel he had so hopefully started in Dean Briggs' class a decade earlier. From his bedroom window he could look across the bay to Eagle Island, the setting for the novel. While his young sons played happily in the tidal pools below and sails dotted the distant horizon, Jerry lost himself in his fictional world. It was on one such morning that he saw a sight on the bay so wondrous that he never shared it with anyone until he wrote his autobiography many years later: "It was a small pure-white whale—or perhaps a beluga or big dolphin—that rolled out several times and then disappeared forever: it is a vision fixed clearly in my mind's eye—the morning silvery blue waters and that shining white shape emerging and diving and finally vanishing . It seemed to me a visitation from another world—like a heraldic creature sent on a sea-god's mission." (*DTW* II, p. 109) His hopes for a career as a writer revived and he faced the blank yellow pages of his notepad each day with renewed enthusiasm.

He had loved visiting Eagle Island even as a boy. It was the kind of self-sufficient community prevalent on islands off the Maine coast in the days before roads and automobiles replaced sailing vessels and steamers. It had been continuously inhabited, mostly by the Quinn family, since 1810, and had a well-established settlement of farms, school, post office, and lighthouse. In addition to farming, the men wrested a living from the sea. They fished for mackerel, built weirs, captured herring in purse seines, dragged for scallops, and trapped lobsters. Some of the old barns along the ridge had been converted into boathouses where, in addition to a few larger vessels, the islanders built mostly double enders. When Jerry designed a nineteen-foot centerboard sloop for Eleanor in 1933, she had it built by Erland and Bonny Quinn on the island. Since Eleanor at that time was a lively lady in her forties, John Donaldson facetiously suggested that it be called *The Roaring Forties*, a word-play on both Eleanor's age and the nautical term for the latitude where the westerly winds strongly blow. The name was immediately adopted. Jerry sailed to the island regularly to check on its progress and was impressed anew at the natural fine craftsmanship of these local builders.

One reason that the community on Eagle lasted longer than some was that the Quinns had early realized the importance of summer guests. In 1900 the Quinns built a boarding house. Until 1915 visitors to Eagle were picked up at nearby Butter Island which had steamer service, but after that ended, the Quinns met them at Rockland or North Haven. Some of the regular visitors built summer cottages. The island was fortunate in having a lighthouse. The children of the civilian keepers kept the school alive and many of the older daughters married natives and decided to remain. The picturesque beacon high on the rocky coast and its warning bell were dependable guides for sailors and fishermen who might find themselves confused by fog.

The rugged beauty of Eagle Island appealed to Brace as both an artist and a writer, and the people who made a difficult living on its forbidding terrain typified the independent New Englanders that he most admired. He was aware, however, that such self-contained communities were threatened by modern technology. He wanted to capture, in words, this world he knew so well before it disappeared. Local boys were having to choose between leaving to get an education or remaining on the island. He created such a protagonist in Edgar, a name he found in the 1900 census of the Quinns on Eagle Island. To Eagle he gave the fictional name Herring Island. Of course, he included other places he knew well: Stonington on Deer Isle and Boston's Back Bay, but it is the Eagle Island of his youth that he most lovingly recreated.

Jerry knew he was lucky to have a position for the coming fall. The Depression was worsening, and unemployment was beginning to reach the lives of friends like Carl Dennett with a wife and four children to support. Carl's marriage itself seemed in jeopardy and Gerald offered them a small amount of money to tide them over. To economize, the Dennetts moved back to the family homestead in East Alstead, New Hampshire, which meant that they would be nearer to the Braces. Once again Carl and Jerry hiked and skied together. One day, knowing nothing of the animal refuge at New Hampshire's Corbin Park, they were amazed to encounter buffalo, stags, and wild boars. They had left their wives in the car below and were happy when they were safely reunited, even though the Croyden Peak fire warden assured them that they had been in no danger.

In July of 1933 Gerald wrote to the Dennetts to try to cheer them up, for without money or prospects they were deeply depressed. He wrote sympathetically, "I was piously educated to consider money cursed filth, one of those Puritan perversions of fact. The lack of it is the real social crime (See Major Barbara & other GBS)." But Gerald never really understood what it was like to be absolutely without money. While others were wondering where their next meal was coming from, he felt deprived because he could not buy the land he coveted. "We pine for a house & lot here. We've studied the whole shore line hoping to find heaven cheap." He had finally found it, "the ninth sphere, the ultimum—in fact The Spot." It was a remote, uninhabited point of land with a pink granite shoreline surrounded by deep water, on the southwest end of Deer Isle. There were about eighty acres of sandy beach, field, and spruce, but the owners would only sell it as one tract. Cost was low, but Gerald realized he would have the expense of building a decent road and finding fresh water, as well as constructing a house. Always eager to be of help, John Donaldson promised to pay for half the land, but Gerald knew that it would ultimately take more to make it habitable than he could afford. It would remain his promised land—a place to sail and picnic, but without the joy of possession.

Gerald continued his letter to the Dennetts with the gleeful news that in his old *Bettina* he had succeeded in outracing the brand new boat that his Deer Isle neighbor, the cartoonist Gluyas Williams, was so proud to have acquired. "We haven't dared encounter Glu since. You don't know how close to the heart such things are. If I had a new boat and some old fossil beat me, I'd feel pretty blasted." To a worried Carl and Catherine it must have seemed of little moment.

When Jerry was re-appointed for the year 1933–34, his salary was reduced by six percent ($150) and he was notified that his contract, like that of several other young instructors, would not be renewed again. Huldah was once again pregnant. In spite of earlier assurances that he would always find a job waiting for him at Williams College, the departmental chairman now had to tell him that they were doing no new hiring. Professor Whicher suggested that Jerry come to Amherst to see if Robert Frost might have some advice for him. Frost was not able to offer any practical help, but he was very sympathetic. He said that he understood what it was like to have a family and no sure plans for the future. He had been in the same situation when he returned from England with no prospects. They talked about mutual friends Sidney Cox and Stearns Morse, and Frost even offered to write him a letter of recommendation if he thought it would help. It reassured Jerry. In later years Jerry would never understand why biographers of Frost described the poet as self-seeking and insensitive to others; he always found him to be warm and considerate.

Jerry rather half-heartedly applied for jobs at Bennington College and Sarah Lawrence, but he really was not eager to teach in a woman's college. Although Bennington had the reputation of being progressive, it seemed to him that the whole interview was about individual students and their problems. Jerry had never had to worry about his students' personal lives when he taught in male colleges.

He and Huldah drove from Bennington to New York to see her sister Jane, and then on to Ridgefield, Connecticut where they stayed in the drafty stone and stucco house in which Uncle Rob and Aunt Bessie had retired. Jerry collapsed again, though this time it was only flu and fever. In a few days he was well enough to travel. It was the last time he ever saw his Uncle Rob. He felt that with his death one more good, innocent man had left his life. The passing of the older generation made him aware that life was changing, but he did not really comprehend how much. Although he read in the papers about soup kitchens and the dust bowl, it all seemed remote from Dartmouth. Even though he had no job prospects, he was confident that something would materialize.

On March 28th, 1934, Huldah gave birth at Mary Hitchcock hospital to a daughter. Huldah had given the boys traditional Brace names. It was Jerry who wanted the girl called Barbara. It was strange that he did not choose Huldah for at least a middle name, because the name had come down in the Laird family for several generations. Perhaps if Jerry had been aware then that his esteemed great-grandfather, John Pierce Brace, had

Barbara with her big brothers

once written a poem to a girl he loved named Huldah, he would have called the new baby by the name that his wife wanted, but never suggested.

Jerry had never skied down Tuckerman's Ravine on the east side of Mount Washington; so in spite of the weakness left by his polio, he was determined to do so before leaving Hanover. On an early May expedition in 1935, he convinced Lincoln Fairley to join him. Spring freshets prevented them from following the regular trail, forcing them to scramble through loose snow and underbrush to reach the Headwell slope. Jerry's fear of heights brought a rush of adrenaline as he poised on the brink before plunging down. Although he never became one of those adept skiers who could drop directly down one of the thousand-foot sheer vertical sides of Tuckerman's giant bowl, he became addicted to the rush and challenge, and for the next fifteen years, he would return regularly. On that spring day, both men became overheated, then chilled. By the time they got back to Norwich, Jerry knew something was seriously wrong. This time he was diagnosed as having nephritus. He was far too ill to complete the school year. Once again Sidney Cox and his other friends added the burden of his classes to their own.

Though still too weak to do the heavy work of moving, Jerry accepted a summer job teaching at the Cummington School of Arts in the Berkshire hills, a position which the ever-faithful Sidney Cox had arranged for him. Lincoln Fairley arrived to move their furniture to Jamaica Plain to be stored in the Laird's carriage house. While a friend of Huldah's looked after the boys, Huldah cared for the baby and took on the responsibility of cleaning the Norwich house thoroughly in preparation for the Mays' return.

Jerry was always fortunate in his friends. At a College Board meeting in New York, Hewette Joyce, who had been a Dartmouth colleague, met the chairman of the department of English at Mount Holyoke College. When he told her about Jerry's need for employment, she suggested that he come to South Hadley for an interview. Jerry could no longer afford to scorn a women's college. Besides he had heard glowing reports about Mt. Holyoke from the Buffum sisters who had all attended it. As soon as he met the two gentle aristocratic ladies, Miss Ball and Miss Snell, who served as alternating chairwomen of the Writing department, there was instant rapport. They offered him a job at $2,100 a year with an additional $300 if he wished to take on extra tutoring. Jerry was able to enjoy his summer teaching knowing that he had a position for the fall, even though it was at a lower salary.

Huldah came back from settling their things into storage in Jamaica Plain and they rented a furnished house for the summer. The Cummington School had originated as a music school, but it had extended to the other arts. Jerry's job was to teach a small seminar of creative writers and to give some talks to the whole assembly. Since his duties were not too onerous, he found time to do the final editing on his novel and to give the handwritten manuscript to Catherine Dennett, wife of his friend Carl, to prepare a typed copy to submit to potential publishers. She laughingly remarked that instead of *The Islands* he should have entitled it *The Weather* as that was what it seemed to be mostly about. The publishers seemed to agree with her, for when in January of 1935 he received his first rejection, the editors praised the writing, but felt that the characters and action were overwhelmed by the long paragraphs of description. Jerry did revise it some, but he hoped to find a publisher who would appreciate that the Maine setting was the true focus of the novel.

Meanwhile both the Braces enjoyed the activities of the school, even though such a collection of artistic personalities naturally led to certain conflicts. Every Sunday, the professional musicians on the faculty and the very talented students put on outdoor concerts which were open to the public. The art department was very modern, and Jerry made a sincere effort to try to understand abstractionism. Like his mother, he preferred harmony and grace to distortion and dissonance, so he always wondered if art in the twentieth century was moving in the right direction. Still he enjoyed being introduced to so many new ways of seeing things and decided that if he couldn't be at Deer Isle, then the Berkshires were a very lovely place to be.

The Braces' home at South Hadley

11
Mount Holyoke Women

One of the most immediate problems that the Braces had to tackle before the opening of the 1934 school year at Mount Holyoke was to find a place in South Hadley to rent large enough for a family of five. Driving the fifty miles from Cummington, they finally had to settle for a rather shabby apartment on the second floor of a rickety tenement across the street from a box factory. There was always an unpleasant odor from the floor below where the owner and his untidy family lived.

One thing that Huldah had learned from Jerry's bout with polio is that a woman must not be totally dependent on her husband. She had promptly learned to drive a car and to handle the family finances. They soon discovered that she had a natural ability for budgeting and planning. Jerry had never enjoyed finances; indeed, he had been brought up to think of money as necessary, but distasteful. It had never been discussed in his home in the years that he was growing up. He was only too happy to turn all family problems over to his wife. On this moving day, she drove alone to South Hadley, cleaned the new quarters, waited until 2 A.M. for the van, which had broken down en route, to arrive with the furniture, and set everything in place before driving back to Jamaica Plain the next morning to pick up Jerry and the children.

They missed Norwich, but they found everyone, especially Miss Snell and Miss Ball, very friendly. Fortunately within a few months they were able to find a suitable house to rent on a quiet side street with a view of Mount Tom, and with fields sloping down to the Connecticut River. It had three bedrooms, and most important to Jerry, an alcove off the dining room that he could use for a study. Here he could write, correct papers, and prepare his courses. It was not an ideal arrangement, for Jerry liked it quiet when he was working and, with three little children playing nearby, it was impossible that there not be some interruptions. Still, it did offer him some sense of privacy.

Teaching in a women's college presented problems—and pleasures—different from those at Dartmouth or Williams. He worked very hard to inspire his students to do independent, serious work. The Mount Holyoke alumnae whom he knew were strong, liberated women, and he wished he could find an approach that would make his present students more serious about their scholarship. It sometimes seemed as if all a Mount Holyoke girl of the thirties wanted was to find a good husband and to raise a family in a pleasant home in the suburbs. Of course, he found it flattering that they often seemed more interested in him than in the ideas he was trying to transmit. These girls were fresh and eager and young, unburdened with children or household chores. He enjoyed their admiration and flirtatious glances. He liked watching their slim figures clad in expensive sweaters and skirts strolling together on the campus. Huldah became jealous if he paid too much attention to the girls, but he assured her—and himself—that he was only trying to encourage them to take their work seriously.

Naturally, there were students who were sincere about their desire to write well, and to them he gave careful advice and consideration. No doubt they felt he expected too much. One girl presented him with a completed novel. He wrote on the title page: "Fundamentally it is still a careless, tentative draft of a novel that has yet to be written . . . I believe you have plenty of intellectual power, but so far at least you are not an artist. You lack the inclusive sympathy, the sure taste, the perception of values that an artist needs." It was harsh criticism and a lot to expect from a girl in her teens, but convinced that talent transcends age and gender, he felt that any novelist with a potential for success must be prepared for rejection and hard work.

While he did his best to keep out of college politics, he found himself inevitably involved. Mount Holyoke actually had two English departments. The writing program for which he had been hired was the one alternately chaired by Miss Snell and Miss Ball. The department of English literature was chaired by Miss Jeanette Marks, a close friend of President Mary Wooley. The latter division considered itself the more intellectual, though Miss Snell was well known in academic circles for her teaching of poetry and the establishment of an annual invitational poetry competition that assembled distinguished judges to hear young poets read from their works. The chairmen took the division very seriously, especially Miss Marks, but Jerry considered it all rather foolish.

He still had a secret desire to be a poet in the New England tradition of Robert Frost. In one of his poems, "Mountain Snow," his sense of awe for nature and weather is clear, but, perhaps because there is no human element, it lacks the wisdom with which most Frost poems end.

> Underneath six foot lies earth
> or nothing: in the everlastingness
> of this icy hour, immortal
> and unchanged,—nothing:

no root nor sap; no spring;
no heart bound, and no breath;
no deep hope waiting, no strife;
nothing muffled, nothing chained;
in the vast moment—no life,
and no death.

On that changeless white there blows
a quiet twirl of dusted snows
and dies; the shrouded spruce alone
are steepled ghosts unmourned;
and coldly the shafted abstract sun
planes the shade and cold gold light,
brushing that remote and stainless white
across each phantom head;
that shadeless light, that intensity
of shade, that immortal gold
is all; the quick is nothing here,
and less the dead.

He experimented with abandoning meter and rhyme for onomatopoetic allit-
eration in another nature poem "April Mud."

That mud sucking bottomless
under April, under sweet sky
smoke blended with hemlock burning
under mapled hills

That serene mud waiting easy
on the town road mounting
west and high, fed sweet
with running snow.

That stretch deep of springs
innumerable and old
and broken under and profound
unaccountable,

That mud too may reach
concrete, the oiled rolling
utopia, wheels unchained
and gone along,

But as it stays deep and fast,
primeval April, waiting easy,

that serene good ooze, that mud,
holds. And all your eight cylinders,
your sixteens, stick deep,
fixed, power and pomp and all.

He had known what it was like to "stick deep" in the mud on a country road, just as he had known the wonder of six-foot snow, but his poetry seems more contrived than genuine. He had chosen verse form as the best way to evoke his feeling for weather and landscape, but poetry was obviously not his medium. He would be more successful with his prose, which he would imbue with lyrical description.

His vivid sense of scene and environment would be a major force in every novel he would write. He was more concerned with feeling than with plot, especially in his early works. In 1949 when he accepted an invitation from Harry Warfel of the University of Florida to be included in *American Novelists Today* (New York: American Book Company, 1951), Jerry wrote, "*The Islands* (which I haven't dared to read since it came out) should have been a poem. The great thing in it is the conditions—i.e. the place, the climate, the requirements of life, the physical arrangements that control so much of behavior. I was in love with the North, and with the people who had learned to fit the northern requirements." He had great admiration for Anthony Trollope, who seemed to have an imagination endlessly filled with plots, but his own approach was very different. A Brace novel always began with characters and settings; only then could he determine how under the stated conditions such people would react.

At the same time that he was writing poetry and completing another novel, he was also thinking of becoming a short story writer. Ed Smith, a friend from his Loomis days, had become a regular contributor to *Saturday Evening Post*. He introduced Jerry to his agents Brandt and Brandt who succeeded in selling one Brace story entitled "Artisans and Models" to *McLean's* magazine (Toronto, Canada, 15 May 1936). The tone of the story is lighter than most of Jerry's writings, though the subject matter is similar to some of his novels. Warren Calderwood, the protagonist, builds model boats of museum quality, but, like the Maine craftsmen that Jerry had known, he works on his orders for full-sized boats on his own timetable and in his own fashion. He fails to finish his client's craft in time for the Halifax races, and he had altered the architect Standish's designs; so he loses the contract. He is undisturbed by the loss of the project, but the client's daughter Barbara, to whom the boatbuilder has given the model, feels her father is making a mistake. When he cannot get his old motor-powered boat started she convinces her father to bring it to Calderwood for repair, and he is impressed when the boatbuilder replaces the carburetor with one he designs on his own lathe. He rehires him, and as they leave, Barbara tosses Calderwood a small package. It is the missing carburetor, which she had removed. No doubt the experiences that Jerry had with Mr. Lewis while designing the boat built in North Haven, Maine, for Lewis' wife and daughter suggested the story. It was so well received that in August it was reprinted in *Fiction Parade*. Encouraged, he wrote a sequel, no doubt hoping to create a magazine serial about Calderwood. Entitled "A Matter of Design" it is about Calderwood—who remains his independent self—and the son of Standish, but the story failed to sell.

Another unsold story, "North Wind," is of a girl, sitting on a rock in front of a lighthouse, watching a lobsterman hauling his traps. She is a typical Brace female, who lures the young man to the lonely island on the pretense that there is an emergency when actually she has everything under control. True love wins, but once again it shows how Brace sees women, no matter how gentle and innocent, as the aggressors in most relationships.

He had written, perhaps while a graduate student at Harvard though the manuscript is undated, "The Goddess of Spring" in which he expressed the fear that he might someday lose belief in that goddess who turns a young man's fancy to thoughts of love. "I found her when I was very young, and since then I have been taught by wise men to look at her so accurately that I shall soon see right through her. And then I shall lose her as those who teach me have lost her." Disillusionment did come to him in time, of course, but springtime and young women would always lighten his heart. Boats and the sea had for him an almost magic quality. His stories seemed hopelessly sentimental to readers of the thirties who were becoming more interested in sex and the gritty side of life. Brandt and Brandt sent his stories "Deep Water Man" and "A Matter of Design" each to nine different magazines, none of which showed any interest. The agents regretfully dropped Jerry as a client. This convinced him that he had better stick to novels as a genre.

Although Jerry was invited again to teach at the Cummington Summer School, even the thought of the extra income was not enough to keep him from Deer Isle, especially since he had the opportunity to rent the Pepper Box again. Life there was primitive and Huldah was not enthusiastic about doing laundry by hand for three young children; so Jerry bought a two wheel trailer for $10 to hitch on to the back of his Studebaker. He precariously balanced their Easy washing machine with spin dryer on it and with great care managed to transport it to Deer Isle. One of his students, a gifted poet named Sara Allen, agreed to spend the summer of 1935 with them to help with the work and children.

They had always coveted a place of their own; so when they heard from a Maine neighbor, Emily Shepherd, that a lovely small farm on Parker's Point was for sale, they immediately investigated. The white clapboarded house had been built about 1890 on a point of land facing Northwest Harbor. There was also a barn, a boathouse, and a large woodlot on Dow Road. Jerry never forgot their first view of the place as they drove down the dirt road leading to its front door.

> Beyond the cluster of buildings the land ended in a grassy and rocky point with rose bushes and bayberry and juniper and a few young spruces, and beyond that the waters of the bay stretched away north and west and south like a designed panorama with countless islands and the range of small mountains on the mainland in the west and a glimpse of the open sea in the south. Two or three hundred yards offshore about west by south from the point a small high rocky island lay like an emblem of the coast, and beyond it to the south the harbor of Deer Isle, Northwest Harbor, opened, and down beyond that the long dark shore of Dunham's Point stretched out against the horizon of the sea. In the afternoon of a summer day the whole place seemed benign and beautiful and very nearly perfect. To the left, on the south side of our point, lay a little beach and the remains of a stone wharf with a grassy lane leading down to it, and a small gray-shingled fish-house at the head of it, and at the very end of our point (jutting westward into deep water) was a rock cliff that stood like a natural wharf with a vertical height of almost twelve feet above low-water level. A wooden walkway had been built from the grassy land out to the rocky point, and I saw at once how I might use the place as a landing for all tides—with perhaps an outhaul and a fixed ladder on the face of the cliff. The whole thing, in fact, seemed to be designed as an answer to our visions. (*DTW* II, p. 126)

Parker's Point, Deer Isle

Each summer for the remainder of his life, he would feel the same pleasure as the house came into view. The owners, Mr. and Mrs Cobleigh, (she was the daughter of the Parkers who had given the point its name), were getting elderly and were eager to sell the property. For what now seems the ridiculously low price of $3,500, the Braces could have the whole property: three acres on the shore, eight acres of woodland on the Dow Road, and all the contents of house and outbuildings including a heavy rowboat, an upright piano, and a large stuffed loon. On the south side of the property, there was a rocky beach which sloped into shallow water ideal for beaching small boats and for the children to play, but it was owned by a Miss Riblet who was unwilling to sell. Jerry's son Loring never forgot a foggy day in July of the following summer when Miss Riblet came "tottering through the woods in her high button shoes and long black skirt tying bits of red wool to trees that she wanted to serve as the divide between the beach part and the house part." Fortunately, some years later, she had a change of heart, and allowed the Braces to purchase the small piece of land needed to make their Eden complete.

The Cobleighs agreed that the Braces could pay for their new house in installments small enough for Jerry to manage by careful budgeting. Since the owners lived in Roslindale, Massachusetts, papers could not be passed until that autumn, but they turned over the keys immediately. Jerry and Huldah eagerly began exploring their new property. Not only was the house furnished with all the household necessities, but the outbuildings were crammed with the oddments of a lifetime, which Mr. Parker, with typical New England thrift, had stored in case something might someday be needed. Every day the Braces made new discoveries. With so little to buy in the way of furnishings, they could concentrate on renovating the rooms. As soon as they were sure the house was theirs, they began tearing the shelves out of a downstairs closet to turn it into a bathroom.

Jerry still had to find a publisher for his first novel. Norman Donaldson introduced him to his friend Coward McCann. Though he was kind in his assessment of the writing, his company did not accept it. In January of 1935 he returned the manuscript explaining that in spite of its fine qualities, it was too long and that the section in which the protagonist moves to Boston failed to come alive. Undaunted Brace next tried Houghton Mifflin but, on April 4, they also turned it down. On May 22, he learned from Macmillan's that because the novel lacked "a single wholly irresistible character," they too did not wish to publish it.

Though increasingly discouraged, Jerry was aware that if an author believes in his writing, he must learn to accept rejections. He decided to try next G. P. Putnam's for no other reason than the great respect he had for a member of the publishing family, Bertha Putnam, who was a historian at

Mount Holyoke. With no intervention by her, the manuscript was accepted by Putnam's in September, 1935, with the proviso that he make certain changes. The editors felt that the plot unfolded too slowly and that the readers' interest needed to be captured earlier in the book. Publication release was postponed until the end of May, when it was learned that Donald Gordon of the American News Company, whose opinion strongly influenced advanced book sales, had given the novel an AAA rating. The publishers felt that it was important for the news to reach all the book dealers to assure that the novel would be widely stocked. Not understanding the commercial importance of ratings, Jerry felt neglected, convinced that the delay meant that the company had little interest in promoting him.

He decided to put the novel out of his mind and concentrate on other activities. He had been invited to write an article for the regular editorial column "From the Brown Owl's Oak" in the June *Writers Monthly: A Journal for All Who Write.* Jerry entitled his article "The Damn'd Profession" which he took from Ezra Pound's lines:

> Lend me a little tobacco shop
>   Or install me in any profession
> Save this damn'd profession of writing,
>   Where one needs one's brains all the time.

Brace had learned from experience that for all the independence and freedom an author has, writing brings with it a loneliness that few people can endure. Each writer becomes an explorer "traversing the unknown all the working hours of his life." Yet Jerry had decided that it was what he must do, and had started his second novel even before he had found a publisher for his first. He concluded, "The damn'd profession! That is the life!"

With the school year at an end, Jerry agreed to a proposal by Leslie Dewing, wife of one of his former Dartmouth colleagues, to sail her recently purchased seventeen-foot racing knockabout from Sorrento, Maine, to Martha's Vineyard. Though she would have liked to sail with him, the lack of privacy in such close quarters made it impossible. Instead, her husband Arthur, an inexpert sailor, would join Jerry for the two-week cruise to Massachusetts. They stopped briefly at Chebeaque Island in Casco Bay to see Uncle Lincoln Hendrickson for whom Jerry had designed a small centerboard sloop which was in the process of being built. As always, it was a thrill for Jerry to see the drawings he had made actually taking shape before his eyes. *Altair* was a sturdy, fast boat and Uncle Lincoln would win races in her until he was in his mid-eighties.

It was not until they reached Portsmouth, New Hampshire, that Jerry was able to buy a *New York Times.* To his amazement, he discovered that *The*

Islands was on the Best Seller list, a significant accomplishment for an author's first novel. Jerry had little time to savour his triumph for as soon as he reached the Vineyard, he had to go directly to New York to correct College Entrance Board exams for three days. Finally he was free to return to South Hadley to pick up Huldah and the children and leave for Deer Isle, stopping for a night at the Lairds in Jamaica Plain en route. *The Islands* quickly went into six printings. By August, 5,764 copies had been sold, with royalties already exceeding the $1,000 advance he had been given. The first check for $396.39 was sent to Huldah, who had returned to South Hadley while Jerry was closing up the place in Maine.

But if the critics liked it, his own family had some misgivings. Both his mother and his prim sister Dorothy wrote to express their displeasure. They were unhappy for two reasons. One was, that as unlikely as it seems today, they considered the book too frank. An even greater reason was that Jerry had based his characters on easily identifiable people. They were especially upset by the character he called Joan whom they recognized as a rather emotionally unstable friend of the family. It is the fictional Joan who tempts the naive protagonist Edgar Thurlow into his first sexual encounter. He cannot resist her advances. "She lay open to him, pliant and easy and sure; her brown eyes had gone liquid and soft, her baby face had achieved a serenity he had never seen in it before; her smile was selfless, beautiful; her body was serene under his touch, as though it had not fully existed until that moment." Edgar suddenly became conscious of a man's power over a woman. "He could play with her, dominate her, be cruel to her, make her happy." (*TI*, p. 262)

Jerry's mother had once cried when she heard that her son was reading *Tom Jones*. Now he himself was writing about sex. She wrote to him in distress about the "disagreeable episode." He defended the scene by explaining what he considered essential to good novel writing:

> For me the episode is neither disagreeable nor immoral—in itself, that is. It may be, of course, just as any other human act may be both disagreeable and immoral. It depends on the intention, its connection with life as a whole. But as it occurs in the book it seems to me a natural and interesting part of the experience of living—and important too. I see no justification in keeping quiet about so essential a part of the whole business of life. There are some disagreeable things in life that one doesn't usually mention because they are relatively minor and lead nowhere. But the whole difficult relationship between men and women is a major part of life, and to assume that the physical part of it is disagreeable and therefore tabu is to turn one's back on a truth that one has to deal with sooner or later. Why not deal with it openly?

He argued that the moment was really the turning point in Edgar's life and showed Joan in a sympathetic light as in this scene she is acting in complete sincerity. He knows that his mother champions virtue, but he argues, "Virtue which is not based on a full recognition of life is not to me virtue at all. Of course, no one can perceive the whole truth of life. But one can courageously try. I see no other alternative."

Yet Jerry himself had been uneasy with the character of Joan. When asked why her fate was left unresolved, he answered that he was not quite sure "except that she was always a somewhat nebulous creature, though derived pretty much from an actual girl. I guess I was glad simply to let her fade away—which is not a very responsible attitude to take." He felt her most unpleasant feature was her whining that she was never allowed to do things because she was "only a girl," though given the times and her place in society, there is some justification to her complaint.

In spite of her disapproval of "the dreadful things" in the novel, his mother was very proud that her son was gaining so much public recognition and that 3,000 copies of the books had been sold even before it had appeared in the bookstores. She wrote him that she had found his descriptions "as vivid as charcoal sketches." She recognized that modern literature demanded a frankness which was different from that of her generation and assured him "I shall not condemn you dear boy."

Of course, many readers felt the way his mother did about modern novels. One fan letter from a Back Bay lady who agreed with the line he had given Miss Everett that "Harvard was just a group of her old friends," praised him for doing a much better job of portraying Beacon Street society than Bernard de Voto had in his recent book *We Accept with Pleasure*. "It is quite true that the old families do throw up a nymphomaniac once in a while, like your Joan, but spinsters like Nancy Everett . . . don't get themselves seduced and if I recall accurately DeVoto concedes chastity to not a single woman in his book." Certainly Jerry had not considered Joan a nymphomaniac, but to a proper Bostonian in the thirties any emotional girl that is the initiator in a sexual encounter must be oversexed.

George Whicher, who had first awakened the pleasures of writing in Jerry, wrote from Amherst to say how much he had enjoyed the novel, but wondered "whether there are enough readers left undebauched by Thomas Wolfe et al to recognize quiet and humorous fineness when they see it." Lincoln Fairley's wife, Margaret, wished that he *had* written more like Wolfe. She wrote to Jerry that she felt she could criticize him as she was one of the few women of his acquaintance who had never fallen in love with him. She wished that he had exploited the character of Joan more. Her first reaction to Edgar had been "Hell, there's a man who must hate a woman because he desires and doesn't love her. And because she interested me I wondered what another man's reaction would have been. What kind of woman he would have made of her." It must have surprised Brace that it was the character of Joan who seemed to arouse everyone's interest, when he had intended Isabel Allen to be the heroine.

Millicent Pettit also praised Joan as the most vividly painted, both physically and psychologically, of all the characters, ("and it was not because I happened to recognize her either.") She complained that the character of Isabel was undeveloped and unreal while Edgar was far too Puritanical. None of the Maine natives she had met had such "a St. Paulish conception of sex." Edgar came closer to representing Jerry's own Puritanical background. Country people had an easier acceptance of human nature.

With her copper-colored hair and child-like appearance, Isabel is based on Huldah as she had been in the days when Jerry first knew her. It is not surprising that he created the character as a minister's daughter, since his early courtship of her had been at Mr. Fairley's church. Like Huldah, Isabel is reluctant to become involved in a relationship and sticks out her tongue at Edgar's importuning. She explains that she is unused to being kissed and then follows a line right out of one of Huldah's letters. "You—you expect me to be something I'm really not, and actually what I am is not what you think it is."(*TI*, p. 301) There is no real promise at the end of the novel that the two will ever marry after she leaves the island for college.

It is interesting that the Reverend James Fairley, who had kept in close touch with both Braces ever since their courtship days at his church in Jamaica Plain, was aware that none of the women characters in the novel were as completely delineated as the men. He wrote from his summer home at Cape Rosier, Maine: "Rose and Joan are modern Eves. I have not felt their seductiveness in my life as Edgar did in his. But then, that proves nothing . . . . Isabel is a dear, and gives great promise of the fulfillment which is implied in the book's dedication to her. Sometime you will give us a picture of a woman as convincing as Edgar is of a man." The Reverend Fairley may not have been a literary critic, but he was a shrewd judge of character. He recognized Isabel as a thinly disguised Huldah, but he also saw that Jerry had not penetrated deeply enough into her psyche to truly understand her and turn her into a well rounded character. Of course, Jerry had been conscious while writing that he must not describe his heroine in such a way that Huldah would be insulted or annoyed.

The Islands is not so much a love story as the conflict of a young man trying to decide whether to leave his island to get an education or to continue the pattern lived by his forebears. Of all the heroes Brace would create, perhaps, Edgar is least patterned after his author. He is neither a deep thinker nor articulate. Until he was taken by Miss Everett to Boston for a proper education, he had known nothing of the society that was Jerry's natural milieu. But the inner conflict created in Edgar by two opposing ways of life led him into the same "bemused state of misery" that Jerry experienced at the end of each summer when he had to return to academia. In his student days especially, Jerry must have often fantasized how much simpler his choices would be if he had been born a sturdy island boy like Edgar.

Edgar's appreciation of the craftsmanship of his Uncle Moses reflects Jerry's admiration for Maine island boat builders.

> Uncle Moses worked with deliberation, never impatient, never seeming to look ahead to the finished job, never expecting to do more than he did. He never had to do the same job twice, he never guessed, or experimented. When he picked up a tool, it was the right tool; when he sawed on a line, the cut was true; when he stopped to sharpen a plane blade, he stopped thoroughly: it was not a temporary touching up, it was a complete act in itself, forgetful of all other acts. Nothing proceeded until the tool was ready. "I remember how Pop 'ud give me hell for losin' the aidge off a tool," he said once. (*TI*, p. 167)

As reviewer Basil Davenport (*The Saturday Review*, 30 May 1936) noted, Down East boatbuilders were among the last Americans to preserve the tradition of finest craftsmanship.

Some of Brace's secondary characters rival his primary ones—especially proper Boston Brahmin Nancy Everett who is so kind and understanding of Edgar. Her sensitivity and unselfishness might seem unrealistic, except that she is modeled directly on Ellen Coolidge whom Jerry described as "the most magnetic and delightful woman who ever lived." Ellen Coolidge failed to recognize herself as prototype, but she did think Miss Everett "a rather pleasant person." She concluded that Brace understood his Maine characters better than he had the Boston ladies. He could get inside his male characters more readily than the females. Sarah Thurlow, Edgar's mother, based on Freddie Sylvester's wife, is not fully realized partly because while Jerry admired hardworking, undemonstrative Maine women, he had never belonged to their world. Though he had observed how years of incessant labor wore them down, he couldn't comprehend what was in their thoughts.

The setting and characters naturally led reviewers to compare *The Islands* with Sarah Orne Jewett's *Country of the Pointed Firs* (1896). This did not especially please Brace, for as a young man he considered her works rather limited and quaint. He rightly felt that he knew far more about boats and boatbuilding than she. He was not yet perceptive enough to realize that by using as narrator a female summer visitor from the city, Jewett had no need for such technical knowledge. The two writers are diametrically opposite in many ways. Jewett centered on the activities of strong island women during the fading Indian Summer of the age of sail. With the young men at sea or working off-island and the old men living in their memories of the past, it is women like matronly Almira Todd and her mother who are the true spiritual centers of the community. Brace was recreating the time of his early youth when there was still vital activity on the islands of Penobscot Bay. Jewett's viewpoint is distinctly feminine; Brace's is very masculine. Perhaps he had the better understanding of the complex emotions of a young boy who must decide whether to venture out into the world or to follow in the paths of his fore-bears, but Brace still had much to learn from Jewett about the rhythm of the lives of women forced to live in an isolated region of Maine.

Surprisingly, there seem to have been few comparisons of *The Islands* with *Silas Crockett* published by Mary Ellen Chase just the previous year. Her novel is actually closer to Brace's than were the works of Jewett. The latter part of her story covers the same time period as his and also has the protagonist leaving college to find work, though his choice has been made for him by the difficult economic times. The three generations of women she created, including that of Huldah, Silas Crockett II's mother, are more empathetically portrayed than the female characters in Brace's book, but she is weaker than he in her depiction of the coast and the details of the strenuous work done by the captains and fishermen and builders of boats.

Brace excels in showing how men are affected by the changing cycle of seasons. "The weather was dominant over all thought, all speech, all of life itself, and even if he were doing nothing better than splitting stove wood, a man must anxiously sniff the slant of the wind and eye the distant streak of fog on the headlands of the outer islands. But a man had a wide horizon; he did variable and venturesome work; weather of the outer islands was relevant. A woman existed only in her kitchen." (*TI*, p. 21)

Local reviewers argued about the location of "Weymouth Island." The publishers accepted Jerry's assurance that it was Deer Isle, but Franklin Lincoln wrongly asserted that it was based on Isle au Haut and that the natives there were very upset that a summer visitor had been allowed to know so much about their lives. It is a tribute to Jerry's knowledge of Maine, that so many people identified the areas described as their own.

Brace began getting his first recognition as a successful novelist. The Maine State Library in Augusta asked him to send an autographed copy of *The Islands* for the Maine Authors Collection. The local bookstore on Deer Isle invited him to sign copies. Beyond the gratification of knowing that his first novel was successful, there was also the extra money it brought in. Jerry may never have given too much thought to money, but Huldah had a practical recognition of its need. Her father had struggled for every penny, and she harbored a fear of debt even in the form of regular payments for a house. The financial returns on *The Islands* convinced Huldah that her husband could be a major novelist, and she determined to create an environment in which he could write. For Jerry, the popularity of the book and the positive responses of the critics were confirmation of his talent, though he found it metaphorically appropriate that he was able to pay in full for his Deer Isle home with the proceeds of a novel entitled *The Islands*.

With property of his own, Jerry had to set a careful schedule for writing or he could spend all day working on the place. Grass had to be scythed, firewood cut, brush cleared, water pumped from two small wells to a storage tank. There was no electricity, gas, or refrigeration. While Huldah aired the house and cleared away the winter's accumulation of dust and mildew, Jerry put out moorings, caulked and painted *Bettina*, and got her into the water. He rigidly adhered to three hours set aside for writing each morning, either on the porch facing the water or in his bedroom. It was Huldah's responsibility to keep the children quietly occupied—easy enough in fine weather when they played out of doors, but difficult when rain or fog kept them in the house. Though she had a college girl to help her, there was always a great deal to do: dishes were washed and dried by hand, lamp chimneys cleaned, and meals cooked on the old-fashioned kitchen range. Even the sails and picnics they enjoyed meant preparing food to take along. Their new home might be all they had dreamed of, but it was a lot of work.

They had to move again in South Hadley. Once again much of the effort fell on Huldah. Jerry was happy with his teaching at Mount Holyoke, but in spite of his efforts to remain neutral he found himself drawn into school politics. Miss Wooley retired, and a Yale man was hired by the trustees to replace her in the belief that a male president would attract more endowment money and give the school a more positive image. Jerry was not especially liberal in his views about women, but he had a high regard for the academic competence of some of the Mount Holyoke faculty. He felt it unfair to hire a man when there were women who could do the job as well. After all, Mary Lyon had founded the school a century before for the purpose of offering women an education equal to that of the best male colleges. She had gathered women of exceptional ability around her, and her five successors had been female. Adhering to strict Victorian standards, Miss Wooley was criticized as too old-fashioned, but it was breaking a century of tradition to replace her with a man.

Jerry had other reasons for being dissatisfied with the change in leadership. The new president, Roswell Ham, felt that he had been hired to raise the quality of the faculty and to demand more scholarly research. When Jerry told him he was actively preparing a second novel for publication, the president's response was "Why in the world are you doing that? It won't get you anywhere academically." Of course President Ham was partially right. Creative writing was still not a recognized field of study in most college curricula and though some universities might appoint a fellow or designate a chair for a major writer whose name would add lustre to their reputation, only rarely was creative writing considered seriously toward tenure. Jerry, however, had no intentions of letting that deter him from being a novelist.

The Islands was still selling well and Brace found himself something of a celebrity at Deer Isle. In August of 1937 he was invited to be guest speaker at the Deer Isle church where he read to a full house his unsold short story, "Deep Water Man." He relished any opportunity for acceptance in the community, though he was aware that he would always be considered one of "the summer folk."

In 1938 Putnam's published *The Wayward Pilgrims*. For this second novel, Jerry chose as his setting the Vermont hills that he had explored during his days as a student at Amherst. It is not as well structured as *The Islands*; instead he wrote a picaresque tale—primarily a vehicle for dialogue—which contains his attitudes toward life, especially teaching. He himself later analyzed it as a "too nostalgic and playful 'open road' tale, with echoes of Borrow and Stevenson and Belloc and all my memories of ventures in the hill country—but it is obvious that I wrote it with the sort of innocence that reflects the time of my youth." (*DTW* II, p. 159) This makes it biographically interesting. He dedicated it to the Dennetts still suffering from the affects of the Depression: "To Carl and Catherine—That can translate the stubbornness of fortune/Into so quiet and so sweet a style."

With sales of *The Islands* reaching over 6,000 copies, Putnam's was interested in selling another novel by the same author while he was still in the public's consciousness. They offered him a slightly better contract, promising 10 percent in royalties for the first 4,000 copies sold, 12½ percent for the next 4,000, and 15 percent after that. Even priced at $2.50, it would have been financially successful if it had sold as well as *The Islands*; however, it never really appealed to the public. As late as 1942 he still had a debit against the thousand dollar advance he had received. The need for money may have encouraged Brace to publish it before he had fully developed his characters, especially Margot, the female protagonist, but nothing could improve upon his descriptions of Vermont. Here he wrote with a sure hand and deep feeling for the countryside.

In an account of his happy days at Amherst which Jerry later wrote for the *Amherst Alumni News* in the winter of 1963, he told them that his novel *The Wayward Pilgrims* had been based on his student days of vagabondage:

a youthful and I hope amusing tale of wayfaring in the hill country: let no word of it ever be taken as autobiography, but the setting and people all grew out of those old escapes and excursions I used to take when I should have been cramming for exams. It may not be wise in any classic sense, and there are no profundities in it, but the gleams and glimpses of life, of farms and villages, and mountain roads and the folk who lived there, all seen in the eyes of a romantic young scholar, was as authentic as I could make them.

It is indeed the minor characters drawn from his own experiences who are the most meticulously created. On a train he meets Mary Butterfield. Her straight talk and family loyalty is reminiscent of the Buffum sisters. At the Carters' pleasant home where the two pilgrims stay on their third night, they receive the kind of warm welcome that Jerry remembered from the nights he stayed at the Hancocks in Jacksonville, Vermont, after hiking all day. As for Mr. Shattuck, who owns the sugar house where they stay, he, like Arthur Johnson from Amherst, has married unsuitably after the death of his first wife. However, he has managed more successfully to maintain his Yankee humor and acceptance of fate. When he falls in a cold mountain stream after accompanying the two walkers part of the way, he struggles out, though he remarks ruefully, "I didn't know no better," unlike his real life counterpart who drowned himself in a mill pond "thoughtfully tying a rope around one wrist so that he could be fished out without trouble." (*DTW*, p. 181) The action in Jerry's fiction often is less dramatic than life itself.

Lawrence Minot, the youthful hero, could well be spokesman for Jerry himself. He remembers fishing trips with his father in the Maine woods, the magic of Christmas, and winter coasting and skating. While he sits in the library reading Burke on the Sublime, he feels that real life is passing him by. "The Lord, he reflected, hadn't meant him to be a student, it seemed to take the starch out of him." (*WP*, p. 7) He finds teaching better than studying, for at least it has some reality, but he views universities like Harvard with irony and scepticism. It seems to him that the academic world masks a kind of fear. "It means behaving in such a manner that no one will find you out. If you keep it up long enough, you never even find yourself out." (*WP*, p. 242) This can be fatal to a writer who must remain close to his inner nature. It seemed to him that "the college teacher only pretends he knows what he's doing. Some pretend so hard that they fool themselves—they talk about their work—covering the ground, you know—as though they knew exactly what was being accomplished." (*WP*, p. 73) Jerry always felt he was an imposter in academia, but unlike many professors, he, at least, was aware to what extent he was a fraud.

The plot of *The Wayward Pilgrims* is simple. Lawrence Minot has been awarded a small grant of money which he uses to walk through the hills of

Vermont studying native dialects. By chance he meets Margot Anton, and the inexperienced young man and worldly, thrice-married woman discuss life as they walk along together for four days, taking refuge in farms or a sugarhouse at night. When in their courtship days Jerry had suggested that Huldah go on a walking expedition with him she had promptly dismissed the idea as improper and unsuitable. If Isabel Allen in *The Islands* was based on Huldah, then dark-haired Margot is her antithesis both in character and physical appearance. Minot calls her predatory and notorious, but the night they spend together in a barn convinces him that he loves her.

Huldah must have known that anyone who knew her at all would not think that the character of Margot was suggested by her, but she feared that they might think it was a description of some encounter her husband had had on one of his long expeditions in the Vermont mountains. Others in the Brace family agreed. They too worried that people would read it as autobiography. Though John Donaldson did not share his wife Dorothy's feeling that Jerry had stepped over the bounds of propriety, he thought that there was some justification for her concern. He wrote to Gerald in May of 1938, pointing out that "the moral questions posed by the book have raised some comment and I cannot help remembering the gist of the first verse from 'La Nuit Blanche' by Kipling." Gerald obviously looked up the reference and wrote out the text by hand on the bottom of John's letter.

> A much discerning Public hold
> The singer generally sings
> Of personal and private things
> And prints and sells his past for gold.

But Gerald then went on to copy out another verse:

> Whatever I may here disclaim
> The very clever folk I sing to
> Will most indubitably cling to
> Their pet delusion just the same.

Huldah never got over her hostility to and disapproval of *The Wayward Pilgrims*. Gerald's mother tried to be understanding though she found it difficult to accept the unconventional behavior of his characters. She chose her words carefully when she wrote to him from her home in California: "Your book gives me much to think about as a story and I see I shall have to modify my standards to be up to date." In spite of her attempts to broaden her views, her son was fully aware that his mother's rigid propriety was unalterable.

Though none of the love scenes are explicit, the weakness of the novel is not in its plot, but rather its failure to clothe the heroine with flesh and blood.

Joseph Lovering, a former student, who wrote a Twayne Series critical study entitled *Gerald Warner Brace* (1981) accurately pinpoints the reason Margot is not more successful as a character:

> There is little doubt that the author wanted her seen as archetypically female. She is drawn to men and attracts men to herself. She has concern for other people. She sacrifices for them. She wants a home but ironically is destined to be on the road. Perhaps the nub of the issue is her quality of mind. For Minot she is attractive not only in body but spiritually. She becomes a foil for him throughout the book as she responds to the philosophical questionings and in doing so she may not be credible. . . . essentially the novel itself is romantic in the sense that the fiction suggests an exploration of the author himself, in his own psychic landscapes, his searching of his own predispositions, his dreams, his illusions, if you will. (p. 43)

During their brief time together, the relationship develops from abstention to a kiss to their final night in the hay loft, but Margot realizes that there can be no future for them. She leaves and Minot is left despondent. "All that remained in the wide silent world was the gray road stretching away downward ahead of him." (*WP*, p. 278) Even more than in his first novel, Jerry eschews the traditional happy ending.

Although Jerry claimed that the book should not be read as an allegory, the parallels to Bunyan's *Pilgrims Progress* are too obvious to be ignored, including the title—though these pilgrims are more wayward than Christian. Margot sees the old road they are following as a challenge to the spirit, "a sort of slough of despond." There are echoes too of one of Brace's favorite books, Robert Louis Stevenson's *Travels with a Donkey*. In his account of a walk across the south of France, Stevenson had expressed his view that "to live out of doors with the woman a man loves is of all lives the most complete and free."

Millicent Pettit, who always gave him an honest appraisal of his writing, recognized the Bunyan overtones. She wrote to him on April 12, 1938, that she had enjoyed the descriptions and thought the novel more poem than story. Margot had never seemed quite real to her, "but taken as an allegorical character, a personification of Experience (such as Christian might have met along the way) or an incarnation of 'Woman the ever mysterious, the ever desirable, embodying all of life, all wisdom, all tenderness,' she was OK."

When the reviews of *The Wayward Pilgrims* appeared in April of 1938, critics were mixed in their assessment, though all agreed that his descriptions of landscape were vivid and authentic. Opinions on characters and dialogue varied, ranging from "honest and witty" to Edith Walton's comment in *The New York Times Book Review* that his "two sententious and improbable pilgrims are pretty hard to take." Nevertheless, the book sold 5,000 copies. Later the book was produced as a radio show in Burlington, Vermont, by Stan Cobb of the Everyday Book Shop. The role of Mr. Shattuck was played by W. E. Aiken who afterwards wrote to Brace telling him how much he enjoyed the part.

The continuing success of *The Islands* and the promise of royalties from *The Wayward Pilgrims* encouraged Jerry to hire his neighbor Norman Pressey, a local Deer Isle man, to paint their Parker's Point house, reputty all the windows, draw the sashes, and put two coats of paint on the trim of barn and boathouse—all for the sum of $36. Jobs were scarce and Maine men were willing to take any work available. The Brace children followed him everywhere. He brought them cookies made by his wife, taught them about boats and rigs, and identified birds and wildlife. Jerry had high admiration for Maine workmen like Norman Pressey who were never daunted by any task, but solved all problems with ingenuity and skill. To become such a craftsman was Jerry's dream and he strove to achieve the same level of efficiency, but he confessed with dismay: "My carpentry was always a bit make-shift, my plumbing tended to leak, my mowing was ragged, my boats blistered and were not tight." (*DTW* II, p. 152) Even the pictures he framed were never quite plumb. He had been raised in a class that had hired help to do the physical work. No matter how many summers he lived in Deer Isle, he would never achieve the self-sufficiency of a genuine native.

Life seemed serene when the Braces returned to Mount Holyoke that fall. When Jerry received word that his 83-year-old father had died, it was a shock, though the family had been aware of his poor health. Since he and his wife lived in Santa Barbara, California, they were not able to see him often, but

Portrait of Jerry's father,
Charles Loring Brace II

Jerry had always had a sense of security knowing that his father was there if he should need help. Charles Loring Brace had been a remarkable parent, offering support and encouragement over the years while making few demands in return. Suddenly the sense of family permanence dissolved. Furniture, books, china and silverware were divided among the next generation. Jerry's mother moved back to New York to live with Eleanor and Muriel Postlethwaite. Now, at age 37, Gerald was the senior male in the Brace family.

He was gaining increased recognition as a writer. In February of 1939,

Touchstone, a magazine produced by Amherst College, invited him to submit an article for an issue to be devoted entirely to reminiscences about Robert Frost. Brace had entitled his modestly "An Unimportant Recollection of Robert Frost" which prompted the editors to add a footnote pointing out that the title had been submitted by the author and did not reflect the attitude of the staff. Brace explained how in his sophomore year he had taken American literature with George Whicher, not knowing that Frost would meet with them for an hour a week for about a month. Students in the 1920s had little awareness of the privilege of being able to study with him and little communication passed between them. "We spoke of him as Bobby with more condescension than affection, we were pleased that he was attached to Amherst—outsiders often mentioned it, we felt that he stood vaguely for some sort of higher culture that we could utilize to our own credit." (p. 21) The students did not appreciate Frost's poetry and they did not find him an especially stimulating teacher, especially as he was not yet the good speaker that he would later become. Surprisingly, Brace then went on to question whether even undergraduates in 1939 had interest in Frost's poetry. He noted that "those who now listen to him with an almost passionate delight are the folks old enough to know no better and convinced that here for once they have the best life offers." This seems a condescending remark from someone who had been a recipient of Frost's kindness and an admirer of his poetry since his own student days. In certain moods, Brace could give unexpected—even perverse and inconsistent—opinions when asked for his views, a fact later noted in several of his faculty evaluations. He had not yet decided to leave Mount Holyoke, but perhaps the negative tone reflects his dissatisfaction and disappointment that those in the college who had the power to determine salary and promotion were showing so little appreciation of his own writings.

12
Boston University

In the spring of 1939, Jerry received a letter, followed by a visit, from Ralph Wesley Taylor, dean of Boston University College of Liberal Arts, offering him a position in the English department with the rank of associate professor and a salary of a thousand dollars more than he was currently receiving. John Milton Williams, a Harvard graduate and Oxford Rhodes scholar, had died very suddenly, and the Braces' old friend William Norton, a member of the history department, had suggested Brace as a replacement. Jerry was not interested. He had considered the university in 1927 before going to Williams College to teach, but when he had gone for an interview he had been depressed by the old red brick building, just off Copley Square, sandwiched between busy Boylston Street and the Boston and Albany Railroad switching yards. He felt he would be smothered in such a noisy, polluted atmosphere.

Huldah wanted him to accept the offer from her old alma mater. She was aware that although he had been raised to the rank of assistant professor, it had brought no increase in salary, and he would never receive rapid promotion at Mount Holyoke where creative writing was not considered of major importance. She liked the idea of being nearer to her family and friends and the prospect of better schools for her children. When Jerry objected that he would be miserable in the city sharing an airless, crowded office with three other men, she knew exactly which argument would persuade him to reconsider. *Bettina* was in serious need of repairs, and should be replaced. Jerry had already designed a sloop that he dreamed of having some day. She pointed out to him that the additional salary would make this possible.

Jerry made one more effort to get the administration to give him a raise. "Deep Water Man," one of the short stories returned to him by his agents Brandt and Brandt, had just been accepted for *The Story Survey* (1939), an anthology edited by his friend and former Dartmouth colleague Harold Blodgett, now an assistant professor of English in Union College, Schenectady, New York. He was a great admirer of Brace's work and had included him in this new collection of distinguished writers ranging from traditional authors like Poe and Hawthorne to contemporaries such as Faulkner and Hemingway. The subject, the eccentric behavior of a boat builder, a deep water man living far from the sea, is typically Brace. Unfortunately, Mount Holyoke was not sufficiently impressed to raise his salary; so, reluctantly, he agreed to go to Boston for an interview.

Boston University was eager to hire a Harvard Ph.D. with two novels and several short stories to his credit. The English department had only one Ph.D., George Sneath, a Yale man who had earned his doctorate at B.U. while teaching there. None of the professors had done any serious publication. The dean promised Brace that if he would accept the position, he would be guaranteed a promotion within a year. If he wished to teach in the late afternoon or evening he could earn up to $3,500, and even more if he wanted to teach in the summer. Financially, he would certainly be better off than at Mount Holyoke.

He had previously met the chairman, Thomas Mather, when he had considered the job there over a decade earlier. Rotund, with thick lensed glasses and gapped front teeth (which he enjoyed likening to Chaucer's lusty Wife of Bath), Mather hid his underlying insecurity under a mockish wit. He invited Jerry to the University Club to meet the others. George Sneath, next in seniority, was a handsome man with a leonine mass of white hair. Though a bit of a poseur, he was kind and affable. Winslow Loveland was a bachelor with a nervous, apologetic manner, always eager to please. Jerry felt that they would be pleasant colleagues.

He was less impressed with the college's facilities. The dingy brick building which housed the College of Liberal Arts at 688 Boylston Street had formerly been the Harvard Medical School, and still had as its largest lecture hall the amphitheater where Oliver Wendell Holmes had once taught. The main entrance led into a large foyer affectionately dubbed "The Marble." Under the wide central staircase, there was a small mailroom where students collected their messages and, in the rear, a tiny bookstore next to the elevator. There were no dining facilities, but there was a room called Gamma Delta where girls could eat their brown bag lunches, and an outer room where boys and girls could sit together. Classrooms, always too warm or too cold, were unattractive and noisy, not only from the traffic and trains, but from an extension of the subway tunnel that was being drilled underneath the building. The library was inadequate, though fortunately the college was located next door to the Boston Public Library. The playing field was so far out in the suburbs that most students never saw it. But with fewer than five hundred students, the school was small enough for everyone on its faculty and staff to feel a sense of responsibility for its direction and destiny. In such a compressed space, almost everyone knew one another, at least by sight, and there was a remarkable feeling of camaraderie and school spirit.

The English department consisted of just two crowded, dark rooms. All that he could see through their small dusty windows was the brick wall of the Soden Building, just across a narrow alley. Attached to the fifth floor of the liberal arts building by a bridge nicknamed the "Bridge of Sighs," it housed the Schools of Education and Music. Four professors had to share the one room; the other was used by all the fellows, lecturers, graduate assistants, and part-time workers. There would be no possibility for privacy.

Jerry signed the contract rather grimly. He had to go through the formality of a meeting with the president, Daniel L. Marsh, who seemed to him like a figure out of a Dickens novel. He spoke pompously, mostly in platitudes, and quoted his favorite poet, James Whitcomb Riley, like himself, a native of Indiana. Jerry wondered what they would ever have in common. As it turned out, it didn't matter, because he would only see him presiding over the ceremonies at commencement exercises in his ermine trimmed doctoral robe and a dramatic round hat from the ancient University of Bologna which had awarded him an honorary degree.

It was left to Huldah to find a house in the suburbs. As soon as the family was settled at Deer Isle, she returned to Jamaica Plain to start searching. She was in good spirits having gotten her way, and when she was happy, Jerry usually was too. On the 14th of July he wrote to his "Dear Best Wife" to say that all was well with the family though he missed her and to send her all the local news. The Strausses and Porters from Great Spruce Island had been to call "4 women & 5 kids." The Brace children had come back from fishing with Eleanor in time for them all to walk back to the harbor. They were learning to swim. The two boys could both go in over their heads and Barbara had announced that she was "almost willing to try." He had not seen a paper since she left so knew nothing of the world. He signed it "With bbls of love from your lorn man."

Huldah found a large, rather elegant, house in Wellesley Hills not far from the Nortons, though she worried that they might find the rent too expensive. It seemed just perfect for their needs. Their furniture was shipped from South Hadley as were the dishes, silver, books and furniture that had been in New York storage since his father's death. The black oak dining room table and ornate chairs, brought from Ireland by Jerry's grandmother, fit beautifully in the dining room and the heirloom grandfather clock added an elegance worthy of an associate professor in an urban university.

Although the Braces only remained in Wellesley for two years, Huldah was pleased to be near her old schoolmate, Mildred Norton, once again. They both became concerned about the wife of one of their husbands' colleagues.

Aurelia Schober, while a graduate student at B.U., had married Otto Plath, her German professor, who was much older than she. He had handled finances and made all the decisions. Now he was very ill with diabetes. As a proper German hausfrau, she had given up all her own independence to be a good wife and mother to their two children, Sylvia and Warren. After his death, Huldah and Mildred encouraged her to realize her own potential. She accepted a position at B.U. School of Practical Arts and Letters and moved to Wellesley. By this time the Braces had left, but the three families continued to see each other socially. Sylvia Plath and the Brace's son Gerald were about the same age, and the three Norton boys were close in age to the three Braces. The young people played games and picnicked together while the parents sat and talked.

By the time she had reached her teens, Sylvia had become a very attractive and talented girl whom young Gerald would have asked out if he had not been so shy. Instead she dated Dick Norton. In later years when she wrote her thinly disguised autobiographic novel *The Bell Jar* she cruelly satirized both Dick and his family. Thus it was Mildred Norton, rather than Huldah, (though the two women shared the same sentiments) who is pilloried for arguing that young men and women should preserve their virginity until after the wedding. As a modern young poet wanting to experience life, Sylvia scorned such pious platitudes about marriage as the formula she quotes in her novel: "What a man wants is a mate and what a woman wants is infinite security." The book, enjoying some success in the United Kingdom, naturally distressed her mother, who unsuccessfully tried to suppress its publication in America. Aurelia Plath's friends realized that her talented daughter suffered from mental illness. When in 1963, at the age of 30, Sylvia committed suicide, they shared her mother's grief.

At Wellesley, the Braces also enjoyed living close enough to West Newton to visit the winter home of their summer Deer Isle neighbors, the Williams. Gluyas Williams was a highly popular cartoonist for the *New Yorker*, and Jerry enjoyed his quiet sense of humor. They were having dinner at the Gluyas home the evening of the Valentine blizzard of 1941. Jerry managed to drive through the blinding snow until his car became hopelessly stuck in a snowdrift about a block from home. They had to walk the rest of the way. The next morning Jerry, with some difficulty, located and dug out the completely buried car.

Jerry could bear city life secure in the knowledge that the boat that he had dreamed about so long was becoming a reality. As soon as his contract with Boston University with its promise for a higher salary was signed, he had returned to Deer Isle to make arrangements to have the designs on which he had lovingly worked so long translated into a new 32-foot wooden sloop.

Jerry captures *Festina's* grace with paint and brush

Maine had not recovered from the Depression and the boatyards were glad to have any work for their men, especially during the long winter. They agreed to build her for the very modest price of a thousand dollars. For an additional twenty-five dollars, Jerry was able to buy a used mast, rigging, boom, and sails that had been stored away in a boathouse at Burnt Cove. The only serious problem was a shortage of lead because of the war in Europe, so iron had to be substituted for the keel. Otherwise everything proceeded smoothly.

The following March after a spring skiing trip to Tuckerman's Ravine, Jerry drove to Deer Isle to check on the sloop's progress. He was prepared to be disappointed remembering his anticipation when *Charmian* was being built at Vinal Haven and how when he first saw her all she had was a keel and stem. But his graceful sloop was all planked and decked waiting for her first coat of paint. He wanted her as natural as possible with no varnish, winches, or motor. She had a simple head and sleeping accommodations for two. Later he would make some modifications, but from the beginning she seemed nearly perfect. He chose for her name the motto of the Venetian Aldine Press, *Festina Lente* ("Make haste slowly"). He soon dropped the *Lente* from her name, for she proved fast even in a gentle breeze.

On that March trip he stayed at the Sylvesters, but he was eager to check on his house even though Dow Road was so buried in snow that he had to wade through waist high drifts for the last mile. He stopped to get a warming cup of coffee at their nearest year-round neighbors, Josephine and Goodwin Thompson. They reported that no one had gone by their house since the previous November. In fact it had been three months since Josephine had seen a living soul except for her husband. She took a grim pride in being able to cope with the loneliness. "'He likes it,' she said. 'He doesn't care if he never sees anyone else'—but she said it without serious resentment." (*DTW* II, p. 143) It is difficult to realize that right up to World War II, island women spent long periods of time in almost complete isolation.

After the slow pace of a wintry Maine, the city seemed more frenetic than ever. Five heavily enrolled three-credit courses, which included some composition, was a normal teaching load. Brace expressed his dissatisfaction with the large classes in an article called "Education's Problem Child." He pointed out that colleges did not recognize the importance of writing in the college curriculum. The best students were excused from Freshman composition. The rest were placed with beginning instructors who were only marking time until they could offer courses in their specialties. Few of these teachers had been trained to teach composition. Administrators and senior professors even questioned whether it was possible to teach writing, and whether it should be considered a legitimate college subject. Brace had hoped that the manuscript might be published by *Harper's*, but it was rejected. Although he did a number of book reviews for the Boston *Herald*, he never had much success in getting scholarly articles published in established journals.

In spite of a heavy teaching schedule, Jerry continued to write. His reputation as author of *The Islands* still brought him recognition. In April, he was invited to be one of the guest speakers at a Boston *Evening Transcript* literary luncheon at the Hotel Vendome in Boston, sharing the platform with other popular writers of the day: Ben Ames Williams, Emilie Loring, Eleanor Early, and David McCord.

Boston University was Jerry's first experience teaching co-educational classes where the women were as serious about their education and future careers as the men. Since every student in the college had to take both composition and literature, professors taught basic requirements as well as courses in the major. Most of the students were commuters from working class homes and held jobs as well as taking full-time classes. They drove taxis, served as hospital aides, worked as janitors, household helpers, and store clerks. They used public transportation to commute—sometimes long distances. They had little time or opportunity for tennis or skiing or organized sports. They may have lacked the social graces of Mount Holyoke women and the athletic skills of Dartmouth men, but most of them were determined to get a good education and have a better future than their parents. Amenities like the teas at Dartmouth's Sanborn House were the products of another world, but Jerry found that his necessary proximity to the students brought him into more sympathetic relationship with them.

After his first year, the administration carried out their promise and promoted Jerry to full professor. His approach to teaching was old-fashioned. He found it difficult to promote discussion and he relied heavily on reading long passages from major works of fiction, but he quietly inspired respect. Reserved, almost shy in manner, he treated each student with a gentle courtesy and focused attention, important to commuting students in a large city university, especially girls, who for the most part, were the first females in their families to attend a four-year college. Young ladies soon began majoring in "Brace," happy to be singled out for an awkward pat on the shoulder or a word of praise. A student from those days, Bertha Carter, now Mrs. Ruark, recalled a half-century later: "He was like a god—but a god who understood, had compassion and bore my intrusion into his life with humor and forebearance." For several summers she rented a cabin on the shore, a couple of hundred yards south of the Brace home, from his Deer Isle neighbor Josephine Thompson. He enjoyed Bertha's companionship, but he refused to become her guru. In the fall of 1941, he gave a light response to her request for advice on teaching English at Presque Isle Normal School in the potato country of northern inland Maine. "Why teach English? . . . Food, diet & health are what count in Presque Isle . . . You might take notes for the Great Potato Epic." He only became serious at the end when he revealed his own insecurity about teaching. "Really if you want advice, consult someone who knows."

His students tried hard to please him. A few considered him egotistical, but most liked, and some idolized him. They were happy just to be near him. A letter from a female student written to him in 1941 exclaims fervently, "I'd much rather sit beside you wherever you are . . . follow dumbly behind you wherever you go . . . you pierce exteriors and reach the person." Huldah read the letters and took the phone calls, sometimes with amusement, more often with exasperation. She knew that flattered as he was by their adulation, he really preferred the companionship of men. When a girl became too much of a nuisance, he left it to Huldah to put her in her place.

While the Braces liked the luxuries the extra money brought them, Jerry missed the rural atmosphere of Mount Holyoke. As late as 1943 he was still seriously considering a return there even though it would mean a reduction in both salary and rank. What may have been the deciding factor in keeping him at Boston University was that in 1941 he and Huldah were able to purchase an ideal house in a perfect setting. They had been looking for a place near Boston with a good school system and plenty of surrounding countryside. They often drove out on Sunday afternoons to explore possibilities. One day on Pinehurst Road in Belmont, Massachusetts, they saw just what they wanted, a gracious Georgian brick house set among big trees, with a "For Sale" sign on its front lawn. There was a garage under a covered porch and several stone walls. One old wall separated the garden plot in back from a country road, once the main route from Concord to Cambridge. It was on a high hill and from the ridge in back of the house, it was possible to see the towers of Harvard and the gold dome of the State House. They knew at once that this was the place for which they had been searching. It was in an area where Jerry had often skied in his Harvard days and was not far from the open fields of the private mental institution, McLean Hospital.

The Braces' Belmont home

Although the Depression was over, real estate was still cheap. The house had been entangled in legal red tape because it had been owned by a couple who had both been killed in an automobile accident. The difficulty in ascertaining which one had died first raised questions about the title. For over a year this had prevented the house from being sold. With money from the trust fund left by his father and a four percent mortgage from the bank, the Braces were able to buy it. Before leaving for Deer Isle in June of 1941, even while the house was still in escrow, they had the rooms wallpapered, floors refinished, and their furniture arranged. The inherited ornate dining room set looked just right in the dining room; there was a perfect place on the wall for the oil portrait of Charles Loring Brace II, and the cases of books were unpacked and put on book shelves in Jerry's study, under the staircase, and lining the hallway upstairs. Two steps led down to a spacious living room which had a big fireplace and plenty of room for their piano. Nicknamed Escrow Hall by John Donaldson, it seemed like a country manor, but it was in close proximity to the city.

In 1941 Putnam's published Brace's third novel, *Light on a Mountain*. Jerry had been delighted when the publishers decided to use his painting of a Vermont mountain on the dust jacket, but he was annoyed that they did not give him credit for it inside the book, on the jacket, or in any of the advertising. Set in the present (the late spring of 1939 to New Year's Day 1940) the novel presents a darker picture of life than his earlier books. War in Europe was threatening Western civilization and the tragedy of the Gaunt family mirrors the decline of society. It was, Jerry wrote, his "utmost effort to deal with the lives and ways of the Green Mountain country—and to do it fairly, with regret for the passing of old times and recognition of the inevitable and even tragic changes." (*DTW* II, p. 159) It is as difficult for an author to choose a favorite from among his novels as it is for a parent to choose a favorite child, but if pressured Jerry always confessed a special fondness for this story of Vermont life. The setting is a composite of the mountain roads and hill farms that Jerry had explored during his years of living in western Massachusetts especially during his Amherst days.

Jerry dedicated the novel to his mother "To L.W.B. with love." Although he and his mother had disagreements inevitable in two people from such different generations, there is no questioning the love that existed between them. Her letters address him as her "dear, dear son" and he respected her moral principles even when they conflicted with his more liberal views. Still he was censorious of her limitations.

> She seldom inquired critically or analytically into the underlying reasons for her beliefs and actions. She had the perfect manners and good taste of a lady, but very little real knowledge of history and literature and the arts: in her day girls seldom went to college and their reading was well censored. She knew only a bowdlerized Shakespeare and was taught to steer clear of the dangerous indecencies of Chaucer and Fielding and Smollett. She read aloud, with histrionic accents, the Uncle Remus stories and *Alice*—over and over, tirelessly, until we knew them by heart. She was vulnerable and fearful, and out of touch with a lot of actuality of modern life, but she had the faith and spirit of a saint and a martyr. (*DTW* II, p. 148)

Perhaps he underestimated her, for she had been brought up in the cultured Brace household and was fairly well read and traveled for a woman of her time. She was the mistress of her home, not its heart, leaving Jerry to search throughout his life for understanding women in whom he could confide: Carrie Johnson, Ellen Coolidge, Mrs. Buffum, and Mrs. Hancock. Huldah had the domestic nature he craved and she was important in assuring that his idealistic nature was grounded in reality, but it might be said of her as Froude said of Jane Carlyle, "She had a terrible habit of speaking out the exact truth, cut as clear as with a graving tool, on occasions too, when without harm it might have been left unspoken." Jerry learned that Huldah's unpredictable temperament often made it unwise for him to confess to her his innermost thoughts.

With two homes to maintain, a new boat, and three growing children, Brace hoped that the new novel would be financially successful. The contract with Putnam was the same as for his previous novel. He would receive 10 percent on the first four thousand copies, but sales were slow. When he wrote to his publishers for money due him to make a downpayment on his Belmont house, he was disappointed to learn that there was only $100 in his account.

Unfortunately, the timing proved wrong for a regional novel. World events dwarfed the problems of one family in a small northeast corner of

America. Some reviewers felt the book tried to cover too much plot in too small a space, though they all agreed that the characters were much more completely realized than in his earlier novels. It was the end of a way of life. The older generation might try to cling to their farms, but there was no future there for the sons and daughters, who were forced to take menial jobs in the towns or to go away to college to learn a profession such as teaching. The two Gaunt brothers represent the separate directions that ultimately divide their family.

The opening chapter symbolizes the transition from the old ways to the new. Mr. Gaunt sells a spruce forest on Stafford Mountain to a lumber company from Rutland to help pay for his son Henry's college tuition. Henry is bitter, not grateful, because he loved the woods. Eventually he comes to the realization that anyone who lives on a farm must learn early that one feels badly about a lot of things. "One got fond of chicken and sheep and cows, and eventually ate them for dinner. It was the same with woods." (*LOM*, p. 4) In his anger, Henry, who has been reading Jonathan Swift, publishes in the school literary magazine a poem he entitles "Vermin." Brace uses the variant responses his characters have to the poem to show their differences. Mrs. Gaunt puzzles over it, Mr. Gaunt falls asleep half way through, his brother Morton ignores it, his sister Sylvia thinks it's wonderful, most of his professors dislike it, but Professor Lincoln McCann is impressed.

The denuded forest mars Henry's homecoming. The scene is written with feeling, for one summer when Jerry had returned to Deer Isle he discovered that Fred Sylvester had sold off the timber from his spruce woods to pay his children's tuition. Jerry wondered how a caring man could destroy a place of such beauty. He remembered how early on summer mornings he had walked to the farm to collect the Brace family's daily supply of milk: "The little road wound along through a stretch of virgin spruce forest, with mossy open glades, and on sunny mornings the bright rays came down through the mists in shafts and planes and turned the forest into a silvery mystery—and there were white-throats and hermit thrushes singing from the secret places." (*DTW* II, p. 10) Fred, amused by such a sentimental reaction, reminded him that a forest is a cash crop like any other, it just takes longer to renew itself.

Each of the three Gaunt children has an experience on the mountain. Henry's solitary climb brings an epiphany when he sees the world spread out below him. As in Frost's poem "The Road Not Taken" he realizes that he is at a turning point. "You could come to the two roads parting in a wood and not see that one was any better or worse," (*LOM*, p. 82) but as he stops at a hill farm precariously perched on the mountain, he begins to comprehend that a writer needs people to give meaning to nature. It is a lesson that Brace himself has had to learn. The author's understanding of these lonely mountain women is seen in a scene where he has Henry listen to Mr. Corwin tell the story of Martha Sargent, whose husband lit out for the South Seas leaving her alone in the isolated cabin. For fifteen years she placed a light in the window each night in case he should return. During the whole account, Mrs. Corwin sits quietly listening and watching with mournful eyes, but the narrator's account is sympathetic to the husband, saying "O' course she was just a woman anyhow—she never did understand how a man feels about them things." (*LOM*, p. 89) Henry sees how one light on a mountain adds new dimension to the wilderness. "Coming into the house he forgave his father for destroying the spruce woods. He resolved to return to college and see the world." (*LOM*, p. 90)

Life in the town as part of a gang of local bullies had brutalized the already coarse nature of Morton, Henry's brother. He goes to the mountain in pursuit of an escaped prison convict. He plans to take life, not find its meaning. He feels superior to the lawmen who are also searching, and has nothing but contempt and anger toward society. In his dissertation for a doctorate at the University of New Brunswick, William Connor discerningly suggested that while the novel does not mention World War II directly, Morton is representative of the type of youth who joined the Nazi movement. Brace felt a responsibility to speak in favor of human decency and against the modern callousness which he sees destroying the world. Connor quotes from a published interview which Brace had at the time with Seymour Linscott of the *Boston Evening Transcript*. Brace's writings were already on a collision course with the directions of modern literature.

> When writers abandoned the old ideas of right and wrong and began to be free-thinkers with a flavor of cynicism and defeatism, then the stage was set for the rise of evil world forces and the downward trend of democracy . . . . all art is moral, whether it admits it or not. ("Teller of Yankee Tales Affirms Belief in Life," *Boston Evening Transcript*, 2 April 41)

Sylvia Gaunt is only eleven when she has her first mountain experience. The dreamy one of the three, she achieves complete oneness with nature. She represents Jerry's ideal woman—intelligent, sensitive, so unselfish that she gives up her hopes for a college education so that her brother Henry can afford to go, yet with enough pragmatism to marry a good man whom she doesn't love rather than to become a slave to her insensitive father and brother Morton. She wants to raise a family and have a home of her own. She has seen what a life of drudgery had done to her mother. In order to keep the family and farm going, Mrs. Gaunt has given up all her own interests, becoming dour and exhausted, and literally working herself to death. Sylvia does not intend to let life defeat her in this way.

Sylvia's adult mountain experience is with Henry's professor Lincoln McCann. Unhappily married and unfulfilled McCann compares himself to Bunyan's Christian come from the City of Destruction to see the Delectable Mountains shining with promise. Henry, who began the climb with them, has twisted his ankle and cut a crutch to help him hobble home just as Jerry once did when climbing with his Dartmouth colleagues. McCann feels that society has failed. He says:

> The fact is that our vision has come apparently to nothing—yours and Henry's and mine, Vermont's and New Hampshire's, Thoreau's and Emerson's, maybe America's. We thought a man could live and let live; we thought nature was on the whole benevolent, that things worked out by themselves—the less control the better. At least it's a beautiful vision—I mean it supposes that every man is capable of living his own life. . . . But apparently we've all failed; we've been simply letting the world go to ruin, as we might let a new car go to pieces for lack of care and oil. (*LOM*, p. 188)

Jerry had been brought up to believe in free enterprise and private charities. Jerry's father and grandfather and Ellen Coolidge devoted their lives to helping others. The Depression had convinced him, however, that there were always some people who could not succeed without government aid. It would have been difficult for most of Jerry's colleagues and friends to accept the fact that he had sympathy for the New Deal of Franklin D. Roosevelt, but if they had known that he agreed with the pacifism of Norman Thomas and had voted for the Socialist Party four different times, they would have been horrified. It was not just Hitler and his colleagues who were reactionary. McCann tells Sylvia that she is the ideal procreator of an Aryan race. He ironically suggests that in the world of the future, liberals such as professors and writers will be shot. He assures her that she will be safe though. "You will be the mother of splendid slaves. They'll take good care of you—they'll probably keep you like a thoroughbred cow, give you a blue ribbon to wear, exhibit you as the ideal American female." (*LOM*, p. 189)

Jerry is less knowledgeable about shallow town girls like Morton's wife Marjie, though he has a certain sympathy for her. She needs lights, and men and fun, but after the baby comes, Morton leaves her at home while he goes off with the men. She is a symbol of what happens to country ways once urban attitudes are introduced. Indirectly she causes Mrs. Gaunt's death and with that passing the central force that has held the family together disappears. The fate of the family, like the war in Europe, echoes the truth of the lines from William Butler Yeats: "Things fall apart; the center cannot hold/Mere anarchy is loosed upon the world."

Light on a Mountain shows more maturity than Brace's earlier novels. He has learned that nature is "as red in tooth and claw" as she is sublime, and that the darkness descending on the world is a threat to everyone. He still sees a good marriage as the greatest hope a woman has for happiness, but, he has abandoned his romantic attitudes. Sylvia wisely chooses her husband in the same level-headed way that a man would select a career. With his fortieth birthday approaching, Jerry was becoming more of a realist.

Professor Brace

13
A Time of Tension

On December 7, 1941, when the Japanese bombed Pearl Harbor, lives quickly changed. Male students enlisted or were drafted into the armed services, soon followed by the younger professors and teaching assistants. Brace had been just too young for World War I; now as a married man of forty, he was just too old for World War II. The teachers who remained at Boston University had to add extra duties to their already heavy teaching loads.

Jerry did not go to Deer Isle in 1942 until mid-summer. Huldah remained in Belmont with the children. The marriage was going through a period of tension. It annoyed Huldah that her husband was still so closely tied to his family, especially Eleanor. She complained bitterly about his rushing over to Dunham's Point every time his sister wanted something done. Eventually the two women would learn to accept one another, even feel fondness, but during the thirties and forties, there was a continuous tug of war between them, which Huldah ultimately won. It took time, too, for her to accept Jerry's female admirers. She had faith in his strict moral code of behavior, but couldn't help feeling the rivalry for his affections. There was also her feeling that her husband was not assertive enough with Putnam, his publishers. She considered Jerry an important novelist, but felt he lacked initiative. Her energetic father had always been able to sell anything, even himself. Jerry was no good at self-promotion. He disliked arguing with deans and publishers to get better deals. If making more money meant administrating or giving up summers at Deer Isle, he was not interested.

Although he felt guilty about leaving Belmont, he knew that only at Deer Isle could he find the environment necessary for his creativity. Since gasoline was in short supply, he went to Maine with his Aunt Leta by train, which during war time was slow and expensive. When he arrived, Jerry wrote immediately to Huldah to let her know that he was missing her. He told her that Aunt Leta had been impressed at how well the children had behaved while seeing them off, and he added sadly, "I thought you were nice too, and I almost cried when we started off & I could see you all waving & waving. And now that I'm here without you, I feel sort of empty and pointless. I've been wandering around mournfully and wondering what you are doing. After I've done so much to spoil our life together it sounds like empty words to say that I can't ever be happy without you, but that's really true. I get to thinking how much you mean to me and realize that it is everything."

That year, Jerry was the only male at the family summer place at Dunham's Point. The main house was being run by four women; and things did not always operate smoothly. Although the property had been promised to Eleanor, Aunt Leta still owned it. Jerry knew that Huldah, who never felt quite comfortable when surrounded by the Brace women, would be pleased to hear of their disagreements. "This is an amusing household—& rather pathetic. I think Mama is pretty fussy, & of course Muriel is always in a flutter, & gets wrought up over the silliest things & Eleanor is terribly fed up with all of them and lays them out right & left. Auntie Leta is good for them, but she isn't always tactful. Anyway they all treat me wonderfully, & Auntie L. is giving me the price of the trip." Although Eleanor and her friend Muriel Postlethwaite had a woman from Sunset to help with the cleaning and cooking, they acknowledged that they all could use a few lessons from Huldah. His sister and wife may not have become as close to one another as Jerry would have wished, but Eleanor did appreciate Huldah's skill in running an organized household.

Jerry stayed in the Trivet as it did not seem worthwhile to open the Parker's Point house. The weather was cold and clear—so cold that sleeping on the Trivet porch, he had needed three blankets. In fact, the Trivet was proving so breezy that Eleanor decided to change its name to "Fair Winds" and even had some notepaper with the new name printed on the heading, but somehow everyone continued to call it the Trivet.

The war made life on the island that summer more as it had been in his youth. There were fewer cars on the roads so he was able to do a lot of running with little concern for traffic. Of course, the gas shortage did create problems. Eleanor needed to have gas to get supplies. She went to the rationing office at Ellsworth where she succeeded in getting extra fuel stamps. Every morning Jerry worked on his novel, but afternoons he and Eleanor went sailing or he took his watercolors out, or he sailed over to Great Spruce Head Island to play tennis at the Porters. He visited the Sylvesters. One day the Sylvester men caught thirty-two flounder; so they gave Jerry five which he filleted and took home for the women to cook for their supper.

War work and fuel shortages had prevented the return of many of the summer residents, although the wealthy St. Johns, who owned the large, handsome house at the top of the Braces' small dirt road, arrived from New York. Their next nearest neighbors, the Thompsons, had been the first of the native Deer Islanders to lose someone in the war. They had no children of their own, but had brought up several nephews. Josephine loved gossip, but normally she was alone all winter with her deaf husband who, like so many down Mainers, spoke only when he had something practical to say. At the news of her nephew's death, all the neighbors had rallied around. Josephine cornered Jerry as soon as she saw him. In a letter to Huldah, Jerry described how when he walked by the house, "Mrs. Thompson fell upon me & talked for an hour solid—poor thing is so excited about Howard she can't stop. The funeral was last Mon & there were soldiers & flags & bugles & guns & everybody was there & Mrs. T. was so thrilled she'll never get over it. She has the relics all fixed up in her parlor, pictures & the flag & 2 framed diplomas from his Army Training School—he was doing fine work & was in line to be made a sergeant. And she talked and cried and talked and cried."

There were other indications of war. After walking down to Stonington boatyard to check on the boats, he wrote to John Donaldson how seeing *Bettina* and *Charmian* there in the midst of freighters, reminded him of the two of them "in this war time world—small, unproductive symbols of a happier time." One day when Jerry was working on his mooring at Parker's Point, an army jeep with two soldiers came bouncing over the rocks to the water's edge and watched him for several minutes. He had noticed tracks on the grass when he arrived and suspected that the soldiers were on a routine patrol, for the army was on constant alert for any unusual activity off the Maine coast.

Jerry was trying to write regularly on a new novel, but he was having difficulty getting started. He wrote to Huldah from the Trivet:

> I'm supposed to be working on my novel now, but yesterday I decided it was no go. It probably means all that work wasted—but maybe someday I can get it started again. Just now it seems hopeless. I really can't feel it strongly enough. It is partly the war and all the modern uncertainties. The book would seem rather quaint and remote and out of touch with reality. So I'm going to try something else, and so far I'm not sure what—but I'd like to make it quite different. Maybe after I finish off this I'll write Chap. 1, page 1 & start once upon a time. I've sometimes had fun with the writing, in spite of the grind, but this story of Maine has been a dead weight.

The new beginning became *The Garretson Chronicle* which many critics consider his finest work.

Huldah thought Jerry should have stayed in Belmont and painted the trim on the house instead of going to Maine; so in all his letters he tries to convince her how hard he is working. He has settled *Festina* more securely in her cradle, covering the rudder with burlap to protect it from the sun. He has located the old buoy six feet below water and substituted a new one. He has emptied the cistern hoping to keep the cellar drier. He has swept the kitchen floor and thrown out some old potato peelings. By now he had learned enough about women to know that when he has gone against his wife's wishes, he'd better make it clear that he hasn't been enjoying it. He assures her that he has been miserable.

> I do miss you. I feel like a hollow shell without you—there's not much point to what I do unless I do it with you or for you. I'd really like to write something good for you, and paint a good picture for you, but I need you to reassure me. If you don't have faith in me anymore I might as well be dead. I hate to have to think about myself so much, but it keeps gnawing and gnawing that I am faithless and self seeking—and I don't like to be like that at all. You don't know what a foolish romantic dream all my youth was—I lived in a mist of illusions, very pleasant sometimes, but very false, like too much drink, and I'm ashamed of its falseness and lack of real values. I want to work back to reality, I want to be secure and faithful; it is only now that I realize clearly the difference between fact and illusion—at least I realize the difference that matters. . . . Life is hard, but as long as I can be with you, and work and play and sleep with you, I like its hardness.

However much he may have yielded to temptation, there is no questioning the sincerity of this letter, though it is difficult to realize that it was written by a man over forty who has been married for years. Over and over in his different letters that summer he blames the "dreams and make believe" he enjoyed as a young man as the reason it has taken him such a long time to learn how much he really loves her. Now he wants them to be together and happy once more. Unfortunately, he never did learn not to spoil the effect by telling in the same letters about all the good picnics and sails he has been enjoying.

Finally, Huldah was sufficiently mollified to begin answering his letters, though only about practical items such as having their oil tank in Belmont filled in case the fuel shortages became more acute. Jerry notified her that he would be returning to Boston early in August to sit on a dissertation oral for Donald Winslow, a young B.U. instructor who had received notification that he would be inducted into the army on the 15th of August. Jerry was first reader of the dissertation on Thomas Hardy so knew it was essential that he be there. He sent a telegram promising to be present.

He had painted a watercolor as a present for Huldah. As usual he was not satisfied with it, and hoped to find time to do another, but he had a number of tasks to complete before leaving. He ran all the way to Parker's Point to check the cistern and lock everything securely. He left the key with the Thompsons where he found Goodwin in a more cheerful frame of mind than usual, though Josephine kept interrupting him with more details about the funeral. He also stopped briefly to see Norman Pressey. He thought he seemed thin and tired. After all the years of not having sufficient work, the boat-builders were now doing war work over ten hours a day in the shipyards.

Rubber was in short supply, so Jerry was delighted to hear that Gluyas Williams had a bicycle tire for him. The Williams had just had electricity installed in their Dunham's Point house and were eager to show it to him before he left. While Jerry's taste in comics ran mainly to the Katzenjammer Kids and Mutt and Jeff, he always enjoyed the cartoons that Gluyas did for the *New Yorker*. The cartoonist was active in the Deer Isle summer colony, and that year he had become an air raid warden. One night he had to knock at the Trivet door to tell Jerry that the light from his reading lamp was showing. Houses along the coast were fitted with black-out curtains as fears increased that German submarines were lurking offshore. The Brace house was too far from the village of Sunset and the Harbor to hear the warning blackout bells, and Jerry, absorbed in a book, had absent-mindedly forgotten to close the shades.

In Belmont, Jerry, too, took on the job of Air Raid Block Warden. Cities along the coast remained on the alert for enemy aircraft, which fortunately never arrived. The one time that Boston was evacuated because of a warning that enemy planes had been spotted off the coast, everything became hope-lessly confused. Boston University closed and locked its buildings, stranding the commuting students dependent on infrequent trains. Subways became hopelessly jammed, and people milled around on all the streets. If it had been a genuine air attack, there would have been hundreds of unnecessary victims.

In the fall of 1942, Jerry's nephew, Johnnie Gilchrist, son of his sister Betty, had to leave the dormitory at Massachusetts Institute of Technology where he was studying Naval Architecture. College dorms were taken over to house the men in the Army Specialized Training Program (ASTP). Betty had never been too fond of Huldah—in fact, in earlier years John, called Johnnie by the family to distinguish him from John Donaldson, felt that his mother had sometimes been actually cruel in her treatment of Huldah. Certainly she had often succeeded in irritating or hurting Huldah's feelings, though this may have been partly unintentional. As the wife of a career diplomat, she was used to the role of great lady and could sometimes be imperious. Nevertheless, Huldah now joined Jerry in warmly welcoming Johnnie to live with them.

Johnnie had always admired his uncle, even more than his own brilliant father who had a distinguished career in both diplomacy and business. It had been Jerry who had first given Johnnie the copy of Skene's *Elements of Yacht Design*, which had awakened his interest in the field of naval architecture at the age of twelve. Jerry himself had learned boat design by trial and error and by asking questions of the Maine boatbuilders. In his youth, designing a boat model had been more of a folk art. "A man could whittle out a half model, shape it by eye, and expect it to prosper." (*BWW*, p. 95) Once he was invited by the great boat designer Starling Burgess to come talk to him about a career, but he never went to see him. It seemed to Jerry's Puritan conscience that to spend his life designing boats would be too pleasant and seductive. Of course, at M.I.T. designing was a serious science. Johnnie had been given a work desk in Jerry's home office, and one day his uncle picked up a heavy two volume text packed with formidable tables and mathematic equations. After perusing it with rather scornful eyes, his only comment was: "So that's what it's come to now."

Johnnie remained with the Braces until 1943 when he was drafted into the armed services. Huldah was a good cook even with the substitutions made necessary by the food shortages. Coffee was mixed with chicory, meat became very scarce, and sugar disappeared from the stores. Unappetizing looking white oleomargarine could be made more acceptable by adding yellow from the little packet of food coloring that accompanied each purchase, though it fooled no one. Johnnie never felt totally at ease during meals. Jerry had been brought up in a family where manners were of greater importance than religion. Now he was equally strict with his own children. Even minor refractions brought sharp reproofs. When Huldah scolded it could be sharp, but soon forgotten. Jerry was coldly cutting, and the children continued to feel chastened throughout the remainder of the meal. Though he sometimes directed comments on serious topics to Johnnie or his sons, Jerry rarely included Huldah in these discussions. This may have been partly to avoid argument, but it was also a throwback to his own youth when serious conversation at the dinner table had been the province of the males. Women were thought to have their own separate interests.

While Jerry was fond of Johnnie, he was often censorious. They enjoyed running together on the old road in back of the house. Tennis was a bit more pressured, for Jerry was annoyed if his partner did not play well, but neither did he like to be beaten. Although Johnnie had been educated abroad during his early years, his parents had sent him to America for preparatory school. Summers he had joined the Braces at Deer Isle. Sailing was the family's true religion. Even Jerry's normally gentle father could sharply chastize any sailing error. Jerry was a natural who moved about a sailboat with the grace of a ballet dancer and knew what needed to be done by instinct. Eleanor was almost as good and was even a better teacher for she did not get as annoyed if a mooring was missed or a sail luffed. Johnnie never became an expert sailor. He lacked instinctive ability and feared Jerry's displeasure. Only Uncle John

Donaldson made sailing pure fun. He was not a natural himself, and felt that any errors simply added to the adventure. No real Brace could have conceived of reacting that way, but Jerry was always amused by his brother-in-law.

Though Jerry did not have John Donaldson's jovial wit, he did have his own brand of quiet humor. Johnnie Gilchrist became aware of that one evening when they were returning from Parker's Point down the Dow Road. Jerry was driving when a woodchuck, mesmerized by the car's headlights, froze motionless in the road. The wheels of the car passed on either side of him, leaving him unscathed, at which moment Jerry turned to John Donaldson and said drily, "Isn't that what a Darwinian would call an example of auto-selection?"

Jerry preferred a regular schedule, but it proved impossible to maintain one under the mounting pressure of work. In March of 1943 the Joint Army-Navy Manpower Commission set up an Army Specialized Training Program at Boston University. By July, six hundred soldiers were housed in Boston's Mechanics Building while they studied in B. U.'s "Foreign Area and Language" program. During the nine months that the ASTP was at Boston University, the forty-five professors had to provide the program with 2500 hours of instruction. This was on top of their regular teaching loads which had been raised to 18 credit-hours a week. Jerry became increasingly exhausted.

New rules allowed students to leave high school in January of their senior years so that they could begin college classes before being drafted. This meant that required courses had to be repeated in each semester. Prior to the war there were few non-traditional students. Most came directly from high school and enrolled in a rather rigid four-year sequence of courses. Now, with students working odd shifts on war jobs and leaving colleges at various times, required courses had to be offered in late afternoon and evenings and in the summer. A six-week Intersession was added to the regular Summer Session so that students could accelerate. Every professor was asked to teach in at least one of these sessions.

Jerry's ability to listen attentively to people provided good material for his novels, but it also meant that he often became more involved in people's problems than he intended. His departmental chairman, Tom Mather, was one who confided his family troubles to Jerry. Even in the days when Mrs. Mather had been Jerry's corrector, she had been nervous and reclusive. During the war, her condition steadily worsened. Their son Tom had serious psychological problems. They lived only about a mile from the Braces' Belmont home and, often at night or in the early dawn hours, Jerry would see the despondent and desperate husband and father walking down Pinehurst Road. Sometimes Jerry would go out to join him and listen quietly to his unhappy outpourings. Mather grew increasingly dependent on Jerry's sympathetic support.

The only time Mather seemed to be able to escape his family worries was while he was teaching his classes. He was a natural performer who never needed notes, not even for long quotations. He would act out scenes with a gusto that his students never forgot. They told and retold anecdotes, sometimes apocryphal, of how his belt had broken while he was engaged in an imaginary sword fight and he had nearly lost his pants, or how in reenacting Grendel's bursting the hinges off Heorot "Swoln as he was with fury/ the house's mouth he rent" he had crashed through the plate glass door of the classroom and emerged in the hall covered with glass. Another time he played Chaucer's amorous Nicholas in love with Alison. Clutching his heart and leaning out the window, he cried so loudly "love me now or I shall die" that someone passing below on the sidewalk called Emergency to report that the overweight professor was suffering a heart attack. None of his undergraduate students dreamed how much his clown facade hid a desperately unhappy man.

On occasion, Mather would drive Jerry home from classes in his old Plymouth, and one day he surprised him by inviting the whole Brace family to dinner. Mrs. Mather must have agonized for days over an appropriate menu. Instead of a simple meal that she and her mother, who lived with them, might have been able to manage, they prepared a turkey dinner with all the fixings. The evening was a disaster. Although dinner was to have been served at six, it was not ready two hours later. Jerry later described the embarrassment everyone felt as they sat with Tom and his daughter, Merrilee, waiting for Mrs. Mather to emerge from the kitchen. "The anxiety of it all was palpable and Tom senior paced in and out with a look of hopeless worry and her daughter made efforts to keep my children occupied, and Tom junior had nothing to say to us at all, and Mrs. Mather was hardly visible and her mother remained invisible to the end. They had clearly planned a major performance for us and the effort almost overwhelmed them: they were exhausted and bewildered while we sat mostly in silence in the Victorian parlor. Their intentions were benevolent but the event itself was full with pathos." (*DTW* II, p. 154) Jerry was unfailingly kind and sympathetic, but he was sorry that he had let himself get so entwined in their darkening affairs.

As soon as his teaching in Intersession was over, Jerry left for Deer Isle, eager to check on his boat and property. He discovered that several panes of glass had been shot out of the windows at Parker's Point and had to be replaced. Once again, Huldah and the children were not with him. Twelve-year-old Loring was helping his mother who had her hands full because young Gerald was ill, and Barbara was away at camp. Jerry stayed in the Trivet. In spite of rationing, food was not a problem on the island as the people there had always been forced to be self-sufficient. The Sylvesters sold fruit and vegetables and milk, Mrs. Haskell had eggs, and, of course, there was always plenty of lobster, fish, and clams. Gerald was a bit scornful of Muriel Postlethwaite's cooking. She would use a megaphone to hail a passing lobster boat in the morning and immediately cook the live lobsters. She would then re-heat them for dinner which caused them to lose their flavor. Jerry felt that even the least experienced housewife should know better than to do that.

His time on Deer Isle was brief, but when school opened in September of 1943, life was a bit easier. Enrollment at the College of Liberal Arts had dropped to a low of 373 students. Not only were most of the males gone, but girls were finding good paying wartime jobs. Of course, this was seen as only a temporary situation. It was assumed that as soon as the war was over women would give up working so the returning men could have their jobs back. Many girls were getting married, often with more haste than wisdom. A man entering the service, not knowing when or if he would return, wanted to have a woman at home waiting for him. *Carpe Diem* became the philosophy of the times. It was easy to meet men in the city. There were USO dances every night. The Coast Guard was stationed in Copley Square, and sororities sponsored weekly social evenings for service men. But it all had an air of impermanence, and the man who took a date out on Friday night might be gone on Monday morning. Some of the rigid rules on sexual behavior began to break down.

Most of the girls at B.U. were not very sophisticated, and Jerry sometimes enjoyed gently shocking them. He read aloud the passage in Thomas Hardy's *A Pair of Blue Eyes* where Steven Knight is left dangling after a fall off a cliff. In front of his eyes he sees the layers of fossils embedded in the stone and chalk. While he ponders the meaning of the universe, the heroine is tearing her petticoats into strips for him to use as a rope to climb back up. Then looking over his glasses and raising an eyebrow at the girls, Jerry commented mockingly, "Think what would happen to a man dependent on a woman's undergarments these days!"

Although never reflected in his teaching, Jerry was becoming increasingly depressed. All hope for a speedy end to the war had been abandoned. Hitler seemed invincible. Boys were dying on far off Pacific Islands whose names had been unknown a few months before. The world of democracy and scholarship were proving impotent against the brute forces of marching men. The future of civilization itself seemed in doubt. Jerry had inherited a natural inclination toward melancholy from his great-grandfather, John Pierce Brace, who had suffered a similar depression during the Civil War. Even earlier, John Pierce Brace had written about his youthful years, "The foolish indulgence of morbid melancholy had become a habit & was almost periodical." With the help of Catherine Beecher and Lucy Porter, who became his wife, he recovered from his early depression, but it seemed to Jerry that he himself was sinking ever deeper.

As soon as his extra duties at B.U. were over, he went to Deer Isle accompanied by Loring. The restrictions of wartime travel and the aging of the older generation meant that the family gathering was much smaller than usual. Only Eleanor, Muriel, and Betty's daughter, Brenda Gilchrist, were in the main house. There were no Donaldsons, "Mama," or Aunt Leta. Jerry felt tired and depressed, unable to get to sleep until the light of dawn and the chattering of the birds filled his room. As a young man he had blamed his father for educating him for a world of idealism that had ceased to exist with World War I. Now another war was changing the world even more. Jerry could see in himself echoes of his own father, while Loring, at 13, was doing the things he had once done as a boy. He realized that every man is part of a continuum. The novel he was writing became increasingly autobiographical. He began to write in the first person, and made his narrator a 44-year-old man like himself, recording memories of his grandfather, father, and his own youth. By using a persona, Brace felt released. As he has his narrator explain: "all my past—and my father's past—comes crowding round me, and I want to embrace it with words." (*GC* p. 7) The novel seemed almost to write itself. He began writing at least four pages a day instead of his usual one or two.

He and Loring accomplished a tremendous amount of work. They sandpapered the tender and gave it two coats of paint. Eleanor came to help them pick cherries. Loring worked on the *Loon*, the small boat used by the young people, while his father cleaned the cellar of debris that had fallen from some toppling barrels that had been left there by the previous owners. Loring dove deep into the icy water off the point to find a lost mooring chain. For two days, they cleaned the garage, and they destroyed and sprayed a large ants' nest. In his younger days, Jerry had taken pride in testing his limits while walking or skiing. Now he felt compelled to work hard physically. He believed, and Huldah concurred, that the back-breaking labor of a farmer or fisherman was somehow more vital than the life of a scholar or writer.

Finally everything at Parker's Point was secured for winter. This entailed great labor. They had to arise at 5:30 A.M. to get the boats ready for lifting. They scraped and cleaned the bottom of *Festina*. Loring was upset because he had left the rudder of the *Loon* on the rocks and the tide had carried it away. They cleared brush and dug clams. Jerry was getting tired and irritated. He complained that Loring was not working hard enough, because he had spent time trying to fix an old victrola instead of finishing his chores. The trip home by train with all their luggage was difficult. They arrived back in Belmont in early August. Jerry was more despondent than ever. It was growing increasingly difficult to face the long days of teaching.

It was young Gerald's turn for Deer Isle the next summer. He had a different temperament from his brother and was not as much a natural craftsman and sailor. Jerry found this difficult to understand. Of course he, too, was expected to work. They picked blueberries, cut trees and brush, lugging it all down to the shore to be burned, and dug clams on their own shore. Although Gerald complained that they were eating nothing but fish, it was a good thing they could, because when they visited the local store there was no meat, crackers, Crisco, oleo, or margarine. Fortunately. when they sailed to Eagle Island, they were given two pounds of freshly churned butter by the Quinns who didn't even ask for rationing stamps in return. They shared a pound with Eleanor, for butter had become an almost unheard of treat.

One day Jerry mowed the grass by hand all the way up to the St. John's house. Then for relaxation he and his son sailed to Great Spruce Head Island where they met Lincoln Fairley and sailed with him most of the way back to Cape Rosier. That night Jerry complained of upper back muscle cramps. He decided they must have been caused by tension or improper posture. Eleanor had been having the same complaint, but had found some exercises that seemed to help. It didn't occur to either of them that the heavy physical work they were doing in their mid-forties and fifties might have something to do with it.

Jerry continued to suffer from insomnia and melancholy. He knew that he was being difficult, but he did not seem able to control it. No matter how much he tried avoiding thoughts of the war, they were ever present. Furthermore, he seems to have been going through what today would be called a mid-life crisis. He still loved Huldah, but he was becoming ever more aware of the differences in their interests and attitudes. She was unhappy with him and punished him by using family responsibilities as an excuse to remain in Belmont during his summers in Maine. He wrote to her sadly:

> I have lived a selfish life and my sense of guilt is uncomfortable. I have destroyed your faith in me and feel bereft. All the things I most delighted in have lost their appeal because we don't share them. This house is so full of you—all the things and arrangements and plans and work we did—that it breaks my heart that you aren't here and we don't share it anymore. The place was what I wanted more than anything, and now I've destroyed it. I ought to be strong enough to accept the verdict and try to go on to something else, but so far I haven't been able to. Maybe I ought to live without such dependence on you, but I seem to be unable to do that . . . my life seems to have broken down.

To add to his problems, Mather had written to see if his daughter Merrilee and young Tom could come for a visit. Jerry did not see how he could manage it. He spoke to Bertha Carter, who was summering on the island and had known Merrilee at B.U. She promised to try to find a place where they could board, but this defeated Mather's desire to have them under Jerry's reassuring presence. The only good news was that there had been premature rumors on the island that the war was over. The European War had ended in May. When news came in the first week of August that atomic bombs had been dropped on Hiroshima and Nagasaki, everyone was sure that there would be an immediate announcement of war's end, but it was not until September 2, 1945, that the formal surrender was signed by Japan aboard the U.S.S. *Missouri* in Tokyo Bay.

14
Recognition

The end of the war brought rapid changes, which Jerry found difficult. The college expanded almost overnight. The previously small, mainly female, classes became crowded with veterans sponsored by the G.I. Bill. Classrooms had to be rented across Boylston Street over the drugstore. New instructors were hired to add to those returning from their military stint. The English department now had two more Ph.D.'s. Donald J. Winslow came back from the Air Force and Irving White was transferred to the College of Liberal Arts from one of the other divisions of the University, the College of Practical Arts and Letters.

The already cramped English office became more crowded than ever. Major Leighton Brewer joined the faculty. He and Jerry immediately became friends. Both enjoyed tennis, camping, fishing, and writing. Furthermore, they were from the same social background. Brewer had published two books of long narrative verse: one on Bermuda, entitled *Red Hibiscus*, and *Riders of the Sky*. The latter recounted Brewer's own experiences in the famed Lafayette Escadrille in the early days of World War I. In 1916, before the entry of the United States into the war, this daring group of young, mostly wealthy, American pilots had gone to fight in the skies over France where they suffered heavy casualties in their engagements with German flying Aces. Leighton had joined the group in 1917 before it was reorganized as the American 103rd Pursuit Squadron. The men treated the war as a personal conflict and paid honor to gallant opponents like Baron von Richtofen, the Red Knight of Germany. Leighton's poem was a tribute to comrades who had sacrificed their lives and whom he now envisioned meeting in a sort of Valhalla. It was the kind of romantic derring-do that Jerry, who had missed both wars, greatly admired. Some of the returning veterans were less pleased to see the Major Brewer desk-plate—it reminded them of the kind of military authority that they wanted to forget.

During the years that Robert Frost taught his informal poetry seminars in Cambridge, Jerry and he frequently visited one another. One night when

Frost had been to a private family dinner at the Braces, Jerry invited Johnnie Gilchrist to join them for the evening knowing that Frost would talk into the late hours. Frost was entertaining and charming, but Jerry was a bit taken aback when after confessing to the poet that in his latest novel he had quoted some of the poet's lines without attribution, Frost responded carelessly, "Oh well, that's all right—I never read novels."

In September of 1946, I became Brace's graduate assistant. Although he had used a corrector for Freshman English papers, he had always preferred to do his own literature essay questions which required thoughtful responses. Now with veterans flooding the classrooms he had to agree to have help. Classes like his American Short Story had over one hundred, mature inquisitive students. Jerry enjoyed them for he found that "they were not discontented or iconoclastic in the fashion of our later time, but they were outspoken and a little grim about their judgments."(*DTW* II, p. l55) He was never a strong public speaker, but his straight-forward lectures and sincere manner won their approval. They knew he was giving them his honest appraisal of what he considered the best in literature.

He had never been completely comfortable lecturing to a class. When Bertha Carter began teaching in 1947, he sent her some "Notes for a beginning teacher." Though light in tone, they are revealing of his own feelings toward teaching and contain a considerable amount of truth as any established professor will attest.

> After ten years you'll be almost as scared as you are now.
> Don't be surprised at anything any student ever does.
> Recollect, for example, that I've just had a year of you.
> Remember that students expect the worst from you. The
> thought is often comforting after you've given them the worst.
> Remember that after you've given them the best, no one
> besides yourself will be aware of it.
> You can't teach anyone you hate, love, or fear.
> Learn to play poker, its techniques will be essential to you.

In novel after novel, Brace would express the view that professors are basically frauds who only pretend to know all the answers, but it was not intellectual insecurity that led him to challenge students to think independently. Brace had firm ideas about a teacher's role. He never pontificated, but encouraged students to think for themselves and express differing opinions.

Jerry and I were becoming good friends. He suggested books I should read and talked to me about boats and Maine. He had once compared his feelings about *Festina* to that of Pygmalian for Galatea, but his power to mold and fashion went far beyond boats, as he himself realized. He cultivated my mind, my tastes, and interests. He suggested the topic for my thesis on "Galsworthy's Concept of Forsytism," for settling his father's estate had made him aware of the importance of family possessions in connecting the generations. The Forsyte trilogy had been published between 1906 and 1921. The account of three generations of one family appealed to him as a valedictory to a lost era. As he wrote in an article for the *Boston University Graduate Journal*: "It was the swan song of a society, an attitude, a code—and even then it seemed irrelevant to the young." He had been brought up in such a society and, though he too had rejected it, he knew it had left its imprint on him. He worried that perhaps he too belonged to an age already past.

Everyone in the crowded English office was aware that Mather's mind and health were deteriorating. In September his son, Tom Jr., finally lost his grasp on reality, hurling rocks and a monkey wrench through the windows of a church. When he was incarcerated in Westboro Mental Hospital, Mrs. Mather threatened suicide. By November, Mather broke down under the strain and had to go to Boston Psychopathic Hospital. The day before his release, Mrs. Mather became uncontrollable and was also committed. His colleagues did all they could to help. They added his courses to their own already heavy schedules. Professor Loveland made young Tom his personal responsibility and for many years visited him in the institution. Jerry wrote to Bertha Carter on January 19, 1947, "At present everything is hopeless. Merrilie looks like a ghost & can hardly speak. Nothing like it outside of Dostoevski. The aged grandmother dodders round the house saying Ruthie, [Mrs. Mather's name] Ruthie, Ruthie over & over."

When Mrs. Mather managed to commit suicide in the hospital by setting herself on fire, Mather became totally dependent on his daughter, not wanting to let her out of his sight. Bertha wrote to ask Jerry if it would help if she invited them to come to New York to stay with her. Jerry thought it would be better if Merrilie went alone, though he doubted if she would. He told how, like the Ancient Mariner, Mather was collaring anyone who would listen to him. "He talks and talks and talks. I've heard every detail of his ordeal from A to Z and back again ten times over. Huldah has heard it. Everyone he can buttonhole has heard it. He goes on with Merrilie constantly—over and over each event, each word, each thought someone may or may not have had." Mather's own mind was slipping over the edge. He drew up a credo of his faith to give him strength noting that "the road to fear is the road to destruction and the first step toward God." He was rapidly going down that road.

Merrilie's friends urged her to take control of her own life, but nothing seemed worthwhile. It was almost a relief when on August 26, 1947, Mather died at the age of 57—primarily from a broken spirit. As the colleague closest to Mather, Jerry was asked to write an obituary for the official records of the

College of Liberal Arts where Mather had taught for twenty-five years. It was also printed in the University magazine *Bostonia*. Jerry described him as a brilliant man destroyed by overwhelming tragedy. "His too sensitive nature was constantly vulnerable, and his honest and tolerant mind could be attacked by doubts and questions; in the end he was overwhelmed by problems harsher than any man can be expected to bear."

Miraculously Merrilie slowly pulled her life back together. Ultimately she finished her doctorate, married and moved west to teach. But the tragedy continued to haunt Jerry. The Mathers reappear as the Quinn family in the novel that Jerry was currently writing, *The Garretson Chronicle*. The physical description is recognizable to anyone who had known Tom with his "immense baby smile, gap toothed and glistening" and "Friar Tuck joviality." The fictional Mr. Quinn too is asthmatic and an insomniac, personifying "the tragedy of all flesh." The narrator confesses some of Brace's own dichotomy of feelings about his involvement with the family's misfortune when he says "I wanted to escape, to release myself from what seemed like a dreadful allegory, a masque of pathetic mortality." (*GC*, p. 270) Marilyn, the Quinn daughter, is pale and silent. Even the embarrassing dinner party is presented in altered form. Perhaps Jerry hoped that eventually love would animate Merrilie as it does Marilyn. Yet for all the miseries the fictional Quinns suffer, their lives never approach the depth of tragedy of the Mathers. Mr. Quinn is able to forget his troubles when absorbed in his watch and clock collection. When Brace had Ralph describe seeing the pieces of the clocks Mr. Quinn was tinkering with spread across the table, no doubt Jerry had a mental image of his own father-in-law who shared the same hobby. Mrs. Quinn mourns for her son, but, at least, he has died an honorable death in the war. Her daughter, Marilyn, in spite of her unhappiness at home, enjoys boys and parties and has moments of lighthearted pleasure denied to Merrilie. Jerry did not dare use the full tragedy of the Mathers for he felt that the truth was too much like a Greek drama to be acceptable to a modern reader. Truth so grim could only be used as plot for a Gothic novel.

Fears that his fourth novel might be too old-fashioned for the post-war world seemed confirmed when Putnam's informed him that they were not interested in publishing his newest work. Once again he had the difficult task of finding someone willing to publish his work. He considered asking advice from Mr. Freedman, a Deer Isle summer neighbor, but when he learned that the man had his milk shipped to the island from New York each week, he decided he was not interested in the views of such a limited mind. Instead he asked Eleanor's friend Elizabeth Otis if she would be willing to become his book agent.

Otis sent the manuscript, typed by a friend with more enthusiasm than skill, to W. W. Norton's, even though they had given up publishing fiction ten years before. George Brockway, the young editor whose job it was to automatically return all fiction submissions unread, remembers how Brace's acceptance by the publishers was almost by accident. Back when he had been editor of the literary magazine at Williams College, Brockway had received a copy of *The Islands* for review. It had arrived too late for publication, but because of his interest in Maine islands, he had taken it home to read. Now, only because he remembered how much he had enjoyed the first novel, he began reading *The Garretson Chronicle*. He was sufficiently impressed to take it to the next editorial meeting. Storer Lunt, who was then the president of Norton, agreed that it had potential. When Lunt discovered that Brace had a family connection with his good friend Norman Donaldson, sales manager for the Yale University Press whose books at that time were distributed by Norton, the author-publisher relationship quickly grew. Brockway and Brace soon considered themselves personal friends, for they had much in common. Brockway had been born in Portland, Maine, and shared Jerry's love for the coast. He had graduated from Williams College in 1936 and did graduate work at Yale. Jerry trusted his judgment and made the rather substantial cuts in *The Garretson Chronicle* that Brockway suggested. The rejection of the novel by Putnam, which at the time had seemed so calamitous, turned out to be fortuitous. Brockway, who later became president of the publishing company, would later read all Brace's novels in progress, making only minor changes in the final manuscripts. Brace could concentrate on his writing knowing that Brockway and Lunt would look out for his book promotions and financial interests.

The initial printing of 10,000 copies of *The Garretson Chronicle*, which arrived at the bookstores in the summer of 1947, was gone in a week, with orders waiting. The *New Yorker* called it the best novel since George Santayana's highly acclaimed *The Last Puritan*. The glowing reviews prompted the Old Corner Book Store to ask Brace to leave Maine and come to Boston for a day of book signing. John Donaldson sailed Jerry, Gerald, and Loring in *Charmian* to Chebeague Island in Casco Bay. From there they were able to make connections for a train to Boston. Jerry had to face the public which his new popularity brought. Several hundred copies of the book were sold that day. Exhausted, he headed toward the North Station to catch the train for Maine. He stopped on the way at a hardware store where he bought himself a jackknife, perhaps as an appropriate memento of the one that in the novel the hero gives to his girl. It became Jerry's good luck charm, and in time he became almost superstitious about it. Several times it was lost, but he was always sure that it would turn up again and miraculously it did. For many years he carried his lunch to his office in a brown bag which usually contained a piece of fruit. An unforgettable image of him is of his deftly paring his apple or pear with that knife, which he kept sharp enough for whittling wood.

By August 25, the novel was a best seller across the country. It was even reviewed on the Connie Forde radio show in Peoria Illinois. Brockway was jubilant. On September 3 he wrote to Huldah lightheartedly: "If I understand Jerry's plans, he is now off fishing, leaving you to close up the summer place. I shan't comment on his apparently irresponsible behavior, but shall confine myself to a brief report on the first ten days in the life of The Garretson Chronicle—out of stock—21,000 more to be printed." A week later he wrote to Jerry who had protested that he had not been off enjoying himself: "Forgive me for my low suspicions of your integrity as a handyman around the house. No man who would undertake to paint his house these afternoons would go fishing just to avoid closing up a summer house." He was one of Jerry's few friends who dared to tease.

Though most reviewers compared *The Garretson Chronicle* to Santayana's *The Last Puritan* or John Marquand's Pulitzer prize-winning *The Late George Apley*, many agreed with Sterling North that it had more warmth and humanity than either. The Cleveland *Plain Dealer* pointed out that it shared more in common with Sarah Orne Jewett's "native plants" than Marquand's "forced flowers." The cultured social class of the Garretsons living in Compton, a thinly disguised Concord, Mass., made the comparisons with Marquand inevitable, but Brace was writing about the "native plants" of his own youth. The original concept for his protagonist, Ralph Garretson, was originally based on Carl Dennett's younger brother, Devon, who had given up the family profession to become a craftsman, but the character soon became merged with Jerry's own. The Garretson family bears a distinct resemblance to the Braces, and Mrs. Kingsley was, as Jerry admitted, a portrait of his Amherst friend Carrie Johnson.

The death of his father, the ugliness of war, and Jerry's own maturing and awakening memories helped Jerry shape the splintered present. As he had Ralph reflect in the novel: "When a man's father dies, the loss is in some curious sense geographical. One stands suddenly on a little hill and looks back at the settled region of his life, the secure homestead, the safety of property, the old order—an order of comforting authority and loyalties." (*GC*, p. 7) These words are followed by the lines that Brace had confessed to Frost that he had used without attribution: "home is where when you have to go, they have to take you in." After such security come death and the division of property.

In 1969, Jerry would describe his writing theories in a book called *The Stuff of Fiction*: "What we have instead of plot in our best novels is mainly biography and psychological probing." (p. 48) This was true of *The Garretson*

Chronicle. Both Brace and his fictional protagonist had been raised "ostensibly in a tradition of liberality and democracy, and actually in an atmosphere of class distinction. (*GC*, p. 10) Neither would ever totally escape.

Ralph's conflicts can be understood only in the light of this heritage. As in Brace's own autobiography *Days That Were*, which began with the three generations of Brace men who preceded him, Ralph begins his account with his domineering Victorian grandfather, and ineffectual father, Randall. Ralph is expressing the self-discovery of the author when he explains: "I emancipated myself from things past, and abandoned them, but more and more I have been bound and made captive by them. I find such binding an essential to continuing life. In a godless world nothing endures but the past." (*GC*, p. 6)

Jerry's own past is suggested throughout the novel. The ignominy Ralph feels when his grandfather sends off those "riffraff and micky boys," the Madigans, caught building a tree house in his yard, is clearly based on Jerry's memories of his mother sending away the Irish boys climbing the beech tree at Ches-Knoll. The memory of her behavior, which had been accepted by the young boys as part of the natural order of society, became increasingly disturbing to Jerry as maturity and experience enabled him to examine the societal views of his family with greater detachment.

Certainly Jerry was remembering his expedition to the summit of Mount Washington with his Williams College friends in the scene where Tommy is killed in an accident on top of Mount Washington. Jerry may also have been recalling his own feelings about the big society wedding of his sister Betty and Huntington Gilchrist, when he wrote about Ralph's sister's large formal wedding with a man of "distinguished social connections." But the most poignant reminiscence in the whole *Garretson Chronicle* is the description of young Ralph meeting Mrs. Kingsley. By the time Brace was writing the novel both of the Johnsons had died, but in his memory Carrie Johnson remained a symbol of warmth and acceptance. Like Ralph with Mrs. Kingsley, Jerry had found in her the surrogate maternal figure for whom he had unknowingly been searching throughout his youth.

Both Jerry and the fictional Ralph are uncomfortable with women of their own age. Jerry has said that before meeting Huldah the only time he tried to kiss a girl was as a young boy in dancing school. No doubt it was in a situation such as Ralph faces when he meets "Beanpole," a girl too tall for the boys in the dancing class. His attempts to console her lead only to deeper embarrassment. Ralph complains that his life is dominated by females. "I'm sick of women. They all say don't do this and don't do that and don't talk that way." (*GC*, p. 163) Shades of young Gerald and his sisters!

Chapter 23 of *The Garretson Chronicle* should be required reading for those who wonder why many men of Jerry's generation had difficulty comprehending modern women. At age 44, he was sufficiently detached to examine what he has learned about relationships. Perhaps he employs first person narration for the first time in this novel for reasons more than artistry. By using Ralph as his alter ego, he can speak with a frankness impossible in an autobiography. Writer and narrator grew up in the years prior to the new freedom initiated during the 1920s. In their youths, passion had been considered "a whisper of evil. Then war, new times, and release—but with the release a deadly ignorance, an inherited fear, a stampede into emancipation." (*GC*, p. 273)

Ralph's words become Brace's confessional. "I was brought up to be nice to little girls. I was taught that they were pure and untouchable. I learned that they lived apart and that it was best for a boy up to the time of marriage to have nothing whatever to do with them."(*GC*, p. 273) After Freud, the new naturalism in literature, and more open discussions about sex, an enlightened few managed to escape from moral bondage. Neither Brace nor his protagonist were among that select group. Like Brace as a young man, Ralph kept his passions suppressed and secret.

> I talked of the folly of innocence. I dreamed of splendid indulgences. I felt lust like an electric charge, numbing my body and burning through my blood. I lived that absurd and secret and terrible life of desire that all men live. I thought everlastingly of fair women and imagined satisfactions beyond the bounds of sin. All my cussed independence, my impulse to be separate and alone and peculiar, was obscurely a part of my secret passion.

> Yet no record embodies that life. Some quality of taste, old habit, cowardice, kept me from experience. No link seemed to exist between dream and fact. I lived outwardly among the forms and manners and words, in the watertight compartment of respectability, and discovered no way out of it. (GC, 274)

When Jerry tries to explain Ralph's passion for Marilyn Quinn he comes closer to clarifying his reasons for choosing Huldah as his wife than he would have dared to do outside a novel, though she was totally unlike his shallow heroine. Like Ralph, Jerry found the girls in his own social set too cool and "nice." Yet he was old fashioned enough to disapprove of the Flappers with their rolled stockings and cosmetics: "artificial color on a woman suggested harlotry." Huldah's high color was natural as were the waves in her red hair. Her manner was forthright. What did it matter to her young suitor that she had little interest in the arts? He wrote her letters, poems, and stories in which he clothed her with all the glory of his imaginative powers. There is little doubt but that he is speaking of himself when he has Ralph say:

I had always wanted a golden princess (so it now appeared, at least);
I had always resented the social arrangements that my family had
made for me; and now at last I had found the lovely creature—in
fact, I was rescuing her, creating her as Pygmalian created Galatea.
Eagerly I thought of all I could do for her, the wondrous ideas I
would put in her pretty head, the books, the art. Even now I had
wrought a miracle. (*GC*, p. 283)

Satisfaction of sexual desire in those days meant first saying the wedding
vows. Jerry's attempts to show his new wife the culture of Europe, and to
interest her in the books he was reading, failed. Passion is enough for a young
lover, but the more mature man yearns for a meeting of the mind as well as
flesh. Perhaps Jerry revealed more of one side of his own marriage than he
intended when he rescues Ralph from Marilyn.

Ralph meets Christina, the Beanpole from his boyhood dancing classes.
Tall, thin Christina prefers art, poetry and music to science, but her Celtic
realism, austerity, and forthright speech is so like Huldah's that at the time of
the celebration of the Braces' Golden Wedding, George Brockway sent them a
card with a passage from the novel which he said proved to him that Christina
was based on Huldah. Typically, neither Brace confirmed nor denied it.

Christina's father runs a drugstore and her Scottish mother has enough
practicality to oppose her marrying a man without prospects. When she takes
her daughter to Scotland, Ralph gives Christina a jackknife as a parting gift.
What he enjoys most about her is the freedom with which they can discuss
anything. Yet even after they have been married for years, he still feels that he
does not understand women. When Christina reads the memoir he has written, " she laughs at what I take seriously and ponders over the items I present
too lightly. Women, she says, will not see the humor of it, nor men the seriousness." (*GC*, p. 382) The two sexes are always on opposite sides of the high-
way of life.

Still, it would be a mistake to see the novel as anything but fiction. As
Jerry would caution in *The Stuff of Fiction*, "The origin of any dramatic character may at first seem unmistakable, but once the character enters the imagined scenes of the fiction he takes on a new function." (p. 83) Ralph is the
same age as Brace and shares many of his interests and characteristics, but the
author is aware that Ralph has not learned some of the lessons that he now
knows. C. Hugh Holman, a former student of Brace's, wrote an introduction
to the paperback edition of *The Garretson Chronicle* (W. W. Norton, 1964) in
which he shows the complexity of the double refraction: "the past, viewed
from Ralph's angle of vision, defines the present, but the fact is not fully per-
ceived by Ralph himself, and thus he is not only the ironic commentator on
his father but also the unconscious object of his own irony" (p. xiv). Brace

apparently accepted this interpretation, for Holman wrote in response to a letter of appreciation that he had received from Brace: "It seems to me that the critic must always stand in questioning humility before the work of art which alone can justify his existence. You encourage me to hope that for once I have been able to achieve some measure of that humility."

Joseph Lovering in his critical study of Brace's writings expresses the view that like Thoreau, Ralph is marching to a different drummer when he leaves the Transcendental theorizing of the older generation to become a carpenter and craftsman. But he remains, however subconsciously, a philosopher and writer. The conclusion of the novel was changed at the suggestion of the editor. In the final chapter, Randall, who finally appreciates his son's views about fine craftsmanship, has mellowed sufficiently to make acceptable Ralph's favorable comments about him in the opening of the novel. The reader learns in a "Postscript" that Ralph and Christina have had a long, happy marriage. This resolution undoubtedly added to the popularity of the novel, but the changes make the ending of the novel ring less true. Brace preferred that the future of his characters be left to the imaginations of his readers.

By December, *The Garretson Chronicle* was third on the best seller list of the *Boston Globe*. The few negative reviews were all by women who may have objected to its male orientation. Some of his former students also felt that he still had a lot to learn about women. Alice Johnson wrote to him from the University of Tennessee at Knoxville. "How does one tell one's favorite professor that he has done a fine job? It reverses the procedure that seems most normal." She did not hesitate to tell him, however, that she did not think he understood feminine psychology. "I find your men charming. Your women, of course, I do not like. That undoubtedly springs from some perversity in myself that refuses to admit that women so patly fit their categories. I see the arched eyebrow now as you read this."

Several former Dartmouth students, now working as editors, expressed interest in publishing some of Brace's short stories, though they were able to pay little, if anything for them. Jerry was negotiating with editors at *Time* who had offered him $250 in advance and $250 more on acceptance for an article on either Sarah Orne Jewett or on the inadequacy of imagination in the modern novel. Once Jerry would have jumped at any chance to have his short stories published. Now that other opportunities were presenting themselves, he was not so eager unless he were well paid.

Some friends worried that reviewers were acting as if Jerry was a one-book phenomenon. Amherst poet Robert Francis said that he had loved *The Wayward Pilgrims*, and objected that reviewers were acting as if his earlier books had just been practice for *The Garretson Chronicle*. Jerry's colleague Doris Holmes wrote encouragingly that she saw the novel as "a sort of

* Translations

annunciation of all the books you haven't written yet." Lincoln Fairley's parents, Uncle Jim and Aunt Elizabeth, expressed their pride in "our Sunday son." His own family too approved the novel.

Sales were unprecedented for a Brace novel and it was being strongly promoted for the 1948 Pulitzer Prize. The $2,500 that his publishers had set aside for advertising was increased to $10,000 and over 25,000 copies of the book were sold. *Omnibook* published it in abbreviated form, which introduced it to a wider readership. Brace was already being contacted by reporters for interviews, when word came that the Pulitzer Prize had been awarded to James Michener for his collection of short stories, *Tales of the South Pacific.* Immediately *Saturday Review* published a protesting article by Harrison Smith about the questionable way in which the prize had been decided. The article ended with a poll taken of twenty-two reviewers of what their choice would have been. Eight chose *The Garretson Chronicle.* The only book to tie it was A. B. Guthrie's *The Big Sky.* Not one chose Michener's book, mainly because they did not consider it a novel.

It was disappointing, of course. Book of the Month Club, which had been negotiating for Brace's novel and might have made him famous and wealthy, changed its mind. Nevertheless, sales continued to be active for the next two years. Studio One, a highly acclaimed television program, dramatized it. The story was translated into German and published by Paul Verlag, advertising on its front cover "Dieser Roman ist einer der grossten Bucherfolge in Amerika." Abridged paperbacks were published in Spanish and French. The United States Information Agency, considering it a good example of American life, published an abbreviated form of it in India in both Telugu and Urdu, as well as in Burma, Pakistan, and Taiwan. Hodder and Stoughton obtained the rights to publish it in England, and Bonniers agreed to pay Brace $200 down and 7½ percent royalties on the first 3,000 copies with 10 percent thereafter for a Swedish version. Brace could truly feel that at last he had an international reputation.

The Garretson Chronicle made enough money for Jerry to pay college tuition for his two boys and to make improvements on the Deer Isle property. He was not eager to modernize the summer place, but Huldah, who had to do the housework and entertaining, wanted her life made easier. They had already added electricity which in time led to a telephone, refrigerator, and, eventually, even a dishwasher. The kitchen range was replaced by an oil burner fed by a fifty-gallon tank of oil in the boat house. Deeper wells were driven with an automatic pressure pump. The barn was turned into a guest house which proved useful when the children got older and had children of their own.

The expansion of the faculty at Boston University meant that Jerry no longer had to teach in the summer sessions. Even before public schools closed for the year, he was able to head for Deer Isle. The family could come later. He always considered the children primarily Huldah's responsibility. He enjoyed taking the boys to baseball games at Boston's Fenway Park and Braves Field, and the whole family had season tickets to the Boston Symphony. Loring played the piano extremely well, and in high school had taken up the trombone. His brother Gerald studied the clarinet for eight years and had the lead position in the school orchestra. Both boys enjoyed skiing trips with their father, especially to Tuckerman's Ravine, and because they had started the sport so young, they both became better at it than he. Now that he no longer had to prove himself by winning, Jerry took pleasure in the challenge of playing tennis with his sons, who were rated number two and three on the Belmont High Tennis Team. Loring had the better ground strokes and serve, but neither he nor his father was as adept at rushing the net and putting winners away as young Gerald. Though their father willingly drove them to social and school events and waited patiently for them in the car, he found communication difficult. He attended their graduations, and one of the few times that he went to church was to hear Loring give the youth sermon. He was supportive, but undemonstrative as his own father had been. He lacked the ability to view life through the eyes of the younger generation. The boys that were so often the main characters in his novels came from his own childhood experiences and times, not from observations of his sons.

Surprisingly, there seems to have been little sibling rivalry between the boys. They shared a car and, for two years at college, lived in the same building. Both Loring who graduated from Belmont High School in 1948, and his brother Gerry who graduated a year later, went to Williams College mostly to please their father, though he had made no attempt to influence their decision. Not only had they heard him nostalgically reminisce about his early teaching years there, but his views were enthusiastically seconded by some of his former students, including S. Lane Faison, who had become professor of arts at his alma mater, and Dwight Little, who with his wife Bunny, ran the summer music camp that Loring had attended. The boys found the school much changed from the place it had been back in the pre-Depression days. The close association of students and teachers and the sense of being close to the institution had been lost as the college grew and modernized. Gerry majored in English, partially in the hope that reading books of interest to his father would lead to discussion of ideas, but the two still did not achieve real closeness. Loring majored in geology; however, when he decided to go to Harvard for a Master's degree in anthropology, his father expressed grave doubts. At the time, anthropology was not a major field in most college curriculums, and Brace was concerned that it would never lead to a financially secure career. Huldah, of course, was delighted that her older son had decided to take scientific courses. Her own scientific interests made it possible for her to understand and discuss ideas that fascinated her son. Jerry would always remain baffled about what Loring was trying to do and why.

After the exciting success of *The Garretson Chronicle*, Jerry found it difficult to get back to writing when he returned to Deer Isle. George Brockway sent him an advertisement for a new novel by Alec Rackowe which was full of back-handed compliments of Brace's writing, providing him with lots of free publicity as Brockway pointed out. The blurb on the jacket of the book, *A Stylish Marriage: A Novel of New York Society 1890–1930* read "Favorably compares with the *Garretson Chronicle* almost the best novel of 1947." Brockway added, "I hope it spurs you on to your work on *A Summer's Tale*." Jerry had returned to his novel of Maine and already had its title, but four hours of work produced only one sentence.

He found physical activity easier. He and Loring helped Eleanor get the *Forties* ready for the water and together they painted *Festina*. By now both of them were feeling the results of their physical labors. Jerry wrote Huldah that "L's hands are badly blistered from his hard work. . . . My neck & shoulders are subject to twinges." But looking with pride at the newly painted *Festina,* Jerry wrote ecstatically, "She looks like a girl ready for her first prom." To him she was more beautiful than any woman. He refused to consider the work on her as the cause for his aching muscles. Even less could he admit that he was getting older. Instead he blamed his stiff neck and twinges on the kitchen chair where he had been writing, saying that the corner was hot in front, but cold on his back.

Encouraged by the success of *The Garretson Chronicle*, Brace thought perhaps he could arrange to have some of his earlier books reprinted, especially as he had received word from Putnam that all rights for *Light on a Mountain*, which he considered his best work, had reverted to him. To his chagrin he learned that all the plates for it had been melted down. No doubt this disappointment added to his writer's block. He felt the need to get away on a cruise as soon as possible. Finally he and Loring were able to get off for several days' sail to the islands of Monhegan and Matinicus in the newly painted *Festina*. When the two returned, they found that they could sleep better and were in much better spirits.

In August of 1948, Jerry was sent an advanced copy of *We Fly Away*, a first novel by an Amherst friend, Robert Francis, whom he had known since Harvard days. The publicity department of William Morrow & Company hoped that Brace might care to comment favorably about the book if he enjoyed it. Although Francis had been regularly writing poems for the *Christian Science Monitor*, Jerry felt that newspapers are ephemeral and a novel would give his work more permanence. Ultimately, it would be the collections of his poems which would gain Francis a more lasting reputation. Brace was enthusiastic about the lightly plotted novel which echoed his own taste. "I enjoyed and admired every phrase of his lovely prose. It seems to me that he combines a modern psychological perception with a simplicity and humor which are in the best sense old fashioned. My favorite book is *The Country of the Pointed Firs*, by Sarah Orne Jewett, and *We Fly Away* kept reminding me of it—but with a nice difference. Robert Francis supplies his own clairvoyance."

At last Boston University began to take notice of Brace's growing literary reputation. The English department had been slow to acknowledge that creative writing was a legitimate part of liberal arts, but students were beginning to demand it. Jerry now had sufficient fame to be put in charge of what would become an important part of the division. In September of 1947, the College of Liberal Arts, which had outgrown its old quarters, moved to new buildings on Commonwealth Avenue west of Kenmore Square. The various colleges which made up the university were widely scattered around the city. It had long been the dream of President Daniel L. Marsh to build a central campus around a replica of the tower in England known as the Boston Stump. Although the tower was never built, the classroom buildings, of Indiana limestone in honor of the president's home state, became a reality. The handsome new facilities offered far more space and modern conveniences, but had some distinct drawbacks. Commonwealth Avenue is a broad, busy thoroughfare with streetcar lines down the center. This is handy for commuters, but make front classrooms very noisy. Air conditioning had to be omitted because of financial constraints; so in summer the only choice was between stifling heat or opening the windows to dust and noise. The five floors, stretching along the avenue, have many staircases and exits that improve fire safety, but students can go for weeks without meeting other classmates. It was all very different from the intimate atmosphere of the old brick building at 688 Boylston Street.

The College of Liberal Arts building was still not finished when school opened. Of its 1,800 students, over half were veterans. Tuition was raised from $340 to what students considered an exhorbitant $400. In order for the faculty to have private offices, the school occupied some old brick apartment buildings beyond the back parking lot. After a brief stay in one building, the English department moved into permanent quarters at 236 Bay State Road. Jerry was assigned a large corner room on the fourth floor. From his windows he could see the sailboats on the Charles River and the Cambridge shoreline beyond. Later the view was partially obscured when Hillel House was built adjacent to the Castle, at that time used as a residence by the university's president. Brace's office was part of a suite of three rooms sharing a common vestibule where there were pigeon holes for student messages and papers. The two offices on either side of him were occupied by his tennis buddies, Robert

Sproat and Leighton Brewer. Jerry filled the bookcases with part of his own library and hung his watercolors on the walls. He even had a couch to rest on between classes. In those days professors did not have to worry about false accusations of harassment, so he had no hesitancy about closing his door to assure privacy during student conferences. There was a trust between student and professor that neither would have presumed to violate.

Edward Wagenknecht, nonfiction writer, editor, and critic, joined the department that fall of 1948. He was considered a prestigious addition, for he not only had a Ph.D. from the University of Washington, but he had edited a number of popular books including *The Fireside Series of Christmas Stories, Ghost Stories, Romance,* and *Yuletide Tales.* He was a leading advocate for the writing of psychographs, a biographical approach created by Gamaliel Bradford. Wagenknecht was a regular book reviewer for the Chicago *Tribune,* and, as one of Brace's staunchest supporters, gave his novels high praise. Though the two men never became close friends, they had great respect for one another.

It surprised Jerry when he found himself becoming a highly respected senior member of the English department. His opinions were sought at faculty meetings and he was elected to the most important committees, though he never joined them gladly. He had narrowly missed being invited to join Phi Beta Kappa when he was an undergraduate. Now that he had demonstrated the qualities and achievements represented by the society, he was initiated on April 23, 1949, as an honorary member of the Boston University Epsilon Chapter of Phi Beta Kappa. Such honors did not mean as much to him as they did to many, but it was gratifying to know that at last his work was being appreciated and that he was becoming widely recognized as both a first-rate novelist and teacher.

Jerry in his B.U. office at 236 Bay State Road

Gerald and Catherine Dennett

15
Great Spruce Head Island

Writing *The Garretson Chronicle* had helped Jerry come to terms with family expectations and his own choices, but he was not quite ready to abandon his nostalgia for the happy days of his youth. He had begun the novel which would become *A Summer's Tale* during the war, but it was too antithetical to his dark mood and the grim times. Now that Norton was eager to publish another book while Brace was still fresh in the minds of his readers, he returned to his earlier idea for a romantic novel in a Maine setting.

Gerald's boyhood summers in Deer Isle had seemed paradisaical, but if all Penobscot Bay had been his Eden, most idyllic of all was Great Spruce Head Island, "the loveliest island in our part of the Bay, with coves and tidal pools and beaches and cliffs and meadows and uncut forest trees and a high rocky summit." (*DTW* II, p. 47) It also had an old farm and a graveyard, for the island had a long and interesting history.

Great Spruce Head had been purchased by James Foster Porter of Winnetka, Illinois, in 1912 as a summer residence where he, his wife, and five children could escape the pressures of a busy life and enjoy a simpler lifestyle in the midst of quiet, natural beauty. Mrs. Porter, a former Bostonian, who was a friend of Jerry's Aunt Leta, always hospitably welcomed Jerry to swim, play tennis, or explore the many trails that had been cleared through the tangled spruce forest. He never forgot "that magic island with Nancy and her four young brothers and her warm-hearted parents and all the innocent ventures and joys a youthful heart could desire. They seemed to live in a state of perfect harmony with themselves and their many friends and their idyllic surroundings—along with a resident staff of caretakers and boatmen and domestic helpers." (*DTW* II, p. 47)

James Foster Porter was an architect, a genteel humanist who represented the values that Jerry most admired. His equally cultured wife skillfully managed the difficult logistics of providing for family and guests on an island retreat while supervising five children. The four Porter boys, Eliot, Edward, Fairfield, and John, were all artistic, athletic and intelligent, though very different in temperament. Nancy, the only girl, was not only attractive, but in both wit and sports was as competent as her brothers. There were usually visitors staying at the house. In the early days there were three steamers that regularly called at nearby islands. The *Catherine* which went to Dirigo on nearby Butter Island was the one most frequently used by their guests. The Porters would come over with one of their boats to meet them. When the Eastern Steamship Company discontinued service after World War I, it became more complicated; guests then had to come by car or train and arrange to be met. Supplies were at first brought in from Camden, but the shortage of gasoline during the war made it easier to go to Stonington on the south end of Deer Isle. This brought the Porters into more constant contact with the Braces.

Jerry knew that if he sailed to the island in the morning, Mrs. Porter would urge him to remain for lunch. He delighted in the lively, informed conversation at the table. Darwinians and agnostics, the family were fascinated by science and natural history. Eliot was a good ornithologist even as a boy. They were all excellent tennis players; so shortly after purchasing the island, Mr. Porter built a concrete tennis court, which got him into difficulty during the first World War. Suspicious Maine natives believed that any mid-westerner who chose to spend his summers on a remote Maine island must have some nefarious purpose. The rumor soon spread that the concrete court was actually a secret gun emplacement. After he had a wireless installed in his powerful motor launch *Hippocampus*, prior to turning it over for use by the U. S. Navy for anti-submarine patrol, the islanders were certain that he was a spy using the boat to communicate with German submarines. Undoubtedly this story, which the family delighted in recounting, planted the seed for the plot of *A Summer's Tale*.

Eliot Porter was closest in age to Gerald. A close observer of nature, he was a fine photographer. When he was eight or nine, his father had given him a Brownie box camera. One day a young heron fell from its nest into a raspberry thicket and stood glaring at him with its plumage all ruffled. Eliot succeeded in taking one of those lucky photographs that every photographer dreams about. His father, recognizing its quality, had the picture enlarged and framed. From that time on Eliot knew he wanted to be a photographer. When the war ended and gasoline was available once more, he would go in his motorboat to all the surrounding islands, carefully examining rocks, tidal pools, and nesting birds. He found Stonington's jumble of weathered wooden houses pressing down the hill to the wharves and boathouses at the water's edge a fascinating subject, and claimed to have taken more pictures of it than of any other place in Maine except Great Spruce Head Island. He became a medical researcher, but in 1939, after having twenty-nine of his prints exhibited at Steiglitz gallery in New York City, he gave up research to do photography full time. By the time Gerald was writing *A Summer's Tale*, Eliot was already famous. Though he rarely photographed people, his intimate relationship with nature can be seen in his close studies of barnacles on rocks, bunchberries, colorful lichen, and birds. Later he would combine the best of these in his loving photographic rendering of Great Spruce Head in the book he called *Summer Island* (1966).

Fairfield Porter, Eliot's younger brother, viewed the local scenery with a painterly eye, preferring to capture the island with oils. To Jerry, who romanticized their lives, the relationship of the members of the family to one another seemed golden. Actually, except for the fact that they all loved and were inspired by the island, they were not especially close. In an article published in *Maine Art Now*, Eliot wrote: "Fairfield was an artist from the time he was born . . . Father and Fairfield didn't have a lot in common. He wasn't even sure Fairfield was serious. Fairfield and I didn't have much in common either until I started doing photography entirely, and then we would both be photographing and painting on the island." Fairfield's paintings are as full of people as his brother's works are devoid of them: portraits of friends, a boy eating breakfast, a pet dog in a doorway. Even when there are no people, they are suggested. Garden chairs wait to be sat in, a wharf invites the viewer to walk down its length to a spot where someone has just hoisted the sail on the small boat at the end. A photograph by Eliot of the same wharf shows it stretching starkly toward deserted boats on motionless water. If Eliot highlights the natural wonders of the islands, the paintings of Fairfield capture the hospitality enjoyed at Great Spruce Head.

While Jerry, who longed to be a first rate artist himself, admired the Porter boys—perhaps even felt a bit envious of them—he also was interested in the local people who lived on the island all the year and made possible the comfortable existence of the summer residents. Monte Green, the caretaker, lived on the island winter and summer and was competent in old time country ways. He chopped wood for the fires, cut and stored the ice for summer use, mowed the hay with a scythe, and dragged brush with his oxen. The Porter children looked upon him as mentor and friend. He built for each of them a two-foot model boat that would actually sail. He was captain of the *Hippocampus* and joined the Coast Guard during the war so he could continue to look after her. In later years Rupert and Lottie Howard came from Eagle Island to live at Great Spruce Head. They brought their hens and cows with them so they could supply the family with eggs and milk, and exchanged the oxen for a horse. True islanders who knew how to be self sufficient, they remained there on the island for twenty-five years.

Ever since 1923 when Mr. Porter had paid Gerald the then princely sum of $20 to teach the young Porters how to sail a small knockabout, Gerald had visited the island regularly. The Porters seemed to exist happily in a world of boats and tides and weather. They explored the rocky beaches, each of which had been given a name, they took him to the Cove, the only place warm enough in which to swim, and they showed him the lichened stone of John Walton with the date 1805 carved on it. Jerry tucked all these details away in his memory.

By August of 1942 when he was considering a novel about the island, he sailed there in the *Forties*. He wrote to Huldah that "I went ashore & said hello to crowds of Porters—Nancy & Eliot & John & their families, inc. all Eliot's sons. We had tea. Then I played a set of tennis with John—& he won 8 to 6, but I was doing all right considering." Although Nancy had long been married, she continued to remain beautiful in Jerry's eyes and he was delighted to see her.

He began to write *A Summer's Tale* set on Great Spruce Head Island. The dedication read "For all my friends who live on islands." Whenever he read the words from Sir Walter Scott's novel *The Pirate*, it reminded him of that loveliest of spots in Penobscot Bay:

Oh were there an island
Though ever so wild,
Where woman could smile and
No man be beguiled,
Too tempting a snare
To poor mortals were given,
And the hope would fix there,
That should anchor in heaven.

These were the lines he would use as a motif for his mythical August Island, so called because it was concealed by fog all the rest of the year. A map of the fictional island that appears on the endpapers of his novel has a different orientation, but otherwise closely resembles the contours of Great Spruce Head.

Although the title was a play on Shakespeare's "Winter's Tale," the plot was suggested by "The Tempest." Once more he showed his affinity to Sarah Orne Jewett. She had used "The Tempest" as a motif for one of the stories in her *Country of the Pointed Firs* in which she had given the name *Miranda* to a ship wrecked in a storm off a strange enchanted land inhabited by gray, ghostly shapes—a sort of holding place between this world and the next. Gerald's beautiful, mythical island is the counterpart of Great Spruce Head—with a concrete tennis court, tidal pool warm enough for swimming, and an ancient graveyard. As in Shakespeare, the novel has a boat wreck, and a wedding party that parallels the masque in "the Tempest." Like Ferdinand, Anthony wonders if the girl he meets after his wreck is human or a spirit, "a professional angel" from another world. There is a Caliban as well.

The many allusions to Herman Melville seem to have little, if any, symbolic significance. The schooner belonging to the owners of August Island is called *Typee* and Anthony's little boat that is wrecked is named the *Doubloon*. When it sinks like the *Pequod*, birds hover above it crying raucously. Anthony is pursued by the evil Doremus, described as "perched on the prow with boat hook poised like a spear. It's the last scene of *Mardi*—pursuers and pursued flying over an endless sea." (*ST*, p. 143) In Mr. Marquis' study there is a model boat *L'Esperance* with glittering windows in the high carved poop that is reminiscent of the glass ship *La Reine* in Melville's *Redburn*. But Brace seems to have chosen these references just for fun, a sort of recognition game for his readers to play.

A Summer's Tale may be pure fantasy, but it is its author's fantasy and thus revealing of his inner thoughts and daydreams. Twenty-seven years after the novel's publication, he wrote me a letter confirming that he had been thinking of his youthful visits to Great Spruce Head at the time he was writing. He added: "There was a June too, whom I fell in love with (she went and married another man)—and she is still there, and still lovely." (21 March 1976) He added that on that island in those magical days only Caliban was missing. June, of course, was based on Nancy Porter.

In creating his fictional heroine, Jerry was able to give free rein to his fantasies. June is descended from Bourbon royalty. She has a natural simplicity and grace. Like all the Marquis family, she scorns affectations of modesty and walks barefoot through the woods or unselfconsciously swims naked with family and friends. "Her body seemed to flow in the light like honey; it was slim and lithe and balanced with classic grace." (*ST*, p. 50) She studied poetry at Smith and is attending medical school at Harvard. She looks "like a poet's vision of a princess," but she doesn't hesitate to express her unconventional views about politics and democracy. She is serious about her tennis game. The story has a fairy tale ending with the newlyweds literally sailing off into a golden sunset. The boy who read Zane Grey and imagined rescuing ladies in distress has clung to his dreams through all the vicissitudes of years.

When *A Summer's Tale* was published in 1949, reviewers described it as light summer reading, but it had a dark undercurrent. Brace was aware that no place, however remote, was free of intrusion from the forces of the outside world. The independent, self-sufficient existence that islanders had lived for centuries would become impossible in the post-war age. In his novel, Brace has the United States government declare August Island uninhabited. The navy is sent to have tests and maneuvers there. Captain Ketcham can see for himself that the little settlement has been in existence for a long, long time, but he can only obey orders. Officialdom is not interested in reason, only in rules.

Not all the evil comes from outside. Lowell, the older son who like Eliot Porter is an ornithologist (though the resemblance ends there), has been convinced by his Fascist friends that he should pursue the family claim to the throne of France. They contemptuously refer to the U. N. as a Punch and Judy show. In the end publicity saves the island, but it brings its own destructive forces as reporters and tourists descend on the once quiet island. Mr. Marquis warns his family that their idyllic world has gone for "the modern world is like a whirlpool that inexorably draws all men into its vortex." (*ST*, p. 279) He feels that while individuals and families may believe in virtue and kindliness, "large groups are tempted by power, and more and more condone inhumanities which the individual conscience would shun." (*ST*, p. 278) Brace saw no other way to explain World War II and its attendant evils.

Reviewers complained that the book was written on so many different levels it failed to be successful with any of them. It had too many literary allusions and too much satire for the popular reader, and was too romantic and fantastic for the intellectuals. Furthermore the sentiments of the book were probably ill-timed. Brace's colleague Edward Wagenknecht labeled the book a comic opera and Utopian novel that burlesqued "fifth columnists, journalists, and the American Navy"—subjects taken very seriously by patriotic Americans. The Cold War and the spreading fear of Communism caused people to view with suspicion any criticism of the United States government and the American way of life. To mitigate public displeasure, the hero, Anthony Wyatt, whom Brace originally had made a Communist sympathizer, was changed to "a sort of socialist" in the final manuscript. In applying for a Fulbright Award, Brace submitted *A Summer's Tale*, his most recent novel, as part of his application. He thought that he was turned down because they considered his novel too frivolous, but it is more likely that they objected to its message which in that paranoid period may have sounded dangerous to the committee. At any rate, he was undoubtedly correct that he might have been more successful if he had sent them *The Garretson Chronicle*.

The failure of *A Summer's Tale* may have had more serious consequences for his literary reputation. After editor George Brockway had read the manuscript, he urged Jerry to put it aside and follow up the success of *The Garretson Chronicle* with another novel of the same genre and scope. Based on knowledge learned from years in the book business he later wrote that looking back on Brace's writing career,

> I felt (and still feel) that if he had published two solid successes back
> to back, he could have gone on and written anything he damned

please and been treated respectfully and read enthusiastically. As I read *The Spire* I groaned for what might have been. He obviously felt a need not to be type-cast but to do something different, for he did the same thing in following *The Islands* with *The Wayward Pilgrims*. Critics, bookstores, and readers haven't time or perhaps ability to puzzle out every writer's quirks, although they'll allow great latitude to one who's 'established.'

Jerry missed the opportunity of being considered an established writer.

It always bothered Brace that colleges and universities did not sufficiently appreciate creative writers. In January of 1949 he published an article in the *CEA Critic* commenting that a well known author on a faculty does more for the college than for the writer, no matter how successful he becomes. "He is viewed with skepticism as one too little conscious of committees, the one who is somehow temporary, a wanderer." Jerry was reaching a point in his life where he wanted to feel permanent.

In 1949 he received notification that he had been awarded tenure at Boston University. No longer need he be "a wanderer." It was a good time for him to learn that he was settled in his university work, for in his private life another tie was broken. He felt a deep sense of loss when he received word that his mother had died. He might complain on occasion that her views were limited and out of touch with the modern world, but the bond between them was strong, and she gave him a secure feeling of family continuity. She had been living happily in New York with her daughter Eleanor and Muriel Postlethwaite. At the funeral Jerry remembered his mother as she had been in the happy days of family gatherings, especially when he saw the grief of his "Uncle" Lincoln Hendrickson, now in his nineties. It reminded Jerry that his sisters had always speculated whether this close friend of the family had been in love with their mother. Lincoln Hendrickson, with old-fashioned loyalty, had remained faithful to his wife, Marion Vaux, through the long years she was confined to a mental institution. He never allowed himself to show more than devotion to his wife's best friend, but he cared for her deeply.

Finances had never been discussed in the Brace family. Jerry knew that his parents had lived comfortably and that whenever he had needed money his father was willing to help. Undoubtedly, he expected the estate to be larger than it ultimately proved to be. John Donaldson assured him that the lawyers were not to blame. It was true that there had been little diversification of investments, but the losses were typical of most portfolios held between 1900 and 1945 which included the years of the great Depression. Once the property was distributed among the many heirs, Jerry discovered that while his share would be useful, it would not relieve him of all financial burdens.

After the death of her mother, Eleanor decided to move out of the New York apartment that Gerald had so long considered home. Her old school friends the Burrages found her a charming house just next door to their old white Colonial clapboard house in an historic area of Wiscasset, Maine. Eleanor's new home was built of antique brick with a trellised entrance over the front door beautifully carved in wood by a master ship builder. Ever-faithful Muriel accompanied Eleanor to Maine, but died of an overdose of barbiturates shortly after they had settled in. She had always been frail and highly emotional, and the prospect of losing the only place she had ever considered home and seeing Eleanor absorbed with new friends, was probably more than she could bear. The Burrage sisters were active in all the affairs of the town and in the local art colonies. Eleanor tried to steer clear of their social entanglements, but she found their frenetic activities highly entertaining to watch.

Mildred and Madeleine ("Bob") Burrage were a remarkable pair. Dynamic and talented, they were also, as Jerry's son Loring remembers, "extraordinary contrapuntal raconteurs." Bob Burrage made museum quality jewelry and her sister Mildred was a fine artist. Both treated Jerry the way Eleanor did, as a delightful younger brother to whom they could speak frankly. When Mildred visited the Braces at their Belmont home, she carefully inspected all Jerry's paintings on the walls, and told him. "Gerald, you should do more oils. They have much more character than your watercolors." While he respected her judgment—she was director of the New England Art Exhibition on Boston Common—he continued to paint with watercolors. He had learned while still a boy to ignore the constant lecturing he received from his older sisters and their friends.

With Eleanor living in Wiscasset, Jerry and Huldah had reason to visit Maine in winter as well as summer. Jerry delighted in the architectural details of the old mansions, the rotting hulks of the sagging schooners near the docks, and the picture postcard loveliness of the village sparkling in snow. He had managed to accustom himself to the frenetic pace

Eleanor's home in Wiscasset, Maine

and noise of Boston, but whenever he turned the car northeast and smelled the salt air of coastal Maine, he felt a quickening of his senses. Even when he did not use Maine as a setting for a novel, it provided an atmosphere conducive to his creativity.

16
Academia

The year 1950 ushered in a decade of fear and paranoia. Never had twentieth-century Americans felt more vulnerable. The Cold War with the Soviet Union continued to escalate and nuclear bombs grew ever more powerful. Preparations in case of attack sound naive today. School children were trained to hide under desks and hold a book over their heads. Families laid in stocks of canned goods and water and were told to stay away from doors and windows when the alarm sounded. Those who could afford it had bomb shelters constructed in their backyards. Jerry's brother-in-law and sister, John and Dorothy Donaldson, had one. Young men were sent off to fight in Korea; at home, Senator Joseph McCarthy had begun his witchhunt for communists. No one felt safe. College professors feared dismissal if a student should report that their lectures or texts contained un-American material. Teachers were forced to sign loyalty oaths in spite of feeling that their civil rights were being violated.

It was an era of expansion for Boston University. The old esprit of the faculty, who, under adverse conditions, had worked together to provide the best education possible, inevitably disappeared with the rapid growth of the college. Jerry mourned that size and complexity were producing "the sort of institutional bureaucracy that tends to discourage individual commitment. It is not so much a calculated dictatorship with a policy of controlling ideas and perhaps a suppressing of some freedoms, as it is a desperate effort to deal efficiently with the whole multitudinous conglomeration of students and faculty and buildings and grounds and all the areas and reaches of human learning." (*DTW* II, p. 153) Educational institutions everywhere were undergoing change.

In February of 1951 President Daniel L. Marsh retired, to be succeeded by Harold Case, another ordained Methodist minister. Originally from Kansas, he came to Boston from Pasadena, California. Donald J. Winslow was appointed chairman of the English department in 1952 to undertake the integration of all the English departments in the university and meld them into one division under the College of Liberal Arts. The task was formidable, requiring great tact and skill. Many of the liberal arts professors were unhappy to see men whom they considered less qualified, but who had earned tenure and rank in their own colleges, now being placed above them in the faculty hierarchy. Brace tried to keep out of faculty entanglements as much as possible, but he could not avoid all of the acrimonious meetings. At least in an urban university, he could escape to the suburbs at the end of the day. He reflected how if he had been teaching on a small rural campus, his life would inevitably be circumscribed by the academic community. It seemed natural to set his next novel in a small college town.

When to his disappointment Brace had learned that reissuance of *Light on a Mountain* was impossible because all of the plates had been destroyed, he decided to resurrect some of the characters in a sequel called *The Spire*. The protagonist of the earlier novel, Henry Gaunt, was made a newly appointed professor at fictional Wyndham College in western Massachusetts. On first appearance the college seems ideal, with the purity and integrity of early New England suggested by the white spire of a chapel in the center of the campus. Closer view reveals that the chapel is now a museum, empty of spiritual meaning. The idea for a church transformed to a museum may have been suggested by the removal of the Congregational Church from the small town of Prescott, Massachusetts, to South Hadley when the Swift River Valley was flooded to form the Quabbin Reservoir in the late 1930s. No longer used for religious services, it became part of the Joseph Allen Skinner Museum at Mount Holyoke College. Nothing in the fictional town of Wyndham is quite what it seems to the outward eye. Even the lovely colonial houses around the village green are, as in Conrad's *Heart of Darkness*, only whitened sepulchers "which indeed appear beautiful outward, but are within full of dead men's bones." (Matthew 23:27)

In an interview with Leslie Horn for the *Worcester Sunday Telegram* (15 January 1950), Brace confessed that his novels were written from personal experience because he did not feel that he was good at making things up. When *The Spire* was published, colleagues from all of the colleges with which Brace had been associated thought they recognized characters and situations, and, indeed, he had taken details from each. His fictional President Gidney shared the problems of President Meiklejohn, who had been resented by the old guard at Amherst College, and caused grumbling among the local townspeople when he failed to pay his bills on time. The unforgettable memory of Carrie Johnson's widower, Arthur Johnson, thoughtfully tying a rope around one wrist before drowning himself so that his corpse could be pulled from the mill pond easily, is used by Brace to describe a suicide in *The Spire*. McAdam, the chairman of the English department at Wyndham, an old-fashioned gentleman with few pretensions to scholarship, typified the professors who began their careers before research and professional recognition were considered essential. Brace later claimed that it was Professor Maxcy of Williams whom he had in mind, but it could as easily have been Professor Sneath, his former chairman at Boston University. Undoubtedly, the incompetent professor in *The Spire*, fired because he has used the same yellowed lecture notes and texts for years, had his counterpart at Boston University where an elderly econom- ics professor not only taught outdated material, but was so naive that every year he insisted on giving A's to such famous names as Harry S. Truman or Ted Williams—who had been regularly signed on to the attendance lists by students in the class. As the president of Wyndham remarked, "There's always one—it's part of the college tradition."

Some of the best scenes in *The Spire* are based on the faculty meetings and college parties that Brace had attended. The jokes told by the professors are typical of answers found on student papers and circulated at the College Board correcting sessions in New York which Brace used to attend; to wit, "Isolde was so full of the milk of human kindness she was able to nurse Tristram back to health." Brace even challenges the reader to guess the answer to a charade he remembered from a party he had attended at Williams. Liz plays the scene where Lady Macbeth attempts to wash the blood from her hands, then is a Chinese coolie planting rice, and finally appears as an African queen decked out in tassels and bangles. Even his family were not told the answer. Son Gerald wrote home from Camp Hidden Valley in Freedom, Maine, where he was spending the summer, to tell his mother that he had been reading *The Spire*, but that neither he nor his friend Bronia could figure out the charade.

Ultimately, identification is less important than what the novel reveals about its author's viewpoints. When Henry is offered the position of dean at Wyndham, it gives Brace the opportunity to articulate his own views on administration. "To a real scholar, a dean is a sort of combination YMCA leader and headwaiter. . . . His job is to apply oil to the institutional wheels, and to keep everyone happy. He is the front man. He works in an office—you can't put a scholar in an office. He makes 'inspirational speeches'—and what scholar wants to waste his time being inspirational? He everlastingly shakes hands—and he fusses round with regulations and punishment and adminis- trative stuff and statistics." (*TS*, p. 96) Many professors share Henry's displea- sure that in the academic world "a handshaking front office personnel man- ager" is considered superior to the faculty.

Brace put forth the message that productive professors, especially those publishing, should receive greater appreciation from their institutions. Although Boston University was intent on becoming a first-class educational institution, it was still not paying high salaries. Brace was one of only four members of the department to be receiving slightly over $6,000. Old-time professors always emphasized teaching over publication as if one precluded the other. When the *Boston University Graduate Journal* published an excerpt from *The Spire* in October of 1952, the editors cogently chose one that had echoes of the arguments offered by such professors that publication is just so much window dressing. President Gidney's response is that "often when a man can do nothing well, he assumes he is at least a good teacher." It is an illusion still cherished by many college faculties.

During the fifties, women were still second-class citizens in academia. Few were elected to tenured positions. Secretaries were expected to be obeisant to their male employers. Faculty wives, especially on rural campuses, lived in the shadows of their husbands, often becoming more moralistic and mean-spirited than the men. Lizzie Houghton, the president's secretary with whom Henry falls in love, is socially shunned because she has served time in prison for having a child out of wedlock. As Henry's landlady observes drily, "There's a law that says a woman can't be immoral—it's all right for a man, I understand." (*TS*, p. 90) Sylvia, the most well-adjusted woman in the novel, is portrayed as a sort of earth mother who would like five or six children. She says, "I don't see how a woman lives without kids. In fact what's the good of a woman without 'em." (*TS*, p. 23) Even the iconoclastic Lizzie takes on new beauty when she becomes the object of a man's attention, and her only hope for happiness lies in marriage. Not that Brace portrayed women as passive. As Henry says proudly about his dead first wife. "She married me—rather than the other way around. She figured things out with incredible clearness: she came to Columbia to get a degree and a man—she wanted both: she wanted a first class degree and a scholar to go with it." (*TS*, p. 117) Brace was convinced that women are more calculating than men and he admired them for it, but at the same time, he considered female dedication to a serious career the purview of spinsters. This attitude was shared by a society concerned that too many married women were in jobs formerly the province of men. Once war work had introduced them to the freedom and pleasure of having one's own money and using one's talents for more than running a household, many had been reluctant to return to the kitchen.

The propaganda of the times exalted the housewife. Movies, magazine articles, even President Eisenhower, tried to convince women that they would be happier marrying and raising families. Like so many men, Jerry could not understand why a woman would choose to remain single. Even though he adored his intelligent, cultured sister Eleanor, who had cared for her aged mother and made a home for all the family at Deer Isle, he considered her life meaningless and unfulfilled.

In these very different times, it is easy to fault Brace for his attitude toward the female sex, but many women themselves in the forties and early fifties shared his views, as is evidenced in a letter he received from one of his former students in 1947, discussing how she felt trapped between the need for money and the desire to remain at home. "Hank doesn't want me to work— I don't want to. I want to be a wife and homemaker . . . but economically its pretty difficult to make the decision. One must choose between the Golden Calf or the Mountain Top—and I kind of think we'll choose the mountain top being both that sort of people." There were still more homemakers like Sylvia than women who opted for careers *and* family.

The Spire was published on August 18, 1952. Brace had dedicated it "TO MY COLLEAGUES: Who live, love, labor freely, nor discuss/A brother's right to freedom." At Boston University, they did not seem to have taken what he had written personally, perhaps partly because it had been set on a rural campus. His friend Leighton Brewer asked, "Is life at a small college really as bad as you portray it or are you becoming more cynical & satirical? This reminds me more of Sinclair Lewis than your earlier Trollopian humor."

Though the faculty at Dartmouth were sure he was portraying the faculty at Hanover and were busily trying to identify characters and situations, discerning readers recognized the generality of the scenes. Wylie Sypher, chairman of the literature and language department at Simmons College in Boston, wrote that while he felt sure Brace had based the novel on either Williams or Amherst, "I'm a little sensitive about some of the difficulties Henry Gaunt faces, since the last semester I have had to deal with a couple of pretty grave problems that come uncomfortably close to *The Spire*. Thank goodness there was no Lizzie to complicate matters further."

Regular reviews were mixed in their criticism. George Brockway sent Jerry a copy of a pre-publication review by Arthur Mizener that would be printed in *Saturday Review* which praised the "quiet variety of judgment which is its most impressive quality." Brockway warned Jerry that the *Times* would be asking him for a different photograph from the one on the dust jacket. Jerry was very willing to comply for he had already written to Huldah, that while he liked the sketch of the spire on the book jacket, he was sorry that they had used "the same old bum picture of me" on the back.

A few days later Brockway wrote again to report that all early reviews had been gratifying. "So far the reactions to the book are embarrassingly favorable. I have Wagenknecht's somewhere and will send or bring it." Wagenknecht was impressed with the internal picture of academic life, believing that "there are few varieties of the academic animal that he has not captured for his zoo." Most critics who knew academia well felt that he had caught the mannerisms and personalities of college people far more effectively than Mary McCarthy in *Groves of Academe*, published the same year.

There were, however, some who found it too tediously talky. One review-er complained "There is scant space for writing because the author exhausts most of his space with conversation, just endless talk." Not surprisingly, The *Christian Science Monitor* took issue with his casual religious views and his use of a symbolism in which the spire had no meaning, the Delectable Mountains were secularized, and nature was described by Sylvia as being sim-ilar to a fudge sundae. This, of course, did not bother Brace as it was exactly the message he had intended. He must have been more disturbed by what was said about him in *The New Republic*:

> When he tries to be meaningful, as in his glorification of fecundity and the old Vermont virtues, he is too often fatuous. And the romance itself is really mawkish stuff. What I resent most, however, is Mr. Bruce's [sic.] efforts to give his novel class, so to speak, by erecting upon it a symbolic structure which it is simply not equipped to support. This he does with frequent allusions to *The Scarlet Letter*, Lady Macbeth, 'American Gothic' and those demonic and death-lusting influences that howl like winter gales through the awful chasms of the New England character. *The Spire* like the author's greatly over-rated *Garretson Chronicle* is an odd mixture of perspicacity and hokum. (*The New Republic*, 25 August 1952)

In spite of a few such critics, the novel sold well and by Christmas it was on the list of ten best novels of the year. The *Los Angeles Times* pronounced it "the best novel of the year" and the *Saturday Review of Literature* included it among its suggestions for Christmas giving. In Charlotte, North Carolina, it was rated eighth in a list that included Steinbeck's *East of Eden*, Hemingway's *The Old Man and the Sea*, and Ellison's *The Invisible Man*. As always the book brought letters from interesting former students. William Loeb, controversial editor of the Manchester (New Hampshire) *Union Leader*, reminded him that he had been in his class at Williams and invited him to bring Huldah for a luncheon at his home.

Although Brace did not try to write creatively during the school year, he did find time for a few reviews. In general he was kindly, but truthful. He him-self worked slowly on each novel, crafting each sentence with such care that he rarely had to make emendations. Even though he praised George R. Stewart's novel *Sheep Rock* (Random House, 1951) when he critiqued it for a New Hampshire magazine *The Freeman* (23 April 1951) he expressed disap-pointment that the author had not taken the time to shape and polish his work into a true work of art. Whatever complaints critics might make of Brace's plots or characters, his writing style was always finely honed.

At Deer Isle he immediately set to work on another book. Mrs. Laird was in ill health and Huldah went to Jamaica Plain to look after her. Son Gerald was away at camp. Barbara had met a young man at the Westergaards who lived across the street from their Belmont home. Dick Gotshalk was a friend of their son, Peter. Dick and Barbara rapidly became friends, so Jerry included him along with Barbara and Loring when he went back to Deer Isle. They stopped at Wiscasset to visit the Burrage sisters and to show Eleanor's new house to Loring and Barbara. Both Burrages had bubbly personalities and kept exclaiming over and over how much they enjoyed Barbara, "how pretty and attractive she was." Neither the Burrages nor Eleanor cared much for Dick, however. Later Jerry wrote to Huldah, "Eleanor's opinion of Dick is positively vitriolic. I never heard her react so violently to anyone."

It was a short visit for the young folk. Loring was going to Wyoming on an anthropology field trip and Barbara had a summer secretarial job in Boston. Jerry was looking forward to having some time alone to write and paint, though as usual he got caught up in the busy life of the island. While he stayed in his own house, he spent much of his time at Dunham's Point. Eleanor had hired a cook for the summer and in addition to Johnnie and Brenda Gilchrist, she also had an artist friend Janet Moore staying with her. Jerry still did his writing on a pad of paper on his knee using a fountain pen that needed to be regularly replenished with ink. One morning he tipped over a whole bottle of ink "fortunately not on a rug or anything valuable. But what a mess!" He wrote to George Brockway requesting fifteen copies of *The Spire*. Since he had dedicated it to his colleagues, he felt that they should each receive a copy. He always had an active correspondence with friends and he was receiving "long screeds" from Margaret Fairley who had separated from Lincoln and was not coming to Maine that year. "Most of the letters are about communism and the state of the world, with a sharp crack or two at Lincoln."

Huldah had decided to bring her ailing mother to stay with her in Belmont, but she was finding it difficult to have three generations in one household. Jerry sympathized, agreeing that in such situations "family relations generally seem somewhat strained because people in close contact with each other usually get to know each other too well." He wished she had Loring there to help her. Her major worry, however, was that the affair between Barbara and Dick seemed to be developing too fast. Jerry wrote that he would be coming home briefly to transact some business, but would return by train to Chebeague, Maine, where John Donaldson would meet him. It did not seem to occur to him that he might remain on to give her support.

Jerry still thought of Barbara as his little daughter, too young to be taken seriously. She was planning to enter Mount Holyoke in the fall and his main concern was whether it was worth buying extra insurance to cover use of the infirmary when she was so healthy. As for Dick, he was intelligent and from a highly acceptable family. His father Dr. D. Walter Gotshalk was chairman of the philosophy department at the University of Illinois and author of major works on ethics and metaphysics. Jerry had never interfered in his daughter's personal life. He was sure Huldah could handle any problems. As for Barbara, family opinion made no more impression on her than it had on Jerry when he was courting.

Barbara was attracted to Dick partly because he reminded her so much of her own father, though he lacked Jerry's immense charm. The fact that he did little talking in a group and expected her to wait on him, seemed to her quite natural. When she went to Mount Holyoke, the separation did not break up the relationship as her mother had hoped. Although both of her parents were unhappy about the relationship, they bowed to the inevitable when they learned that she and Dick had decided to marry. A private wedding was performed by the Unitarian minister in their Belmont home. Since Dick was studying for a Master's degree in philosophy at Harvard, Barbara transferred to Boston University, where she would receive free tuition as the daughter of a member of the faculty and be able to stay near her husband. At the end of the year, she left college to have a baby. Her father was deeply distressed—he felt she was taking on the responsibilities of wife and mother before she had had the opportunity of enjoying the pleasures of girlhood. He thought of the wonderful freedom and romantic dreams of his own late teens and early twenties before he had to settle down to family and job. Barbara's impetuous behavior would deprive her of all that. Although he recognized that Barbara had much of her mother's competence and pragmatism, he found it difficult to accept that she was no longer his little girl. It didn't seem very long since he himself had been the younger generation. This was especially true at Deer Isle where he and his sisters and John Donaldson still sailed and painted and built ship models and picnicked and searched for osprey nests as they had since they were young. Their children were physically part of this never-never land, but life at Dunham's Point seemed fixed in time, in spite of muscle aches and twinges which sometimes reminded him that he was growing older.

Brace was disappointed not to receive a raise in the spring of 1953 though his department chairman had recommended him highly. He had begun work on *Bell's Landing*, but, as so often, the early stages moved discouragingly slowly. Fame was creating interruptions. A Mrs. Westerfield had sent him a six-page family history that she thought he might be interested in turning into a book. She and her husband came from Camden to talk with him. Jerry was unfailingly courteous, but he was not interested in writing other people's stories.

He had increased responsibilities at Boston University. He was made a member of the department Curriculum Committee and also the all-college Committee on Courses and Concentration, both of which were very time consuming. His chairman suggested in the annual report to the administration that perhaps Brace should either be given a lighter teaching schedule or released from extra duties. He pointed out that Brace always served on committees conscientiously though he was often inconsistent in decision making. "He is sincere and direct in his expression of opinion, but he is quite unpredictable as to the particular position he is going to take on a particular subject." Brace was a subscriber to Emerson's theory that "a foolish consistency is the hobgoblin of little minds."

One reason that Brace found it difficult to take too seriously the problems being discussed at faculty meetings was that he was distressed by greater world events. Although Josef Stalin had died in March of 1953 and the fighting in Korea ended with the signing of the armistice at Panmunjom in July, the Cold War continued. Vietnam and the French were at war. President Eisenhower was trying to keep America from being involved, but many felt that eventually the United States would be forced into the conflict. In February of 1954, young Gerald was drafted into the army and sent to Fort Dix. He applied as a translator since he knew French well, but with typical military logic, he was sent to Stuttgart, Germany. Six months later, Loring was drafted. Initially trained at Chesapeake Bay, he was sent to an atoll in the South Pacific, a crucial spot, for in March of that year, the first hydrogen bomb, hundreds of times more powerful than the atom bomb, had been exploded at Bikini. Gerald senior had escaped two world wars, but now both his sons were in the middle of events.

In the winter of 1954, Brace was invited to speak at a New England Writers Conference dinner at Durham, New Hampshire. The talk was published in the March issue of the *New Hampshire Alumnus*. He chose as his topic "The Great New England Novel," a twist on the more usual debate as to whether there will ever be a great American novel. Though New England is a microcosm of the larger world, none of the great writers of the day— Theodore Dreiser, Sinclair Lewis, John Dos Passos, William Faulkner, or John Steinbeck—had come from New England. It was a gap that Brace himself wanted to fill, but he found it difficult to articulate the history and values that set New England apart. "It's like being in love and yet trying to deal objectively and fairly with the object of the love—and this we know is a contradiction of terms. Yet the artist must do just that. He works with what he loves, and he has to work with a kind of detachment and perspective which the very act of creating almost denies him."

If New England did not have a definitive novelist, it did have its spokesman in poetry. In May of 1955 *New Hampshire Profiles* published an article by Brace on "Robert Frost's New Hampshire." Much of it was a defense of Frost's negative attitude toward academic life, for Brace had learned how difficult it is to combine teaching and creativity. "Frost wrote that he had a lover's quarrel with the world, but it would be more nearly accurate to say his lover's quarrel is with the colleges. He is a man of learning, but more profoundly he is a poet, and he knows that learning can smother poetry—smother it even with well meant kindness."

What Brace liked most about Frost's poetry was that it evoked a New England now gone: an age of oil lamps, scythes, horses, sleighs and all the old hand ways, "crystallized forever in the poems." Brace felt that civilization becomes a poorer place when man loses direct contact with the soil. He then went on to discuss how he and Frost shared an admiration for Dean Briggs as probably the wisest dean that Harvard ever had. After Frost married he had enrolled at Harvard to study Latin and Greek, but soon discovered that college was not for him. When he went to the dean's office, he was surprised to have Dean Briggs agree with him, an empathetic response which Frost never forgot.

Though Brace was frequently asked to write and speak about literature, he received only rare recognition for his paintings. Thus he was delighted to have the B. U. Chenery Library mount an exhibition of his watercolors and oil paintings from April 30 to June 6 of 1954. Though not of truly professional quality, his New England land and seascapes are pleasant to view and attempt to evoke much the same feelings as his novels.

In 1955, Boston University initiated a sabbatical plan which would allow any professor who had been there seven years to have a semester off at full pay or an entire year at half-pay. Jerry was one of six professors who applied and were granted leave that first year. He took the whole year because he had been offered a visiting professorship at Harvard for the second term at a salary far higher than he was receiving at B. U. The additional money allowed the Braces to spend on some extra luxuries, including a bay window in their Parker's Point house from which Huldah could watch the birds at the feeder

The new bay window — 1955

and be able to glimpse the boats in the bay. A new bathroom was installed upstairs as well.

Barbara had brought her son Lincoln, now twenty months old, for a stay on the island. It seemed to the proud grandparents that the baby was perfect in every way. Jerry was upset though by the changes that Deer Isle was undergoing.

Along Dow Road, lumbermen were stripping woods already devastated by a hurricane. But the big news of the summer was that the old party-line phone system was being replaced by dial. Jerry worried that the native women would lack entertainment in the winter now that they could no longer listen in on their neighbors' calls.

In his latest novel *Bell's Landing*, Brace returned to problems reminiscent of *The Garretson Chronicle*. In a doctoral dissertation on Brace written for the University of New Brunswick, Herbert William Connor made the cogent observation that *Bell's Landing* is actually a revised treatment of the theme of *The Garretson Chronicle*, reflecting the differences in characters born twenty years apart. Both books deal with the same social and cultural background and the pressure that this puts on the male protagonists. "In fact the most striking difference between *The Garretson Chronicle* and *Bell's Landing* is that the latter presents a fundamentally bleaker, more pessimistic view of contemporary life than does the former, which, for all its irony and autumnal conception of New England culture is on the whole a fairly cheerful novel." The older generation of Redferns had been able to live life fully and well, but in this alienated and uncertain world, it is no longer possible. The death of the aunts and the decay of the house symbolize the end of the old civilized way of life.

Bell's Landing was published on August 29, 1955, with Brace receiving his usual $2,000 advance. Royalties would pay him 10 percent for the first 5,000 sales, 12½ percent for the next 5,000, and 15 percent after that. This would be the standard contract he would sign for all his later books. He was sent a small extra sum when both the San Francisco *Examiner* and the Canadian *Montreal Star* published the novel in condensed form in their magazine sections. The setting for *Bell's Landing* had been suggested by a visit that Jerry had made during his Harvard days. He and Lincoln had gone to Beverly, Massachusetts, one Sunday to attend the Unitarian Church where Mr. Fairley was serving as guest preacher. Jerry had distant cousins, the Lorings, who lived in affluent Prides Crossing. When he saw an austere dignified lady dressed all in black sitting in the front pew, he suspected that it was "Aunt" Katherine Loring. He checked with an usher who was obviously a bit in awe of her, but assured him she would be pleased if he spoke to her for she was "really quite democratic."

"Aunt" Katherine, who fondly remembered his Aunt Leta and Aunt Emma, invited him and the Fairleys to follow her chauffeur-driven limousine to her home. Passing through imposing stone pillars and up a long drive, they arrived in a gravelled turning place before a big Gothic house facing the sea. The scene imprinted itself indelibly in his mind. They stood "staring out at the blue horizon and down at the rocks and beaches below us where the small breakers rolled in. There were beds of spring flowers about the house, and very green mowed grass, and flocks of white pigeons flew round the cupola of a carriage house and barn that was somewhat below and behind the main house." (*DTW* II, p. 59) This was the scene he recreated in *Bell's Landing*—complete with pigeons, driveway, sea, and chauffeur. Of course, he made fictional changes. Aunt Katherine had been a friend of Henry James and Sarah Orne Jewett. The protagonist's aunts had known Kossuth, Mrs. Stowe, and Sargent. The first two had personal meanings for Jerry as he thought of his grandfather's defense of Kossuth and imprisonment in a Hungarian jail, and the portrait of his great grandfather, John Pierce Brace, in Harriet Beecher Stowe's novel, *Old Town Folks*. The plot, once again, reflected the conflict between two brothers, one who enjoyed scholarship while the other preferred manual work.

If the setting came from the Lorings' estate, the two sisters bear more resemblance to the Dodd sisters with whom Jerry and Lincoln had boarded in Cambridge. Aunt Evelyn, who takes in Will and Harold Redfern after their father commits suicide during the Depression, is the one who holds the place together as long as possible. Like Annie Dodd who was "vigorous and downright" she administered the house efficiently until poverty and old age took its toll. High-minded Aunt Lucy is like Annie's sister Jean, "a sweet and rather helpless and spinsterish lady who lived in the shadow of her strong minded elder." (*DTW* II, p. 24) Both Jean and her fictional counterpart live the kind of ineffectual existence which as young girls they had been taught to consider proper.

A new element in this novel is an awareness of the immigrant population in America, a subject to which Brace had given little thought before coming to Boston University. He had touched upon the Slavic population in Waltham in *The Garretson Chronicle*, but now he focuses on the Greek Anthonakis family, based partly on neighbors of the Braces in Belmont. Pop Anthonakis is a philosopher who views life pessimistically. He must work in a machine shop instead of playing the violin as he had hoped he could do in this land of opportunity. His granddaughters too are not completely assimilated, and Sally, whom Will loves, marries an unsuccessful artist. The inspiration for Sally, who loves poetry and music, and for her sister Althea, may have originated from two girls of Greek heritage in Brace's classes. Whenever he had student conferences with the Verenis sisters, Betsy and Mattina, he was aware of their dark beauty and suggestion of foreign mystery.

For the first time Brace attempts to deal openly with sex in a novel, though he never could bring himself to write frank details. As he has Will explain, "I know that writing about sex is in effect paradoxical. The aim is candor and simplicity and freedom from superstition; the result is often a magnifying of the eroticism it has set out to dispel." (*BL*, p. 144) He has already concluded that there will always be need for a "sacred mystery" to swear by and against, and that "the secrecies of sex are the best ones we have in a time when heaven and hell are failing." (*BL*, p. 133)

Having just served in the Navy during World War II Will Redfern has had enough of mass activity; so he decides he doesn't want to follow the crowd of veterans enrolling in college. It may have been Brace's decision to discuss the problems of a returning veteran from this branch of the armed services that prompted the United States Navy in September of 1957 to order 427 copies of the novel for their ships' libraries. When Will returns to *Bell's Landing*, he discovers that Sally is married, rather unhappily, and his aunts, with only James, their faithful and unpaid retainer to look after them, are in a bad way physically and financially. Aunt Lucy takes refuge in the past. Aunt Evelyn's struggle is more heroic. She even takes on some of the characteristics of Brace's better Maine characters, but she never achieves their self sufficiency. A cousin sends her daughter Betsy to help out, and Will is attracted by her good sense and cool irony. Though appearing a modern woman on the surface, she has been trained in perfect manners and physical hardihood. Brace endows her with the coolness that always made him uneasy with girls from his own class. She treats men as equals, but in so doing she loses the mystery and passion found in an immigrant girl like Sally. When the aunts die, the property is left to Will, who, forced to face reality, reluctantly concludes that he has neither the money nor the temperament to maintain such a large place. Although Will's future is left unresolved, he is enough of a realist to survive. Jerry had become aware of the demands of property first from reading Thoreau, but later, from experience. In his fifties, he was reluctantly learning an even more difficult lesson; one must eventually loosen the hold of one's past.

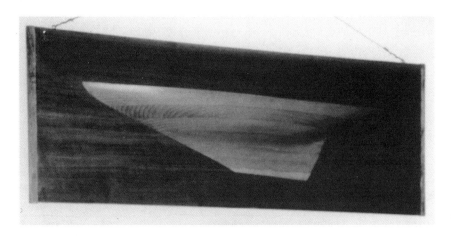

Two of Jerry's boat models

17
From the Mediterranean to Penobscot Bay

Having a sabbatical in 1955 allowed the Braces to remain in Deer Isle until late in the fall and then to embark on a Mediterranean cruise by Norwegian freighter. It had been a long time since they had been abroad, and in those early days they had been on a very limited budget. Jerry dreamed of shipboard, though they both well knew of Huldah's propensity to seasickness. All the days at sea were joyous for Jerry. He saw whales and "innumerable beautiful porpoises that leaped through the air like arrows." They stopped at Casablanca and Beirut. At Istanbul they visited the university and the Mosque of Suleyman the Magnificent. Jerry haunted the waterfront where the boats reminded him of Noah's ark. They bought Christmas Cards to send their friends noting that, in spite of the Turkish scene on the front, the sentiments were printed in French as the Turks considered Christmas "a heathenish affair." The seas were rough on the way home and Huldah was too ill most of the time to leave their tiny cabin. The constant vomiting seriously exacerbated her hiatus hernia.

They had rented out their Belmont home for the year. The furnished house at 146 Albermarle Road in Newton that they had found to live in while Jerry was teaching at Harvard in the spring semester would not be available until February; so they set off for California. They drove along the Twain-Harte Trail in Calaveras County where Jerry reported that while he supposed there were still frogs, he had seen no jumping contests. They visited Sutter's Mill to see the spot where on January 24, 1848, James Marshall had found the first flakes of gold, triggering the gold rush. Jerry was awed by the pristine beauty of snow-covered Yosemite, though deepening drifts in the high Sierras made driving difficult. San Francisco was wet most of the time they were there, but the weather improved as they headed back through Death Valley and along the Grand Canyon.

They arrived at their temporary home in Newtonville in the early part of February. Since Newton was an easy commute from the city, many of their B. U. colleagues lived there. They soon received dinner invitations from the

Wagenknechts and the Winslows as well as the Nortons in nearby Wellesley. They had enjoyed their travels, but psychologically and physically, Brace's world remained limited by the boundaries of New England.

If Jerry's life centered in the local region, the same could not be said for his offspring. Loring was still serving with the army in the South Pacific, Barbara was at Penn State where her husband was teaching philosophy, and Gerald, instead of returning home after his January discharge from army duties in Germany, was "adventuring" in France where his company had been briefly stationed the year before. He sent his family a photograph of himself sporting a full red beard. As a summer job he was selling perfume and commuting to Paris by scooter from the suburbs, where he had a whole house to himself in return for the care of two boxer dogs while the family was away. It amazed Jerry how his family had scattered across the globe, while he was so contented with New England. He commented "My own youthful adventures were very conservative and unimaginative in comparison to my sons." Huldah did not take her son's decision to remain in France as lightly as his father had. She was upset that he was not coming home and removed his name from their home address in Belmont, essentially disenfranchising him. No doubt she was sincere when she said she considered it the only honest thing to do, but her actions also reflected her displeasure. She would have been even more unhappy if she had realized that France would become her son's permanent home.

At Deer Isle, that summer of '56, Jerry was getting ready for an influx of visitors. *Festina* was in the water and he had painted the porch and bathroom and laid rubber tiles on both the bathroom and kitchen floors. He took pride in being his own handyman though it did not come easily to him, and he frequently became frustrated. Barbara, Dick and young son, Lincoln, arrived, and Loring wrote that he would be coming sometime, though at the moment his life was complicated by a boat and a girl. He was due to be discharged from the army in September and had already accepted a research job at the Jackson Memorial Laboratory at Bar Harbor, Maine.

Jerry had finally gone against all his principles and given in to Huldah's pleas for an outboard motor for *Festina*. It was only powerful enough for auxiliary use, but he had to admit that it made it easier to come back to the mooring in a light wind. Any mechanization was a major concession for someone who believed that sailing should be kept pure. Being becalmed or caught in a rainstorm was part of the challenge. Many of his guests who were not sailors did not feel the same way, and now with a growing family of young grandchildren he felt he must accept the inevitable.

I usually joined the Braces for a week or two each summer. Together, with Eleanor, they introduced me to the islands that they loved so well. Jerry took me to Long Island to photograph hatching gulls; to Fling and the

Porcupines to see osprey nests; to Hurricane (not yet part of the Outward Bound program) to search under the enveloping underbrush for granite columns and carved stones, abandoned by quarrymen when the operation shut down; to Eagle where, except for a few summer visitors, only Marion Howard and old Mr. Littlefield lived on alone after the mechanization of the lighthouse in 1959; to Crow for picnics; to Brimstone to

Festina at anchor off Fling Island — 1960

gather basalt stones, and to Isle au Haut, to climb high enough above the spruce forests to see the lobstermen hauling pots in the cove below. Sometimes the Havilands took us in their lobster boat to explore inlets where a sailboat could not go. Once ashore, Huldah dozed in the sun under a big hat to guard her from sunburn or prepared the food for our lunch, while we explored the islands from tidal pools to spruce covered crests. On foggy or rainy days we sat in the warm kitchen or before the living-room fireplace listening as Jerry described the islands as they had been in his youth. Although Huldah was sometimes jealous of Jerry's admirers, she recognized the need he had for an audience. Like the storytellers of old, he wanted to make sure that his personal Camelot would not be forgotten.

In the summer of 1956, Edward K. Graham was appointed dean of the College of Liberal Arts at Boston University. Ralph Taylor, the outgoing dean, was an old fashioned, low-keyed, courteous gentleman; Dean Graham was totally different. He was brilliant, but mercurial and sometimes difficult. He had a Ph.D. from Cornell where he had served as assistant to the President. He enjoyed terrorizing the meeker professors and the young secretaries. With his pipe puffing forth an aromatic apple tobacco scent, he would remove it only long enough to smile warmly, showing his gapped front teeth, or to roar with disapproval. His orders were often signed Captain Ahab, an appropriate pseudonym, and to make sure no one could read his private messages he wrote them in Anglo Saxon. Jerry, who found the new dean intelligent and amusing, was neither cowed nor angered. Ed Graham soon found himself relying on Brace's wisdom and calm, and chose him to serve on a committee made up of the most distinguished senior members of the faculty. It would be their responsibility to make decisions on all the major business of the college.

Brace, who had always tried to avoid college politics, now found himself in the thick of things.

Creative writing was no longer considered a frill at the college. When Brace returned after his year of sabbatical, Boston University awarded him its highest accolade. He was chosen university lecturer for 1956, an honor given each semester to one professor for outstanding writing or research. On December 11, Hayden Hall, the university's largest auditorium, was filled with students, friends, and colleagues to hear Brace lecture on "The Age of the Novel." Later published as a monograph, it not only discussed the history of the novel, but also expressed concern that the novel was becoming an anachronism. Once both the mirror and educator of society, fiction, he said, had lost its purpose in an age where men no longer agree about God, duty, and the role of society. With the loss of man's spiritual commitments "the only meaningful experience is his limited self, the little circle of his ego, and his only hope of effective originality is self expression." This, of course, was before the electronic media and demands for ethnic studies eroded the position of the traditional novel even more. Though he recognized that business and science were replacing the humanities, Brace still hoped that art would regain its greatness, and mankind its higher beliefs.

At this same time an article appeared in *College English* (Dec. 1956, No. 3) entitled "Gerald Warner Brace: Teacher-Novelist" written by former student Arthur S. Harris Jr. In discussing Brace's place as a writer, Harris tried to answer the question often asked by critics as to when Brace would be recognized as a major American novelist. Dry wit and precise perfectly shaped prose were earmarks of all Brace's novels, but because they suffered from a slow pace and an enclosed environment they failed to achieve the popularity and stature they might otherwise have had. Harris continued his article with an accurate appraisal of Brace as a teacher: "Brace is no magnetic teacher, trying to dazzle students with knowledge and entertain them with classroom wit. He teaches with quiet confidence and resists even approaching the stereotype of a college professor." Jerry always deliberately avoided the jargon and pose of an intellectual.

In a lecture Brace gave to the Epsilon chapter of Phi Beta Kappa, he reminded his listeners that it is not facts and formulae which determine an educated man. The true scholar is one who has learned how to live and has a knowledge of human values. He felt that some of the wisest men he had ever known were old-time country folk who lived close to nature and had learned about life from the struggle to survive in a sometimes hostile environment. Many were beaten down by hardships, but the best among them became strong and self-sufficient. These were the people who became models for the novel he was currently writing.

In *The World of Carrick's Cove,* published in 1957, Brace went back to the earlier way of life that he had heard described by the older men on the islands. For a setting he used Isle au Haut, perhaps one of the loveliest of all the Maine islands. Today three-quarters of its spruce forests and rocky coastline are under the jurisdiction of Acadia National Park, assuring that its beauty will remain in its pristine state for future generations. Though busy in summer, it is sparsely inhabited in winter, and deer still roam its woods. The small island is only about six miles long by two and a half miles wide and from its rocky heights, a climber can, on a blue sparkling day, look down on the lobster boats and sailing craft, but in fogs and storms the ledges can be treacherous.

Jerry himself could remember when the island was a busy lobstering and fishing community with three or four hundred permanent residents. Since it is only six miles south of Deer Isle, it had always been a favorite destination for a sail. Most of the inhabitants lived near the thoroughfare on the western side of the north shore. There was a church that had been built in 1857, a post office, and an old factory later turned into a boatshop. The island had been a tourist mecca since 1880 when Ernest Bowditch, grandson of the author of *Practical Navigator*, had bought land there to establish a fishing club at Point Lookout to be used by fifty wealthy families from Boston, New York, and Philadelphia. Over two dozen cottages connected by boardwalks were built, along with three or four boarding houses. However, the rocky terrain made communication difficult between the tiny clusters of houses at Rick's Cove on the northeast, Head Harbor on the southeast corner, and Duck Harbor on the southwest coast; so these areas had remained isolated from the summer colony.

Jerry liked to anchor at quiet Duck Harbor. In his youthful days there was an old homestead back from the shore occupied by a family named Hamilton who had a fleet of boats—peapods and dories and, the ultimate prize possession in Jerry's eyes, a Friendship sloop used for lobstering and fishing. Ben Carrick, the 82-year-old narrator of Brace's novel, recalled when these sloops were being built by Wilbur Morse in Friendship, Maine, but like the clippers and Gloucestermen they "came to glory and then disappeared." (*WCC*, p. 52) Jerry knew the Hamilton family only slightly and his novel is not about them, but based more on the Quinns of Eagle Island. The setting is clearly Duck Harbor as he remembered it from his youth, but he had learned what island life was like in the late nineteenth century, and captured the intonation and flavor of the Down East speech by listening to the reminiscences of old timers.

When nets were laid across the narrow mouth of Duck Harbor, it became a natural herring trap, penning in the shoals of fish. Old Ben Carrick remembered his sense of awe when the fish arrived:

> It was a great thing when the herring first began to come in, like a supernatural force under the water. It would be dusky, or maybe

dark, and you could see the thousands and thousands of little flash-es below the surface. It was spooky, in a way: not a sound anywhere except the quiet of the sea outside sort of rising and falling, and the moan of that buoy way off the Old Man, and the water surface of the cove would seem pretty black, but with silvery ripples in it from the starlight, and then you'd see the flashes way down—it seemed like millions and millions, all flickering by. If it was dark that's all you'd see. If it was twilight you might see the moving shapes under water all going and going. And then you'd begin to hear the little splashes like a rustle all over the cove, and you'd feel mighty strange about it as if things were going on you couldn't understand. It was like a different place altogether. (*WCC*, p. 36)

Jerry did not consider himself formally religious, but sometimes his writing takes on a spiritual power. The men at work had little time to savor the wonder. To get the net across the mouth with weights and floats and then to dip the fish with long handled nets into the dory took skill and hard work. Ben's Pa was more energetic and enthusiastic than careful. His nets were rotting and set up in slipshod fashion, allowing the herring to slip through. Perhaps in this busy world, Brace's loving attention to such details are no longer what readers demand, but they evoke a feeling of magic in those who take pleasure in country ways.

Jerry was thrilled to see men still employing this method of trapping her-ring at Duck Harbor on one of his last trips to the island. He had moored *Festina* for the night and was just preparing to sleep when Andrew Gove, a Stonington fisherman, came in with a seine boat and crew. Jerry awoke in the early dawn hours to the sight of myriad flashing shapes of herring beneath his sloop. On the shore he could see red deer browsing and an eagle soaring over the rocky crags. The fishermen opened their nets just wide enough to let Jerry's small sloop slip out. It was a scene that could have come right out of *The World of Carrick's Cove*.

Ben Carrick's Pa never learned one of the main rules for survival on an island. Neighbors have to help one another. He was forced to rely on his neigh-bor Henry and his steer after he had killed his own horse, Joker, by beating it with a branch because it refused to pull too heavy a load. In contrast, Ben recalled how efficiently Henry handled his steer with just a little stick with a cod line on the end, and "all he had to do was give a light flick here or there, port or starboard, and say a word or two so quiet you hardly noticed it, and that steer would move six inches one way or the other just as easy as though he was run by electric power. He never had to strain or lunge the way a horse does; he just leaned a little and moved along steady and sort of delicate."

(*WCC*, p. 32) Here Brace was remembering how beautiful it had been to watch his friend Fred Sylvester control his pair of oxen, Star and Bright. As Fred spoke to them "quietly and affectionately" they would listen carefully before moving steadily forward to their tasks.

Although Jerry had once taken for granted the part that island women played in keeping a home together, he had come to realize how difficult it could be, especially for those brought up in areas where they had had access to books, piano, and friends, who then found themselves isolated from civilization. Ben Carrick explains:

> You can talk about galley slaves, but I believe no human creatures ever worked harder and longer than women did in those times. We didn't think anything about it; we supposed it was the way it had to be, like the tide coming or going or the seasons. She lugged in stove wood and tended fires. She made and mended all our clothes, and washed in a galvanized tub with a scrub board—and no decent wringer. . . . As for water, we had a well up above the hen house and a hogshead to catch the roof water, and she'd had to fetch it in pails and set 'em on the stove to heat. . . . If we had chickens she tended them. Same with the cow. In lambing season she'd be out with the bottles of warm milk. . . . I remember when we were small she'd take us clamming, with a pair of Pa's boots on and her skirts pinned up. And berries—all kinds: she gathered pails of 'em and made sauce. (WCC, pp. 18,19)

Jerry knew that even on well tended farms, the women's work was never done. One of Fred Sylvester's daughters, Neva Beck, remembers a life that would seem unbearably difficult to a modern wife. "Mother did all the cooking for the boarders, besides picking berries (which she loved to do), making butter, washing the clothes and the bedding and all the other countless things that had to be done on a farm and at a boarding house. We milked the cows along with Dad, twice a day and of course, we had our chores in the house too. We had to wait on tables, clean the rooms etc." Neva remembers it as a happy existence, though it seemed to Jerry that Mrs. Sylvester lived "a life of quiet but somewhat ironic desperation." (*DTW*, p. 11) Observing all that country women were expected to do, it is no wonder that he thought that the women in his own family had easy lives.

A Maine boy comes of age when he has proved himself by completing a worthwhile project. For Ben it was finishing the sloop that his grandfather had started many years before. Brace endows Ben with his own feelings when he has him say:

I can never pass by a model of a boat of any kind; if I see a man framing a punt I want to stop and observe it, and it's the same with every other vessel. There's nothing nicer than to see the first strakes go on to a timbered-out sloop boat when you can admire the work in her and take note of the lines. She's all new and strong and able, and you think to yourself that she'll do better than any boat that ever was: if you had to name her right then you'd name her Hope. (*WCC*, p. 52)

A boat is like a man's first love, even if later—like a wife—she doesn't live up to all his dreams. "If you handle her at all, you always think of her as alive—you get mad when she's stubborn or cranky and you talk to her and argue with her, and when she does well for you, you love her like a bride." (*WCC*, p. 129)

Jerry had learned the importance of sharp tools one day at Sylvester's when he had casually touched his thumb to Freddie's ax and drew blood. It is a lesson that Ben's Pa never learned, but that his neighbor Henry teaches Ben. It seems to Ben that if he wants a practical education he will learn it best from observing experienced boatbuilders. Like Edgar in *The Islands*, he elects to leave school. The older men tell him that education is a civilizing force, but they agree that unless manners are taught at home, they won't be learned in any school, a message that Brace felt modern society could well note. Ben's brother Willy does finish school, but he never really amounts to anything. He becomes the type of independent, eccentric, odd-jobs men once found so often in rural New England.

Readers hoping for sentimental romance or explicit sex would be disappointed by the love scenes. Ben and Cora are more apt to wrestle than to couple, and family responsibilities keep them apart for years. Ben merely tells the reader near the end of the novel that he and Cora married, had two children, and that for the remainder of her life she worked hard by his side indoors and out. Now a widower, he seems to remember the tragedies of losing his wife and his sloop with equal grief. But he is satisfied with the life he has led. He has done the type of work for which he was best fitted with no overseer except his conscience. He concludes "That was the way of it and I can't reasonably ask for anything better." (*WCC*, p. 308)

Ben represents Brace's philosophy that the hard, wintry coastal region of Maine creates strong, independent people. "For those who could cope with it, the harsh challenge of the old northern coast, on both land and sea, produced moral and physical strength, and beyond that spiritual serenity." (*BWW*, p. 62) It is this strength and serenity that Ben has achieved, though as a lonesome elderly widower his reflections are tinged with sadness. This worried some of

Brace's editors, who thought readers would want a happier ending. By now George Brockway had become a close personal friend and Jerry had no hesitancy about defending the tone he had adopted. "I thought the mood of it was about right since the old man would inevitably be melancholy, and I thought it put the whole thing in the right perspective." After rereading the manuscript several times, Brockway agreed that the book stood up well just as it was written. Brace might not always be an astute businessman, but he would speak out when it came to his writing.

"The World of Carrick's Cove," Isle au Haut, Maine

18
Teaching Creative Writing

Conscientious as he was about his academic work, Brace frequently felt stifled in the city. After a long morning of teaching or listening to the politics of a faculty meeting, he was eager to get back to the office suite to discuss baseball scores, camping, and sailing with Leighton Brewer. They arranged tennis matches together, and one summer Leighton and his wife visited the Braces at Deer Isle. Jerry took them sailing in *Festina*. Mrs. Brewer was an animated conversationalist, an asset at a dinner party, but now it spoiled the sense of freedom for the two men. They began discussing the possibility of finding a remote spot where they could go camping together. At first it was just idle talk, but gradually their plans took shape after they discovered that there was still a large unmapped territory in Quebec. In 1957 they travelled to Canada and paddled by canoe into the wilderness. They felt as if they were the first white men to camp in those virgin forests. It brought back memories to Jerry of a trip which as a young boy he had taken with his father in the Maine woods north of the Rangeley Lakes, and the thrill he had felt when their guide had pointed north toward land which he said no man had ever explored.

It was the idea of the frontier which had been the basis for the American Dream, and Jerry worried what would happen when there were no longer new areas to be discovered. During his own lifetime he had seen roads built into remote regions, trees felled to meet the demands for lumber, rivers dammed and harnessed. When a dozen years after his Canadian venture, he wrote a writers' handbook called *The Stuff of Fiction*, he mourned the passing of the wilderness.

> Some take comfort in the ideas that the frontiers have moved on to outer space—cold comfort at best. Some may point to the unknowns of the psyche, the inner space where mystery and originality still beckon the explorer. Doubtless we must make the best of our limitations. But the loss of the vision of the wildness and vastness of the natural world is a hard loss for someone to bear,

especially I think for Americans who have lived so long on a still virgin continent.

Few of the creative writing students in his classes at Boston University had had the opportunity to explore the wilderness. They were from working class backgrounds with neither money nor leisure to travel. Even for those who longed for nature, finite local woods would have to serve. Because of its size and large number of commuters, Boston University was often spoken of deprecatingly as a warehouse for students, but the educational opportunities it offered were the key to a better life. John Gilgun, who graduated in the class of 1957, later wrote an autobiographic poem which well expressed the situation of many of his classmates:

> . . . I was born into a class
> Destined from 1830 on for the Dark Satanic Mills,
> But by 1950 they had all moved South for the cheap labor
> Leaving only one mill open—Boston University.

Brace enjoyed teaching creative writing, but he always wondered uneasily whether it was a subject that could be taught. In his unpublished autobiography, he analyzed the limitations. "What a teacher of writing can actually do is so involved with idiosyncrasy and temperament that no clear course of instruction can be counted on to achieve success." (*DTW* II, p. 156) He worried that an intellectual atmosphere might stifle creativity. He had no special formula, but offered his students the same encouragement that had been given to him by George Whicher at Amherst and Dean Briggs at Harvard. Although he had not known personally his predecessor at Boston University, Dallas Lore Sharp, he had heard much about him from former students and colleagues, and endeavored to teach in the same tradition. Of the three men, he thought that perhaps Sharp, who had written charming books and familiar essays on nature, had been the most professional, for he had always strongly encouraged his students to publish. In Brace's later years, after creative writing became a separate division of the English department and major professional writers such as John Malcolm Brinnin, John Barth, and John Cheever had been hired, Sharp's works would seem quaint and old fashioned, but the principles of good composition and the needs of students never change. Brace felt it his mission to direct young writers toward the best in literature and to encourage them to persevere in their lonely endeavors.

Brace was proud of students like John Gilgun, though he was modest about taking any credit for their successes. When John was on the staff of *Patterns*, the college literary magazine, he wrote to Brace, who was on sabbatical, to request a review copy of *Bell's Landing*, and asked if he would be willing to write an explanation of his writing process to be published with it.

Brace promised to have Norton send a copy of the book, but wondered what kind of quotation he had in mind as he always found it difficult to explain his creative technique:

> I'm always surprised at how seriously articulate some authors are about their own work—i.e. Joyce Cary or R. P. Warren, to name two. Probably I write more by impulse than by calculation, which isn't anything to boast of. The novel simply accumulates until it reaches a sort of end. I get to feeling that the characters are writing, or acting, on their own. I suppose in B.L. one of the technical little problems is the first person narrative. And I suppose the variations on the theme of old age have some calculation to them. The familiar problems of what to do with tradition is another theme. Good luck to you anyway.

Students not accepted into Brace's writing classes often brought their creative endeavors to me. While he was always willing to help serious writers, he was intolerant of vague abstractions and empty words. His written suggestions of what I should tell one of these students in conference show both his irony and careful critical analysis.

> I think his poem is nothing but pretentious nonsense. He has some misty notions about Truth and Self Search and Life, but none of it has any valid connection with experience. He has hypnotized himself with empty language (Depth Strength—specially Lubricious Night, a phrase I never saw the beat of.)
> Tell him as sweetly as you can that the poem is no good.
> Tell him it is based on vagueness and abstraction.
> Tell him (sweetly) it is sentimental and weak-minded.
> Tell him it has no warrant of experience (Thoreau's phrase)
> Tell him not to use so many capital letters.
> Tell him to try to write a poem with one level of meaning in it.

> Later (morning)

> I thought if I slept on it I might feel better, but I don't. I dreamt I went to a restaurant and waited an hour and got nothing. Then I threw the crockery at the waitress, beat up the manager, raised general hell till they promised to bring me a steak. An hour later they brought a plate of frankfurters. It was the worst dream I ever had. You can see how grim things are, and if my view is depressing & dyspeptic, don't take it too hard.
> Put it down to the end-of-the-year bad temper.
> Damn everything, especially students, poems, stories, and papers.

> Maybe it doesn't sound like it, but I *tried* to find something nice to say about it.

The tone is meant to be light, but the anger and frustration are just below the placid surface he always showed to his classes.

The creative writing program at Boston University was now prestigious enough to attract major writers. Although Brace continued to teach the prose creative writing, the poetry seminar was conducted by Robert Lowell, 1946 winner of the Pulitzer Prize for *Lord Weary's Castle*. Lowell's seminar attracted a number of extremely talented young poets: Sylvia Plath, newly married to English poet Ted Hughes, Anne Sexton, George Starbuck, a talented poet who later chaired B.U.'s creative writing program, and Donald Junkins, who became head of the writing program at the University of Massachusetts.

Brace had known Sylvia Plath since her childhood at Wellesley Hills, but since then she had suffered from mental problems and been at McLean Hospital. Plath and Sexton both found Lowell's teaching style loose and uninspiring at first, but they enjoyed the class discussions. As Anne Sexton later wrote: "We talked death with burned-up intensity, both of us drawn to it like moths to an electric light bulb." Both girls had already attempted suicide and were in psychotherapy. With a free hour between class and Sexton's appointment with her psychiatrist, she would drive Starbuck and Plath in her old Ford after their Tuesday afternoon seminar, to Arlington Street for drinks at the Ritz Carlton Hotel. It was while illegally parking her car in the hotel's loading zone, that Sexton made her oft-quoted quip that it was all right because the three of them were "going to get loaded." It was a period of great poetic ferment in the Boston-Cambridge area, and if some of their lives ended tragically, the impact they made on American literature was enduring.

Two decades later, after Sexton and Plath had both met death at their own hands, most of the rest of the class were at the Boston Church of the Advent to attend the funeral of Robert Lowell. In a commemorative poem entitled "Robert Lowell, The Church of the Advent, Boston" Don Junkins skillfully interwove visions of the living poet with the funeral service. Lowell, a manic-depressive who regularly returned to McLean Hospital for treatment, was often erratic in his behavior. Junkins' lines recall how

> Once he fell asleep reading one of my poems in his office, just before class on Gerald Warner Brace's couch: 'Do you mind if I read it lying down?' he asks, finishing a sandwich, propping himself on one elbow, His eyes close almost instantly. I leave him, for class.

Lowell was the antithesis of Brace, who took student conferences seriously, yet each man had something special to offer the budding writers under their tutelage.

The year 1957 was an active time for the Brace family. Barbara presented them with a second grandchild, a little girl she named Diane. Loring had returned from the South Pacific and proposed to Mary Louise Crozier, known familiarly as Mimi. He had met her at the Harvard Museum of Comparative Zoology where she worked. Her family was well known at Deer Isle for her aunt Jean Crozier came there each summer with her friend Kathe Wilckens. Mimi was accustomed to academic people. Her father was Harvard professor William Crozier, and her uncle was Hudson Hoagland, professor of physiology at both Tufts Medical School and Boston University. It was difficult for Huldah to part from her "first born" but when she saw that the marriage was inevitable, she threw herself into the arrangements with her customary energy. On June 8, Mimi and Loring were married in a formal ceremony at Harvard Chapel and went to Rockport on Cape Ann for a honeymoon. Their first night was spent at the Clipper Ship Inn in a room called "The Flying Cloud" which caused Jerry to comment wryly: "I hope it was appropriate, but you never know. No one ever tells."

He began a new novel even before his previous one was in the bookstores. As so often, he had difficulty getting started. Writing me a letter gave him the excuse to postpone facing a blank sheet of paper. "I've made a beginning, a very drab and dreary affair of commuting on the B&M. I'll have to consult you about technical details. The first copies of The World of Carrick's Cove appeared, but the whole works are being held up till the Book of the Month makes up its mind whether it wants to use it for its January selection. The fateful decision will be made day after tomorrow." To his disappointment, his novel once more just narrowly missed being chosen and he wrote to me ruefully two days later, "We'll have to keep the old Mercury for another year."

Like the *Garretson Chronicle, The World of Carrick's Cove* was chosen to be translated and distributed in Asia as an example of typical Americana by the United States Information Agency in Washington D.C. Over the next four years, five thousand copies were published in Pak Bengal, five thousand more in a condensed version in Hindi, two thousand more printed in Marathi, and four thousand, seven hundred-fifty in Arabic. It was also published in Argentina as *Cronicas de la Ensenada Carrick* and ten thousand copies were published in abbreviated form in France as *Je Me Souviens d'une Ile.* It gave Gerald pleasure to look at the shelf of his books that for the most part he couldn't read—he could only wonder what the translators might have done to his book and what people of such different cultures had understood.

By August the novel was in all the bookstores. At Deer Isle it was greeted with delight. The little local weekly *Island Ad Vantage* pointed out: "To read it is to read the immediate past history of our own island and its people." The local Methodist Church invited him to speak to a full house. To be sure some of the critics outside of Maine thought there was more about sailing and weather than the average reader wanted to know. Orville Prescott complained in the *New York Times*: "*The World of Carrick's Cove* is filled with detailed description of how to make a lobster trap, how to sail a small boat, how to build a sloop all by yourself when you are only 16 or 17, and how to launch it. All this material is mildly educational and bristles with technical jargon." (2 September 1957)

Other reviewers were kinder. Granville Hicks wrote in *The New Leader*: "Brace had made himself the novelist of New England especially in examining how the values of the New England past have lived into the present." (2 September 1957) Many once again compared him to John Marquand, George Santayana, Sarah Orne Jewett, or Mary Ellen Chase. The book met with enough favor to be nominated for the National Book Award, but once more it lost out—this time to John Cheever's *The Wapshot Chronicle*.

Although Cheever had already gained recognition as a talented short story writer of the *New Yorker* school, *The Wapshot Chronicle* was his first full length novel. To have him receive the prize for his account of two New England brothers—one sensitive, one aggressive—caught between their nineteenth-century heritage and the twentieth-century world, must have been especially galling to Brace. He may well have considered the novel a parody of his own, especially *The Garretson Chronicle*. Reviews of the two books may explain the reason for the judges' preference. While *The World of Carrick's Cove* is described as leisurely paced, nostalgic, and dryly humorous, Cheever's work is seen as ironic, bawdy, and uproariously comic, "taking the complexities of sex in a cheerful, twentieth-century stride"—an attitude in tune with the spirit of the fifties. Once again critical appreciation had eluded Jerry's grasp.

Jerry continued to be involved in family life. He wrote that on Friday the 13th in June of 1958, in spite of fifty mile an hour gales, *Festina* had been launched, rigged, and sailed to her mooring, and Mimi had been rushed to Blue Hill Hospital where she had given birth to a 6 pound, 13 ounce boy named Charles Loring Brace V. Two days later they were all gathered in front of the fireplace, but what with babies, boats, and weather little writing had been accomplished.

In spite of rain and fog, he and John Donaldson went on a cruise to Seal Cove, the domain of Samuel Eliot Morrison. They returned to Northeast Harbor in a heavy fog, but he had enjoyed going there to see how the yachting crowd lived. He was sure that Seal Cove was "the most elegant yachting center in Maine & has free moorings, free garbage collecting, free morning paper & tide table delivered to each yacht: and lamb chops cost 87 cents apiece in the local market. I love to go there and see Life." He was competitive even on a leisurely cruise, and was delighted that *Festina* had been behaving well and outsailing everything she encountered.

The weather remained bad into July, and Jerry became very annoyed with the weather forecasters complaining "I can understand that predicting weather is hard even for professionals, but I wish someone would instruct them to look out the window before they tell us what is going on." He was being a little unfair, for Deer Isle is often enshrouded in fog while the sun is brightly shining in Boston or Bangor.

Jerry received a letter from Dean Graham asking if he would be willing to appear on television. As an author, he was aware that interviews helped sell books, but he doubted whether he had the right personality to perform. He recalled that once at Mount Holyoke the drama coach had asked him to try out for the lead in a school production. "I said I was no good, & she said nonsense & insisted on making me try. She came to our house with the play. I tried & that's the last I ever saw of her. I'm willing to do my duty up to a point; but my histrionic talent is zero."

Huldah had taken up rug hooking, and Jerry designed canvases for her, often on a marine theme appropriate for an island home. They now had all the amenities in their Deer Isle home, but the house maintained its old-fashioned charm with a Franklin stove in the dining room and the stuffed loon still surveying the living room with his watchful eyes. The family was growing. In 1959, Barbara and Dick had a third child, a son named Ralph Walter for Dick's father.

Through the years, Brace had maintained his friendship with Robert Frost, and frequently visited him in Cambridge at "his dismal little house on Brewster Street," where he was watched over by Mrs. Theodore Morrison. When Frost was invited to speak at Boston University on October 30, 1958, Brace drove him to the talk and back and introduced him to the large crowd gathered in Hayden Hall. The microphones had been positioned in such a way that while the audience in front could hear well, Brace's voice did not carry to the back of the stage where Frost was sitting. When the poet came forward to acknowledge the applause, he told the assembled crowd that he hadn't heard a word said about him, but he was sure they should discount most of it as he and Gerald Brace were old friends. Jerry always remembered with pleasure how Frost said it twice to give it emphasis. Frost loved an audience and that evening he was in a particularly mischievous mood. When in his deep New England tones he elongated the words "Provide, provide" he seemed to be mocking the whole Yankee ethic.

Everyone knew that Frost was a night person who loved to talk. Brace hosted a reception for him on Bay State Road after the performance. Robert Lowell was present, accompanied by a quiet unobtrusive young man. Frost was in high form and in his usual non-stop monologue got on the subject of Ezra Pound, who had been one of the first to recognize the worth of Frost's poems and generous in his reviews. Now a number of writers, including Frost, had been working to free the poet who had been indicted for the treasonous broadcasting of Fascist propaganda to the Italians during World War II. Tried in the United States he had been confined to a mental institution to save him from possible execution. His friends were trying to collect enough money for him to return to Italy to live out his remaining years. Nevertheless, that evening Frost made some very unkind comments about Pound. During a break in the monologue, Lowell softly announced that he would like to introduce his guest, Omar Pound, son of the poet. Everyone was embarrassed except Frost, who promptly launched into another monologue—but he did change the subject.

19

Stepping Into a New Age

The decade of the sixties opened on a note of hope. The election of the youthful president Kennedy energized the nation. Brace felt an almost personal involvement when his old friend Robert Frost was asked to read a new poem at the inaugural. The elderly poet could not see in the glaring light so recited another of his poems from memory, but he enjoyed the public acclaim. Youth and age seemed to unite in the promise of better times ahead.

Jerry and Huldah had settled into comfortable domesticity. While Mimi and Loring went to Milwaukee for a job interview and to find an apartment, the grandparents looked after toddler Charlie in Belmont and then took him to Deer Isle with them. Like many proud grandfathers, Jerry seemed more relaxed with Charlie than he had been with his own children. He wrote, "I hesitate to try to present the facts about Charlie, but the evident truth is that he is a perfect child. He is beautiful, happy, intelligent, & whatever else a 2 yr. old should be. He loves to ride in cars, sail in boats, visit, sleep in strange beds, chat with strangers, play with big dogs, take baths—whatever he is doing seems to delight him & he looks like a classic cherub." Not long after Loring and Mimi had settled in Wisconsin, they added another son, Roger Crozier Brace, to the growing new generation. The most disturbing family news was that Barbara and Dick were planning to be divorced. Although it was not totally unexpected, the parents worried about the problems she would have to face as a single mother with three children, two of them still practically babies.

Amidst all the upheavals in the world, it pleased Jerry that some of the Maine islands remained relatively unchanged. He loved to tell tales of islands like Matinicus, the outermost inhabited island in Penobscot Bay, and Matinicus Rock where wild storms had been known to carry away buildings and maroon its inhabitants in the lighthouse for days. It was here that seventeen year old Abby Burgess had once kept the light burning in the lighthouse tower for four weeks when a storm prevented her father from returning from the mainland. In the sixties, Matinicus was still the self-sufficient, thriving community that Brace so movingly described in his nonfiction book, *Between Wind and Water.*

> Of all the little sea kingdoms of the coast, the mellowest, most prosperous, and the farthest from the main, is Matinicus; which seems to retain its vitality in spite of the modern changes. Good lobstering keeps them going there. It is not a rocky outpost of fisherman shacks and wharves, but rather a gentle little country of meadows and gardens and white-painted clapboard houses with doorways of old New England grace. There are formal parlors and family Bibles and the sacred bits of good china and furnishings passed on from early times, along with treasures touched by the romance of the wrecks of long ago. There is a well-tended country cemetery, with stones marking the life and death of Youngs and Ames and the older royal lines of the island. There used to be cattle, mowings, plowed land and a network of little roads and paths with barred gates and stiles—now all changed, with automobiles on the roads and milk and fresh food sent by the mailboat from Rockland. But nowhere on the coast do you feel more vividly the evanescent past, the old self sufficiency of a world of the oar and sail, of the ax and saw, of life sustained by farming and fishing and the work done by hand. . . . Wherever you look, in the whole circumference, you have glimpses of the sea like a bowl of blue light. And the horizon line is always level, always straight, always there, like an assertion of pure logical truth. (*BWW*, pp. 29,30)

The poet Harold Vinal was born on the island, and Edna Saint Vincent Millay wrote some of her most delightful sonnets about it. Millay's mother had been a midwife in Camden, who boarded island women while they were awaiting the birth of a child. Later, Edna had been sent to stay on Matinicus in the hope that the sea air would improve her delicate health.

Gerald had begun writing a new novel even before *Winter Solstice* was in the stores.

> You can see from the paper [lined, three holed notebook paper] that I'm evading my morning duty. I've sort of begun work on a novel, but the going is discouraging. The early copies of Winter Solstice have come, & I hope I've done right to send one to the Dean: publ. date is set for Aug. 22. So far no advance interest in it anywhere— & one early notice complains that it is too dismal. So it is!

Not only was Jerry's own winter solstice mood behind him, but he sounded almost euphoric. He was full of enthusiasm. "Summer is now beginning, with sails visible in the bay, cruise schooners in the offing etc. Havilands on hand. Donaldsons—picnic planned for today, a bright and breezy day. *Festina* is fine, & the new sail is good." Huldah was about to return to Belmont and together with Loring they planned to go to Penn. State to help Barbara move. Then they would go to Vermont to pick up a bureau and parlor organ, part of the ancestral furniture that Loring wanted. Jerry remained in Deer Isle to cruise and enjoy himself.

In July of 1960 Jerry enjoyed a solitary junket in *Festina*. "Spent 2 nights at Isle au Haut (Carrick's Cove). 7 this A.M. fetched out to Matinicus Rock & admired the puffins & other wonders (no whales) & am now tied up at a mooring in the harbor."

A couple of days later he confessed that he had lost all track of time so couldn't date his letter. He had found Matinicus as beguiling as ever, though he couldn't find a place to leave mail on a Sunday.

> Of course there is a US Post Office there, with a large sign over it (the general store)—but nowhere to mail letters. I asked a girl how they mailed letters on Sunday and she said they didn't. The mail didn't go out on Monday anyway so why mail letters on Sunday? All I could do was to leave the cards on the doorstep with a stone on them. After that I took a walk—first northward to a lovely sand bathing beach I had never seen before, a perfect half circle of white sand with youngsters playing. Twenty years ago no inhabitant of Matinicus would have gone into the water for pleasure—now the kids have fins and snorkels.

He continued his walk around the island admiring the "lovely purple-blue orchises everywhere—a feature of Matinicus." It pleased him to think that one

Home after a sail — Deer Isle, Maine

island was maintaining its old way of life. He returned home the next day, "past Hurricane Island & through Leadbetters Narrow & the Thorough-fares—& it was one of those incredibly brilliant days like the one we had for the Hurricane trip. It is the prettiest stretch of waters on the Atlantic coast."

He was rereading some of the sea novels of James Fenimore Cooper, but he was finding him "the worst stuffed shirt who ever wrote novels." Although Jerry had thought he would accomplish a lot of work while Huldah was away, when he wasn't cruising, he was being invited out to meals. He wrote that even the new neighbors the Trowbridges had ask him for a meal "at 5:30, they said. I looked a little surprised at the time & said something about it (they being city people of some elegance): Oh, sez he, we just start drinking then. A splendid policy, I said."

It was obvious that his mood was far different from what it had been while he was writing *Winter Solstice*. Teaching at Boston University had raised his consciousness not only of working families, but also about the problems faced by women. When he compared the lives of individuals trapped in the arduous grind of commuting by public transportation to the city each day in order to earn a living, with the earlier harsh but independent existence of farmers and fishermen, it seemed to him that more had been lost than gained. The freedom of choices achieved by women brought also new fears and responsibilities. *Winter Solstice*, the least autobiographic of his novels, had been a major departure for Brace, especially since it focused mainly on a female character. When he had written to congratulate John Gilgun who had just had his story "A Penny for the Ferryman" sold to *New World Writing* by Jerry's agents, McIntosh and Otis, Brace confessed that he was not happy about his own soon to be published book: "It is a dismal suburban story, and I doubt if many would want to read it. I'll be glad to get through with it."

The title *Winter Solstice*, of course, refers to the darkest day of the year, and the action is circumscribed between one dismal December 21st and the same day the following year. It is a time of darkness of the soul as well. Each day Mary Kyle Eustace and her father make the commute to the city on the train. Each winter day begins the same:

> the long morning march up the platform, the steady shuffle of boot-ed and rubbered feet, the grim facing forward to the city, the queer silence of separate people moving shoulder to shoulder in a kind of daily oblivion. It seemed like night still under the platform roof, and yellow lights made whirls in the misty air. Sprays of rain blew in from the side. Diesels hummed or roared aloud. No one seemed to speak or show human feeling. They marched intently with closed faces." (*WS*, p. 12)

The same passage is repeated at the end of the novel as life continued its dreary cycle.

All of the characters are overwhelmed by problems. Mary Eustace is an intelligent, unmarried twenty-nine year old who reads Proust on the train. She is independent, but dissatisfied with her life. While several men are interested in her, only married John Rossiter engages her heart. Rossiter is a prime example of how Brace developed his characters. In physical appearance and temperament he is like Boston University's Dean Graham. He has gapped teeth and is always smoking a pipe. A compulsive talker, he has charm, tremendous energy, and a quick temper. The name John Rossiter is taken from Harriet Beecher Stowe's *Old Town Folk* which has a fictional character of that same name who is a thinly disguised depiction of Jerry's great-grandfather John Pierce Brace. Rossiter's occupation as a social worker who places orphans on farms is reminiscent of Charles Loring Brace. Ultimately, the strands merge and the character develops a personality of his own.

When John and Mary become trapped in a snowstorm, it gives Rossiter the opportunity to expound his views on life and women. There are no absolute truths in his "Rossiter's Law." "Truth is self-corrupting . . . You take the vision of peace on earth—it is the kingdom of God, the ideal, the very truth of man's hope, but it is false to man's nature." (*WS*, p. 72) The natural condition of man is one of discontent and desperation. He also believes that it is hokum when women are told that they will be frustrated if they never have a lover or a child. "Love and motherhood are all very well, though they achieve as much misery as they avoid—maybe more. If I had to pick the ten all-round best women I ever knew, six of them would be virgins—but try to tell Hollywood, or try to tell the department of psychology at the university of yours; they are all professionally committed to the dogma of sexual frustration and are thereby doing incalculable harm to half the gullible women in the nation." (*WS*, p. 63) Knowing intelligent, satisfied, single women such as Ellen Coolidge and his own sister Eleanor had finally convinced Jerry that there are other acceptable goals for women besides marriage.

The novel demonstrates that while adversity may temper the strong, it destroys the weak. When Mr. Eustace has a heart attack after struggling home through a snowstorm, he is content to spend his time staring at the television set, even as he complains of its mindlessness. "If that machine gives us a reasonable facsimile of this nation, and I don't see why it doesn't, then I tell you we are doomed. What we fatuously refer to as the great American way of life is nothing but sex, salesmanship, and permanently arrested development." (*WS*, p. 103) Except for ball games and the news, Jerry himself had little interest in television. No doubt Mr. Eustace becomes his spokesman when he has him criticize the immensely popular, innocuously pleasant, music show "Hit

Parade": "We used to talk about wet dreams when I was young—that's what comes over the air hour after hour. Wet dreams set to music, purveyed by pimps and crooned by luscious little whores. There it is, the soul of a great nation made visible and audible." (*WS*, p. 104)

Brace was consciously trying to deal with modern women and their problems in a more open way than he had ever attempted before. Mary's sister, Patience, is a psychology major who considers herself a sophisticated realist, proud of her emancipated views. As an unmarried woman she is nervous about having sex, not unusual in those days before the birth control pill. The night of the storm she becomes pregnant, but doesn't tell her lover for she knows that his career will be ruined if he has to give up his education to support a wife and child. Her friends urge her to have an illegal abortion. She believes in free choice, and does not see why religious people make such a fuss about such things, but she would rather commit suicide than have a back alley operation. She feels her sister could never understand her predicament, as she "went to a nice girl's college and they all had money and families and social weddings—they were respectable and dull and their only idea was to settle down in the suburbs with two cars." (*WS*, p. 127) Patience's problem is conveniently solved when her failed suicide attempt brings on a miscarriage.

Though for the first time Jerry was trying to look at life through women's eyes, he maintains some of the stereotypes. When Mary reacts personally to Rossiter's abstract philosophizing she explains that she is just being a female; nevertheless, when the very proper Harold Chivers apologizes that he would never have taken her to see the Tennessee Williams play, "The Pink House" if he had known it was about a brothel, she reassures him. "The fact is that funny or not funny, sex is much more important to women than it is to men—and by women I mean all women. I think women know more about it and think more about it and accept the realities of it more openly." (*WS*, p. 134) While she thinks that girls are supposed to know how to deal with proposals of marriage "just as they are supposed to be able to lie and deceive . . . and take delight in the skirmishes and duels of sex," (p. 192) she finds it difficult to refuse Harold. Patience is more realistic. She points out that getting into bed is the easiest part. "But living with someone day after day, talking and eating and planning and going places and just passing time—that's the part that counts."

Mary not only turns down Chivers, but also Professor Heath who could give her a comfortable, safe life. When Rossiter is killed trying to break up a gang fight, she feels she must carry on his work. She joins the choir of the liberal church where he had sung, and goes to work for Children's Aid. Brace had come to believe that, for true fulfillment, it is not so much a husband that a woman needs as a purpose.

Critics' reactions to the novel were mixed. Granville Hicks wrote in *Literary Horizons* that Brace was showing the different forms that Thoreau's "quiet desperation" could take. Others were harsher. Lou Manning in the *Daily Olympian* found it "a plodding and often boring account of an aging career girl's quest for a purpose in life." Nothing better demonstrates the sixties cult of youth which found everyone over 30 suspect than this suggestion that a career girl of 29 was too old to be a sympathetic heroine. Some felt that the views on abortion and suicide were too liberal and that there was too much questioning of the role of God. A review in *The Cresset* commented: "Possibly this agnosticism is responsible for the distasteful frequency with which they take His name in vain, and certainly it makes a search for enduring values more difficult." Others recognized what he was trying to achieve, like Donald Warman who wrote in the *Little Rock Gazette*: "His moods of winter's isolation, then thaw, exultation, and the thoughtful autumn are an evocative and illuminating frame for an unabashed love story that achieves dignity and human affirmation." Strangely, none of the reviewers commented on the remarkable change in subject and attitude of an author struggling painfully to understand modern day problems.

Brace had been thinking of Anthony Trollope while writing *Winter Solstice*. Mrs. Eustace, Mary's mother, found that she could only escape her desperation by reading the novels of Anthony Trollope. Though she enjoyed Jane Austen's novels, they seemed parochial compared to the wider world of Trollope. In 1961, Brace wrote an article entitled "The World of Anthony Trollope" which was published in *The Texas Quarterly*. He disapproved of the way critics were always trying to rank authors. "The great writer is one who has earned the right to be in a class by himself; Trollope is unquestionably such a writer. He may be inferior to Fielding on Fielding's ground or to Austen on hers; if he is an elm, he can't be expected to produce acorns, but on his own ground he is uniquely and perfectly himself and no one is his superior." He sagely prophesied that Trollope would eventually be better appreciated, for "his hold over the future is as sure as Chaucer's." He foresaw rightly, for Trollope's novels were not only serialized on television, but his works were increasingly read and appreciated during the final quarter of the twentieth century.

Because Brace had to return to autumn classes, he missed an opportunity to meet John Steinbeck with whom he shared the same literary agent. Over the years Elizabeth Otis Kizer had become a good friend of both men. She had known Eleanor Brace a long time, and for the past thirty years, she and her companion Beulah Ascarelli, the assistant headmistress of Miss Hewitt's exclusive finishing school for girls, had rented the Trivet for a week or two each summer. They befriended Brenda Gilchrist, Jerry's niece, who enjoyed the touch of sophisticated city life that Elizabeth brought to Deer Isle. To quote Brenda, "She was tiny, elegant, tottering in her high-heeled black sandals along 'root 7' Uncle John's name for a bumpy path between the big house and the Trivet, carrying the latest novels by her authors under her arm, a Reynolds Price or a Walker Percy." John Steinbeck dedicated his novel *Sweet Thursday* to her. When she heard that he planned to convert a pick-up truck into a camper and drive it across America, accompanied only by his French poodle, Charley, to experience the United States first hand, she told him he must begin at Eleanor's house on Deer Isle, for in Maine he would still find evidence of the country's true roots.

Eleanor and her poodle Joey

Comparing his quest to that of Don Quixote, Steinbeck christened his camper Rosinante and set off as soon as the Labor Day traffic was over and hurricane Donna had blown itself out. He traveled Northeast from his Sag Harbor home on Long Island, viewed the brilliant foliage in New Hampshire and Vermont, and arrived in Maine where he was greeted by Eleanor and served fresh Stonington lobsters for dinner. It was an uneasy meeting. As he grew more hearty and profane, Eleanor became increasingly the proper lady. Still she and the rest of the family were eager to read what he would publish about the visit in his book *Travels with Charley*.

He said more about her cat George than he did of her. George had been distinctly unhappy with Charley and no friendlier to his master who wrote:

> I never did rightly see George, but his sulking presence was every-where. For George is an old gray cat who has accumulated a hatred of people and things so intense that even hidden upstairs he communicates his prayer that you will go away. If the bomb should fall and wipe out every living thing except Miss Brace, George would be happy. That's the way he would design the world if it were up to him . . . Miss Brace admits that for the purposes of a cat, whatever they are, George is worthless. He isn't good company, he is not sympathetic, and he has little aesthetic value.
>
> "Perhaps he catches mice and rats," I suggested helpfully.
>
> "Never," said Miss Brace. "Wouldn't think of it. And do you want to know something? George is a girl."

Steinbeck could only conclude that George was descended from the days of the New England witches "because if ever there was a familiar, an envoy of the devil, a consorter with evil spirits, George is it." (*Travels With Charley*, New York: The Viking Press, 1962. p. 47) But George had just the kind of wild, independent spirit the Braces admired, and Eleanor considered him handsome enough to hook his likeness into a rug.

Steinbeck was impressed with the mysterious power of the island which he likened to Britain's Dorset and Avalon. Seeing the dark spruce and rock bound coast, he concluded that the fierce individuality of the people was the product of the landscape they inhabited. "Everything stood out separate from everything else, a rock, a rounded lump of sea-polished driftwood on a beach, a roof line. Each pine tree was itself and separate even if it was part of a forest." (*Travels With Charley*, p. 49) To Jerry nothing proved a man an outlander more than not being able to distinguish a pine tree from a spruce, although it is a natural mistake for those who know Maine as the Pine Tree State. At least Steinbeck's error offered confirmation to Jerry that Deer Isle was still uniquely his territory.

Dow Road, Deer Isle, Maine

End of the Road
The Braces

20

The Sixties

The promise of better times for the world soon faded. In spite of Kruschev's talks with President Kennedy about test bans, fear of the atomic bomb did not diminish. The building of the Berlin Wall was a visual reminder of the Iron Curtain of Communism, and some of the glitter of Kennedy's Camelot became tarnished by the fiasco of the Bay of Pigs. Boston University was not immune from the unrest of the times. For the emotionally unbalanced, the spreading fear of communism could lead to paranoia. Brace was unfailingly kind to troubled students. Typical was his concern for Frank Fitzgerald, a former undergraduate who had returned to Boston University to earn a graduate degree in the writing program. Burton Cooper, who later became a dean of the College of Liberal Arts, was a classmate of Frank and remembered how attached he became to his mentor:

> He was one of Jerry's groupies. Frank was a witty, interesting person, though he was often difficult and hard to bring down to earth. His life was full of sordid adventure, but there was no one more generous or compassionate than he. He committed suicide in the early sixties. In his last year or so, he had peculiar and awful fears and fantasies. He was certain that 'they' were spying on him and were about to do terrible things to him. He was safe, he felt, only riding in a taxi or in the presence of Professor Brace. At about the time Jerry published his novel, Frank wrote letters—mad tangled letters—to the Nobel Prize Committee. He went all about the city (in taxicabs) stopping at bookstores and buying up all copies of Jerry's novels. On any occasion when he was able to see Jerry or talk with him on the telephone, Frank lapsed into lucidity. But it was only that presence or that voice that recalled him. Nothing else availed.

As with Mather, Jerry had the ability to soothe a disturbed inner psyche that no one else could reach.

The spring term of 1963, Jerry had a sabbatical semester at full pay. Though he had not been feeling well, he recovered sufficiently to drive with Huldah by way of Texas and Arizona to visit Loring and Mimi on the West Coast. The year before, in 1962, Loring had completed his Ph.D. at Harvard, and had been appointed assistant professor of anthropology at the University of California in Santa Barbara. He was already a world authority on dentition of hominidae, a subject that fascinated his mother, but his father found totally incomprehensible.

Jerry wrote that Santa Barbara was "elegant and beautiful" and suspected that "a jury of travel agents & editors of *Holiday* would choose it as the most beautiful large community in the country." He added "It also abounds in Jaguars, Rolls Royces et al. I confess that it all seems like a bright kodachrome possibly made out of fibre glass—even mountains, sea, and flowers. I note that most of the yachts in the harbor are fibre glass too. Even the weather seems ceramic; we had a moon for two weeks every night." He was reading *Two Years Before the Mast* and was amazed how in spite of urban growth, the shore was still exactly as Dana had described it with even the mission still there. He was happy with his writing which was "going to beat the band. Pages and pages of stuff. Nothing else on my mind. Moral—if you want to work, leave home."

He and Huldah spent several days in Claremont visiting friends. She went to Disneyland, but he refused "which gives you some idea of what an old dope I am. I 'wrote' instead, and must report that since my previous boast, the writing has gone very hard. I should have known enough not to invite reprisals from fate." He was feeling better. He and Loring climbed a mountain together and he even gave a lecture to a writing class in Loring's college. He marveled at his son's physical and mental energy. Loring had signed contracts for two books and had agreed to write chapters for two others. He was writing reviews and he had been invited to present several papers.

The weather in California was very cool, which surprised both Jerry and Huldah as the palms, orange trees and cacti suggested a much warmer environment. He felt cold even when he was inside, and Huldah became ill with pneumonia. Jerry also developed a virus which he couldn't shake, but by May they had recovered enough to take a trip north to see Crater Lake and the redwood forests of Washington. There was just time for a brief visit on their way back to see Lincoln Fairley in San Francisco and to stay with Charlie's widow, now Mrs. Helen Philpott, in Denver where they planned to see Dean Graham.

They arrived back in Belmont in late May and stayed with their neighbor Rachel Westergaard while they were preparing to leave for Deer Isle. Both Huldah and Jerry were still suffering from bronchial infections. Slowly she recovered, but Jerry continued to feel as "limp as a wet rag." They were stoical

New Englanders who believed in weathering through illnesses, but the slowness of their recovery was discouraging. There was always so much to be done at the beginning of each season and he found that he could work for only brief periods of time. He confessed, "I can't seem to do anything vigorous without subsequent relapse so most of the time I don't do much at all. The writing goes very reluctantly. But I've sailed a good deal & *Festina* is as delightful as ever . . . Today I actually spent several hours sitting in the sun doing nothing but listen to birds even though it was a perfect sailing day." He was almost overwhelmed by all that needed to be done: a tree on the barn roof, trouble with the well, the house needing paint, trees ready to crash down if there should be a big gale. Life in Maine was no longer unadulterated joy.

They tried to maintain their usual routine. Barbara and her family were with them, and Eleanor had a household full of Donaldsons and Gilchrists. They all mustered up enough energy to take part in a hobby show to benefit the Deer Isle Historical Society. Jerry displayed some of his watercolors, Huldah put in her hooked rugs, John Donaldson had a display of his boat models, and Eleanor showed her rug with her cat George design and a copy of Steinbeck's *Travels with Charley*.

When Jerry's Aunt Bessie died in Ridgefield, Connecticut: "Huldah and Eleanor bucketed off to do their duty & were gone a week—terrific labor of cleaning out the house and all." Jerry remained at home with Barbara's friend Bonnie Hall, a former student who was devoted to him. "Bonnie & I consoled ourselves with some fine sails—& I got her to work on the *Forties*." Huldah was always somewhat jealous of Bonnie and she could not have been pleased to leave her behind with her husband while she took responsibility for his family matters, but Jerry always seemed blissfully unaware that anyone would worry about his relationships.

Jerry's health gradually improved and he was feeling slightly better by the time he returned to classes that fall. In November, he gave a talk to the College English Association on the College Novel. He was including Bernard Malamud's *A New Life,* which had been promoted as "Life found magnificently in the haystacks, classrooms & bedrooms of a small northwestern town." While Jerry appreciated its competence, it was not the type of academic novel he especially enjoyed. As he wrote to Bertha Ruark who was then living in Oregon, "I can't keep up with the proliferating bedrooms & classrooms—& haystacks." On November 22, 1963, came the shock of President Kennedy's assassination in Dallas, Texas. With Kennedy's death, something hopeful and trusting in the American people died, too.

On September 23, 1964, Jerry's sixty-third birthday, his tenth novel *The Wind's Will*, was published. Although it has his familiar theme of a boy on the threshold of manhood, it was autobiographic in neither time-frame nor setting. The fictional South Portage, Maine, was similar to many shabby river towns that he had visited, but had not actually experienced. It was a compilation of several places: Gardiner and Randolph on the Kennebec, Bangor and Brewer on the Penobscot, and for "Bateman's Castle," a spot just below Wiscasset on the Sheepscot. He had gotten the idea from stories he had heard of the boyhood of Edward Arlington Robinson who had used Gardiner as his bleak "Tilsbury Town." Back in 1958 Brace had been invited to Maine by Mildred Burrage to take part in a program of readings of the poems of Robinson and a discussion of his life at the Lincoln County Cultural and Historical Association.

Brace in 1964

Mildred had brought all her usual enthusiasm to the event and had written a long column featuring Brace for the *Kennebec Journal* (4 January 1958). Jerry had long admired the poet, but this helped to re-awaken his interest, and led him to wonder what it must have been like to be young and living in a degenerating Maine river town.

His agents foresaw that the book might have problems. They suggested that he cut some of the dialogue and make Joanna Wexler, the Lilith of the novel, less irritating. They also recognized that some of his terminology was out of date and pointed out that he should not refer to the three female classmates of his protagonist as "sex kittens," though the expression is somewhat indicative of how Jerry saw high spirited teenage girls. Brace did make some changes, and his publishers accepted the book under the same contractual agreements as his previous one: a $2,000 advance, royalties of 10 percent for the first 5,000 novels sold at retail, 12½ percent for the next 5,000, and 15 percent for any sold after that. The book would sell for $4.50 instead of the $3.95 charged for *Winter Solstice*. His books had become successful enough that he was worried about income tax; so the publishers agreed to pay him in installments of $8,000 a year with the proviso that if in any year royalties came to more than $40,000 he could ask for the whole sum. The informal friendly relationship between Brace and Brockway is evident when on May 21, 1964, the publisher returned page proofs to him suggesting that they could be donated to a library as a tax deduction "or you could paper your ceiling with them and lie on the floor and read the book whenever the spirit moved you."

Jerry's agent, Elizabeth Otis, considered his contract a more than fair arrangement, informing him that most publishers required that 10,000 copies be sold before moving to 12½ percent, but she did feel that Norton had not done enough to promote sales of his previous novel. She suggested that perhaps he should consider an offer that had been made by Little Brown. Although Huldah pushed her husband to be more aggressive and consider other options, he decided to remain with Norton, because by now both George Brockway and the president Storer Lunt, a close friend of Jerry's step-cousin Norman Donaldson, sales manager of Yale University Press (whose books Norton then distributed), had become trusted personal friends.

Brace might have done better to follow his earlier custom of setting his novel in the past. Instead, as in *Winter Solstice*, he tried in *The Wind's Will* to deal with sex more openly and to create more modern women characters. In his attempt to be more contemporary and less personal, he lost some of the authentic voice of his earlier novels. It was difficult in the free wheeling sixties for readers to believe that a minister could die from a sense of sin or a woman be hounded out of town for illicit behavior, even in a backwater Maine community. It was equally impossible for modern readers to accept that any young man graduating from high school could be as innocent as the young protagonist, David Wayne. He is far more typical of the youth of Jerry's own generation.

David is full of love and fear of the girls in their shorts and airy dresses who come into the store where he works, "a graceful girl made flames inside him, the play of her skirt about her knees set his head whirling. And he let himself dream of fantastic deeds, rescues and victories and passions, and beautiful idylls." He ends up dating a girl his own age who is competent and bossy, not at all like his romantic visions. It is not surprising that he weaves his fantasies around Albertine, a teacher from across the river who seems to know all about sex.

Brace believed that men and women are basically different in their desires. Albertine is amused when David takes her to his secret cave, exclaiming, "The perfect hideaway. Girls dream of satin coverlets and running water, boys dream of caves." It is a surprise to David to learn that older people have sexual longings and desires. He can not imagine his own parents having sex. Though he knew, of course, that his quiet mother with her twisted hip had conceived a child, "he could hardly believe that his father had taken part in it." (*WW*, p. 39) Albertine mocks his Puritanism and tells him the Catholics have a much easier time in letting the church take care of their consciences. Jerry had so little real knowledge of the Catholic church that one of the readers from McIntosh and Otis had to correct his confusion of the "immaculate conception" with the "Virgin birth."

It is Joanna Wexler who educates David about sex. She is a foreigner who goes to his father's church. She too is older, but he romanticizes her as a lonely princess. "She was quiet and deep, like a stream of clear water. She was the mystery of life, the secret that beckoned and called, the sound of music, the silver of moonlight, the blossoming of spring." (p. 122) It is with her that he has his first sexual experience, and while he is repelled by her sagging breasts and marks of age, he is also captivated. His world comes crashing down when his father, a minister, is discovered having sex with her at a camp meeting. Then the two run off together, abandoning David and his mother.

Remembering Robert Frost's use of "A Boy's Will" from the Longfellow line, "A boy's will is the wind's will," Brace chose *The Wind's Will* for his title. Though released from some of his old repressions, the novel with its talk of heaven and hell and loss of innocence, seemed old fashioned to a new generation. Reviewer David Read wrote in the *St. Louis Post Dispatch* that David would never have emerged such a thoroughly nice boy. "That this is not the way it should have worked out will be apparent to any reader who has ever been a boy or close to a boy in the last 20 years. Evidently Mr. Brace has not been a boy for a long time, and the result is a curious novel, full of a kind of romantic nostalgia about growing up that went out with the Armistice, was buried in the depression, and was prevented from coming back to life by World War II." It is an apt observation, even though the same reviewer did refer to the title as "The Wind's Mill" which he thought a "neat" choice!

Other critics also found David unrealistic. In the *Winnipeg Free Press* John Olsen observed that Brace had only "a foggy memory of boyhood. He has made his hero, David Wayne, into a modern version of Huck Finn, floating down rivers and hiding in caves." Mary A. Steele reviewing in the *Chattanooga Daily Times* commented on how far Brace had lost touch with the changes in boys of the sixties. "Boys will grow up and common sense will prevail, Mr. Brace tells us, and no doubt these things will prevail. But they would have seemed a good deal truer to me if the characters had been somewhat less wooden, if the scene had been something less of a backwater, and if the time had been 1919 instead of 1960 some odd as it purported to be dated." Others, unkinder still, compared it to a soap opera with unbelievable plot and characters, and a fuzzy philosophy. The book that for Brace had been so daring already was out of fashion. Brace saw his dream of being the great New England novelist getting ever further from his grasp.

The Wind's Will took off with 8,000 copies sold in the first three months, but after that sales slowed down. Though it was recorded as a "Talking Book" for the blind, it never really became popular. Brace's disappointment over his poor financial returns was somewhat mitigated by the decision of W. W. Norton to bring out a new edition in paperback of *The Garretson Chronicle* with an introduction by C. Hugh Holman. At the time of its first publication, *The Garretson Chronicle* had found an audience eager to believe in both individual freedom and continuity with the past. By the sixties, attitudes had changed. Fearing that his novels were out of touch with modern society, Brace decided to abandon fiction for a while to write factually about such immutable subjects as literature, Maine, and sailing.

Jerry Sailing

21
Mirroring Life's Experiences

By the 1960s, Gerald Brace had become worried about the future of the novel as a genre. The times seemed incapable of producing any great contemporary prose works. Self-confession had lost the power to shock. Though Brace knew that he could never plunge as deeply into the depths of his own soul as earlier writers like Conrad and Melville had, he did try to reflect life in the mirror of his own experiences and proffer to his readers whatever lessons he had learned. At age 64, he had lost many of his own illusions, but he was convinced that people still longed for heroes. Caught up in the elaborations and mechanization of modern life, mankind became entrapped by the very machines produced to make them free. Perhaps fear that the age of the self-educated, independent man had passed forever, created a need to read about men educated in a log cabin or planting a bean row like Thoreau. It seemed to Brace that novelists were needed to help an increasingly fragmented society find shape and meaning in life.

In the spring of 1965 Brace published an article entitled "The Essential Novel" in *Texas Quarterly* in which he reflected on the problems that the genre was facing. He thought perhaps no great contemporary novels were being published because self-indulgent authors had lost sight of the need for revelation. "If our arts are becoming simply permissive, if anything is given a place simply because it exists, then the principles of selection and evaluation on which art has been based no longer hold and we have given up our age-old hope that human life can have order and significance." (p. 37)

He refused to accept that the novel as an art form was totally doomed, but he recognized that its function was changing. Although he could not foresee the later blurring of the genres of fiction and nonfiction, he did consider John Steinbeck's *Grapes of Wrath*, published in 1939, the last great documentary novel. Television can document information to a much larger audience with far greater impact and speed. He appreciated the genius of a novelist like James Joyce, who in his search for new methods had abandoned the dramatic tension used by writers like Dostoevski, instead making the climactic meeting between Bloom and Stephen Daedalus in *Ulysses* intellectual rather than emotional. "Mainly we see that Joyce is being very facetious, displaying his facility with parody, irony, allusion, and cross-reference." (p. 35) Brace questioned whether the future of the novel was being advanced by such techniques, for while Joyce wrote brilliantly, he broke all the traditional rules. The opportunity for critics to hypothesize and analyze the symbolism leads to a concomitant loss of emotional feeling. As literature increasingly becomes associated with academia, the tension between studied methods and intuitive creativity makes it difficult for novelists to become wholly successful at either.

Brace envied Margaret Fuller who in the nineteenth century could say "I accept the Universe." He would have felt satisfied if he could have said "I accept mankind." He firmly believed that no matter how much anger or contempt a writer may reveal, he must never reject the human predicament. "Man himself is the beginning and end of the artistic effort—more than that, for I must assume that man is of primary importance and that his struggle toward order and wisdom is the major motive of his existence." (*Texas Quarterly*, Spring 1965, p. 36)

The words struck a responsive chord in those who deplored the directions of modern literature. The United States Information Agency had the article translated into Korean where 5,000 copies of the scholarly journal *Nondan* published it, and into Japanese for *Nichibei Forum* which had a subscription list of 7,000. Like Robert Frost, Brace was articulating a need to create "a momentary stay against confusion." Many older people in those angry, rebellious times agreed.

Jerry accompanied Huldah in the spring of 1965 to her Boston University Fortieth Class Reunion where they had a nostalgic luncheon on the Marble, the old 688 Boylston Street first floor main hall, which before the move to the new campus had been the meeting place for countless CLA students. Everyone there was aware that the building was about to be razed to make room for a new wing of the Boston Public Library.

The next day, Sunday, the Braces drove to North Dartmouth, Massachusetts, for Jerry to receive an honorary Doctor of Letters degree from Southeastern Massachusetts Technical Institute. He treated the whole affair lightly—later he did not mention any of his honorary degrees in his autobiography—but in spite of his self-mockery he was rather pleased. He wrote, "I seem to be making like a reputable author this year, what with an hon. degree and other flatteries. Maybe I should begin to take myself seriously, though it is probably too late for me to pick up new habits." He shared the platform with Massachusetts ex-Governor Peabody (whom he advised to run for office again), and Arthur Fiedler, conductor of the Boston Pops Orchestra. "Fiedler was the prima donna. No one asked me for an autograph. He is no better than a mountebank, of course—but I suffered for him when they murdered the Academic Festival Overture."

When Jerry returned to Boston University that fall of 1965, he was tired and run down. He managed to attend his classes, but a month later his health had not improved. He was deeply discouraged, though his doctor could not seem to find anything seriously wrong. He had not felt really well since his trip to California two years before. He lacked ideas for another novel. Instead he began a valedictory look back at his happy years on the coast of Maine in a series of essays which seemed almost to write themselves. These were combined into what became his most self-revelatory book, for though ostensibly about sailing and Maine, they expressed his views about life, both past and present. Published under the title *Between Wind and Water*, the book gave him the opportunity to achieve another ambition. He had always wanted to be an artist and for this volume he painted all the illustrations himself—scenes of boats and coastline that were indelibly etched into his memory. The original paintings still line the stairway of his Deer Isle house.

He was aware that in evoking the days of his youth he might be accused of sentimentality. "Our modern temper in general is inclined to be cynical, and assumes that human nature is as bad at one time as another. And of course it sees the primitive country life of other times as quite irrelevant to the realities of the present." (*BWW*, p. 10) He believed that true freedom had been lost somewhere after World War II. The post-war generation has a constant need to act, to accomplish, to be entertained, to travel, to discover. Even the so-called sexual freedom created pressures unknown in earlier times. Brace and the people surrounding him at Deer Isle represented a more puritanical era:

> The flagrant indulgences, if any, were to be kept to a minimum and carried on in secret. In this ethic everyone, native and non native alike agreed. . . . In our simplicity we felt that restraint and self-control were the way to happiness. The fewer demands, we thought, the greater freedom. We had no intimation of the Freudian revelation that the virtue of the puritans was a more sinister evil than the sins of the unregenerate. The fact that we were on the whole happy in our self-imposed suppressions, and even free in a naive sort of way, is simply one of the persistent delusions of the pre-Freudian world. (*BWW*, p. 11)

He had seen tremendous changes during his lifetime. Skis, horses and sailboats, which once served practical purposes, had become simply recreational pleasures. Landscape was compressed into regulated parks, ecology replaced Transcendentalism, and nature, once considered the source of an orderly chain of being, became increasingly terrifying as scientists continued to learn more about the ever-expanding universe.

Jerry admired the old-time Maine natives who remained free and independent, no matter how difficult their lives, for "men living apart are naturally anarchical; they do what they want to do. But in Maine they have kept the balance better than most." (*BWW*, p. 22) Their moral code was strict and their kindnesses untouched by profit motive. In spite of the hidden passions gnawing at the foundations of New England respectability which form the bases of the plays of Eugene O'Neill, Brace firmly believed that they got through their sexual ordeals better than those living in a post-Freudian society. "The institution of marriage worked better than it does now, but of course required greater restraint and loyalty and less self-indulgence. No doubt some were injured or even destroyed by sexual fear and hypocrisy, and there was more illegitimacy than was ever admitted." (*BWW*, p. 43) The harshness and self-discipline of their lives may have destroyed the weak, but for those who managed to cope, the challenge strengthened and led to a spiritual serenity. This had been the underlying philosophy of *The World of Carrick's Cove*.

While Jerry had early learned the importance of women to country life, he still saw their roles as clearly defined. "A man could win victories, small or large, over land or sea, against the weather and the natural properties he handled; he could take pride in his mastery. A woman, whose labor was longer and often harder had the vision of family strength and support; she linked generation to generation in a great chain." (*BWW*, p. 4l) He had noted how men without wives degenerated, with homes dirty and in disrepair. He even recognized that a woman might work in the fields or in boats beside her man, but he still considered her chief responsibility to be his helpmate.

The society of the summer visitors was once neatly stratified. The very rich, like the Rockefellers and Watsons, had great estates. The old families had large country "cottages" interspersed with the smaller houses of clergy and teachers. The spinsters rented tiny summer camps. With the exception of the very rich, most, like the Braces themselves, lived in a "beautiful Emersonian world, with money enough to be comfortable, but never ostentatious, with faith in the harmonies of nature and devotion to both beauty and duty." (*BWW*, p. 74) Perhaps they were a bit smug and self-satisfied, but they had strict ideas of propriety and a genuine high mindedness. By the mid-sixties when Brace was writing this, most families no longer had the luxury of spending several months in Maine. The summer scene was changing. He felt that only the spinster would always remain to assist at fairs and food sales and join rug hooking groups. He failed to foresee that she too would change. The unmarried female continues to exist, of course, as professional career woman, divorcee, lesbian, single parent, or free spirit, but the spinster as type has practically disappeared.

Gerald's real love affair was never as much with people as with boats. His devotion to *Festina* remained unaltered. "I look at her with the inward bewilderment of a man who wonders how he ever got himself into his particular matrimonial trap, but once she is off and moving, sheets tight in, rail down, tiller gentle to the hand as she eats out to windward, she is wholly beguiling." (*BWW* p. 101) He was constantly concerned with weather as all good boatsmen must be. "In foggy times your world turns mysterious, strange distant sounds haunt the air, you withdraw into yourself in secrecy; in storms you share the old legends of the sea, and remember the exploits of brave seamen; in fair weather you rejoice in the flashing brightness of sea and land and you push off once again on your never-ending quest for adventure among the islands." (*BWW*, p. 125)

To Brace's surprise the book that had been such a pleasure to write turned out to be the best selling of all his works except for *The Garretson Chronicle*. It sold over 10,000 copies in the first six months and continued to have steady sales after that. Nelson Doubleday Condensed Books published a long excerpt from it in the *Best in Books* in 1966. Later the complete book was brought out in paperback by Down East publishers. His colleague Edward Wagenknecht was undoubtedly correct when he pronounced it the best written of all his books.

The knowledge of boats and boatbuilding revealed in *Between Wind and Water* prompted the *New York Times* to commission a 3,000 word article for their magazine section on a replica of a Hudson River sloop to be designed by Cyrus Hamlin. Brace was to receive an advance of $150 and another $400 when the article was accepted. He did a great deal of research and wrote a fine article, but it was never published because ultimately Hamlin was not the naval architect chosen and, to quote the letter from the editor, it had been learned that he "is indeed not one of our eminent architects," a fact which, it would seem, the paper should have ascertained before commissioning the article.

Many readers empathized with Brace's dismay over what people were doing to Maine's once pristine environment. No longer could one walk out on the shore and dig a pail of clams in twenty minutes; fish were declining, as were bald eagles and osprey. Even warblers and thrush were heard less often. Only the scavengers—crows and gulls and cormorants—increased. "More and more nature has to be invented and cultivated and preserved by tricks of stagecraft: in a not too remote future we may inhabit a vast Disneyland, and take our pleasure in observing pneumatic wildlife and plastic mountains." (*BWW* p. 210) Jerry had always scorned ski lifts, artificial snow, stocked ponds, and crowded marinas. They seemed to take all the challenge and adventure out of his favorite sports. To be sure, woods and quiet coves with rocks and mosses remain for those who seek them out, "but the old natural pantheism of the romantic poets and philosophers has gone the way of all religion. It is still a beguiling sentiment, it evokes hopes and dreams in simple hearts, but the weight of modern scientific thought, whether positivistic, behavioristic, or existential, is solidly against it. Man's chief business from now on is to master his surroundings and redesign and rebuild them for his own uses. And of course in the process he will inevitably redesign himself." (*BWW,* pp. 217, 218)

Jerry was aware that there was something artificial, perhaps even foolish, in his attempt to cling to vanished ways—to write with a fountain pen instead of learning to type, to prefer not to have even an auxiliary motor in his sailboat, to improvise and repair his own equipment. His beliefs and feelings were more closely allied to Whittier, Emerson, and Thoreau than to a reading public moving into an electronic age. The simple truths he had once espoused no longer seemed to work. Certainties became undermined by complexities. He no longer knew where he should stand on problems such as the Vietnam War. He was a pacifist who sympathized with the protestors, but he also felt that America had responsibilities. He tried to explain his rather confused views to John Wiggins in an interview for the *Boston Globe:*

> I'm not a Utopian. Human nature is so imperfect that nothing much can be done about it. That's a kind of cynicism, I suppose. That means that it doesn't do much good to hope or protest or pass legislation. It all comes back to the fallibility of man, which is very great. When you get to be 65, you don't kick and scream about life.
>
> As regards Vietnam. I'm baffled and bewildered. It's deplorable and tragic and very bad to have suddenly a war that has no clear objective, but I don't know what we do. There's much evil on both sides. That's not a very useful opinion to offer the world. As in all such cases you read drastically different opinions about it and find it hard to arrive at truth. I'm not enough of a president or general to say what ought to be done. (*Boston Globe,* 22 January 1967)

The idealism of his youth had been replaced by an uncertainty that was willing to leave decisions to political and military powers. This widened the gap of understanding between him and the student activists.

In 1967 the Braces drove to Pennsylvania through a snowstorm to spend Christmas with Barbara who since her divorce was not only a single parent to her three children, but helping as well to care for the three children of her close friend, Leah Fletcher Seeley, who had died the previous July of a blood clot following exploratory surgery. Ralph Seeley, the bereaved widower, suggested that they combine their two households into one. It would mean meshing two families of teenagers approximately the same ages. To complicate matters further, both she and Ralph had a son Ralph, though that was solved easily by calling her youngest son by his middle name Walter. Still she was unsure. Jerry wrote that she was having as much difficulty as deciding upon a new car! Ralph, a graduate of Duke with a Master of Science in Electrical Engineering from Pennsylvania State, was an associate professor of engineering research at the University's Applied Research Laboratory. He enjoyed outside activities— especially canoeing and cross country skiing—and he had the ability to view life with a detachment that fitted him in well with the Brace family. Barbara had known and liked him for a long time. Finally she said "yes" and they were married on May 21, 1967.

That year, 1967, was Jerry's last as a full time professor at Boston University. He was given three honors: he received the Shell Faculty Publication and Merit Award for *Between Wind and Water*; a former student gave the University a $1,000 scholarship to award in the name of ten professors of whom Brace was one; and the college set aside a sum which would provide two $100 prizes each year for two students chosen to receive Gerald Warner Brace Awards in Fiction and Poetry. The Mugar Memorial Library requested that he add his papers to their extensive research collection. It gave a much needed boost to Jerry's ego at a time when he was feeling discouraged and at odds with the times.

Encouraged by the popular acceptance of *Between Wind and Water*, and driven by the need to create, Brace returned to novel writing. He had once tried to analyze why writers, in spite of disappointment, continue to produce. The article which he entitled "The Writer's Talent" had been published by the *Boston University Journal* in the Spring of 1965. In it he had reflected on all the talented students he had had over the years and how few had become professional authors. However creative, they soon discovered the need for sufficient money to provide for cars, wives, rent, and children. Writing alone rarely provided that. To earn a living and continue to create takes energy and perseverance, for writing is a long and lonely business. "The impulse to create lies below the level of reason and understanding. It manifests itself in images, the spontaneous mind-pictures of scenes and people; it is promoted by desire and it often becomes an obsession."

If writing can be a force greater than hunger or sex, it can also be a source of fun. Brace allowed himself some of this playfulness in what would become his final novel, *The Department*, an ironic look at the various English departments he had known so well. All of the characters were given the names of shore birds though the book is not an allegory nor were the names really metaphorical. He was fully aware that everyone would be seeking to identify himself and his colleagues, though he protested that his characters were types, not particular people. He appended an Author's Note in which he quoted Tobias Smollett's cautionary apologue at the beginning of *Roderick Random*: "Seek not to appropriate to thyself that which equally belongs to five hundred different people. If thou shouldst meet with a character that reflects thee in some ungracious particular, keep thy own counsel; consider that one feature makes not a face, and that, though thou art, perhaps, distinguished by a bottle nose, twenty of thy neighbors may be in the same predicament."

Brace arranged with W. W. Norton to send each of the full-time English department faculty a complimentary copy. In spite of his admonishings, the most popular pastime at Boston University became trying to guess who had been a model for each character. Colleagues from his former colleges also believed they recognized people. The verisimilitude had been strengthened by a narrator who seemed to be based on Brace himself. Robert Sanderling is a rather diffident professor on the verge of retirement nervously planning his farewell speech. Subconsciously Brace revealed more of himself than he had intended. He had been surprised to receive a letter from Mildred Burrage scolding him for being too harsh on himself as scholar and husband. His immediate response was that Sanderling was purely fictional, but later he realized that there was a certain truth in her observation. "I think Mildred may have been too severe in her reaction—at least I thought so at the time. But I confess that in a way she was right. She saw a part of me that I hadn't intended to reveal." (*DTW* II, p. 164)

Brace uses Sanderling to express his own difficulties in writing about sex. Both enjoyed reading Chaucer and Lady Chatterley, but found it difficult to write openly about the subject. As Sanderling says, "I am not competent to reveal our secret lives—or perhaps I am reluctant, or simply afraid. With all my readings and observations, I live in isolation like a hermit, remembering the ways of my youth when sin and virtue were obvious and black and white. The idea of an open and proficient indulgence in sex just for the fun of it torments me with a kind of horror, even though I can appreciatively read about it in the pages of *The Golden Ass*."(*TD*, pp. 133,134) The repressions of a lifetime are not easily overcome. When Judith Samaris, an intelligent young prostitute in Sanderling's class comes to him for advice, he is too innocent about life to offer any practical suggestions. He finds himself wondering about the men she has known and has an overwhelming desire to penetrate "the mystery, the meaning, the truth of all that sexual activity," (*TD*, p. 165) but he is aware that the secret will never be revealed to him.

Every man feels a need to know that he is admired, especially if he is made to feel incompetent at home, and in a college there are always students, especially in the graduate division, ready to fulfill this role.

Any university is full of them. They haunt the waiting rooms and offices, they confer, seek advice, discuss—or they assist, type, copy, file—or they lie casually in wait—or follow you about—or leave little offerings on your desk—or write perky notes. Among the hundreds who come and go are all imaginable varieties of human female, and it is a commonplace to say that no man is safe. You can defend against the predatory ones, or the calculating ones, or the wicked ones, but not many men can withstand the wiles of high-minded innocence. True love overrides all considerations—for awhile, at least. (*TD*, p. 135)

The male is an unwitting victim enmeshed in feminine wiles. The wonder is not that some professors succumb, but that so many of their marriages survive.

In the romantic days of Sanderling's youth, he surrounded the girl of his dreams with all that he had learned about love from popular songs and fairy tales. Such sweet delusions cannot be sustained, of course, in the prosaic world of marriage. Sanderling respects his wife for her energy and intensity. He counts on her to rescue him from those predatory females that are dangerous and unscrupulous; though their two lives have grown increasingly separate and they rarely physically touch each other any more. Age does not change a romantic, and even at retirement, he still envisions the woman in a tower waiting to be rescued by her true love.

Jerry no doubt believed that in Harriet Sanderling he had created a very different character from Huldah. Certainly the idea of a vivacious wife who has a martini waiting for him when he returns home at the end of the day could only have been wishful thinking, but, of course, the tensions between husband and wife and between mother and daughter come out of his own experience. From his own psyche too comes Sanderling's response to family problems. "What can a father and husband do? Obviously great strength and courage are needed in these crises, and I had neither." (*TD*, p. 198) For all the substantial differences between the Sanderlings and Braces there is more similarity than probably the author ever intended.

The professors in *The Department* are types found in academic departments everywhere. Brace had known them in every college with which he had been associated: Dartmouth and Williams and Harvard and Amherst, but especially Boston University. Facing his own retirement, Brace empathized with Sanderling. Their views have fallen from fashion, so what can either of them use as final remarks? Sanderling muses,

My program, if any, would be simply a re-stating of all the too-familiar values: the use of reason, restraint, common sense, common decency, common honesty, the effort to be patient and as brave as possible in accepting what must be, the effort to do things well and beautifully. It is what you used to hear in small-town commencement addresses; it is not the thing to say to philosophers and intellectuals. And though it is really the only program in life I can subscribe to, as it were, I have the uneasy feeling that it is all much too naive. The critics who write for the intellectual journals (some of my colleagues among them) are arrogant in their certainty that man's spiritual and psychic problems are insoluble. To all who inhabit the earth, today whether they think or feel, life must be a tragedy." (*TD*, p. 155)

The routine of academia merges one year into the next with little to distinguish the "classes, committees, conferences, exams, papers—day after day and year after year." Requirements and curriculum are endlessly discussed, with each new generation discovering anew what the previous one has already discarded. No one knew better what academic meetings and oral examinations were like than Brace, who had spent a lifetime quietly observing them.

In the earlier days, senior professors sat on most Ph.D. Orals though gradually the Braces and Sanderlings found themselves replaced by younger men. Such exams could be frustrating—even embarrassing—especially if the student was ill prepared. Brace had sat through many of these Orals often with barely concealed impatience. He said little, but he never suffered fools nor limited thinkers gladly. Dean Burton Cooper, formerly a Brace colleague, remembered one such occasion when Brace was chairman of the examining committee:

> The candidate was a priest and he had written on Graham Greene. Bob Sproat was first reader. The candidate had written the dissertation three times; the committee did not have the heart or the moral energy to ask him to do it all over again. It was a pretty dismal piece of work. During the questioning the candidate informed the company that Greene was the first writer ever to use the detective-fiction form to promulgate a large moral theme. I asked him if he was certain that no one had. I asked him if he had read anything that Greene had written about his own reading. He said he had not; he had restricted his reading exclusively to the novels treated in the dissertation. Jerry began to look out of the window. I persisted, asking the candidate about other earlier novelists who wrote serious detective fiction. It went on for a long time. Suddenly Jerry turned. "Mr. Cooper wants to know" he said in a tetchy voice, "if you ever heard of Dostoevski. Have you ever read *Crime and Punishment*? "The

candidate confessed that he had not read Dostoevski and did not know if Greene had. It did not matter, however, he told us, because Dostoevski was Russian and was not Catholic. Jerry just buried his face in his hands.

There is wisdom in academia, but there are also petty jealousies and vanities. At Boston University, Brace's colleague, Professor Winslow, assigned his Eighteenth Century course the task of writing a parody in the verse form of Alexander Pope. A graduate student, George Lane, responded with a cleverly written, long political satire entitled "The Adlaiad" based on the Stevenson-Eisenhower campaign. When Brace saw it, he realized how easily a student could use such an assignment to expose an incompetent professor. It suggested to him the scene in *The Department* where a paranoid professor takes as a personal affront the satire that a student has written for a class.

Sanderling learns how much modern literary tastes have changed when he teaches a course in creative writing. Students admire Faulkner, Joyce, Camus, Proust, and Beckett. They want to write about self and sexual lust. What can an old-fashioned professor hope to teach the young? "I find myself relegated to the status of cultural fossil. My hopes for mankind are derided. My notions of virtue are in some way repressive and sinister." (*TD*, p. 289) In 1983 Phoenix Press, a division of the University of Chicago Press dedicated to rescuing out-of-print books too good to disappear, republished *The Department*. The editors of *Fiction, Literature, and the Arts Review* headlined my review of the novel, "The Professor as Cultural Fossil." It seemed an ironic epitaph.

Gerald Warner Brace

22
The Darkening Years

Although Brace always believed that his academic work had prevented him from being a more prolific writer, when he was made Professor Emeritus in 1967, he found himself unhappy at the thought of no longer teaching. The word "emeritus" seemed to carry a suggestion of finality—a note of sadness. The goals he had sought may have been beyond his reach, but he was not ready to be consigned to insignificance and oblivion. He was delighted when he was invited to continue teaching his course in creative writing.

In spite of the changes in the world, he felt that his years of experience as teacher and writer had given him useful knowledge even if students might find some of his ideas outmoded. At least he could offer suggestions for books a writer should read and basic facts of composition. He prepared a text on writing which he entitled *The Stuff of Fiction*. Sections of it had previously been published in *The Boston University Journal*, *The Bay State Librarian*, and *The Massachusetts Review*. He dedicated his handbook "To the memory of LeBaron Russell Briggs, the kindest of all teachers" from whom he had learned at Harvard how important a teacher can be to a young person stumbling uncertainly into the future.

The Stuff of Fiction is written in simple terms, and has no complex theories of criticism. It is more than a textbook, however. The sadness of loss is there too, especially the end of the frontier. Already the Maine of his youth and the mountains of Vermont and New Hampshire had lost their remoteness, and he foresaw that the future would only accelerate the inroads made by an ever-increasing population.

> The virgin wilderness will go. The mystery and originality will go. Species of bird and beast will vanish. The space itself will dwindle. Roads will come, and cars and trucks and people with their necessities. In the wild west no place is very far from a highway; the mighty forests are called tree farms and the wildest rivers are dammed and harnessed. In my lifetime both poles have been reached and Everest has been climbed. (*SOF*, p 16)

But it is not only the physical frontier that has been lost; the human psyche too has been so much analyzed and explored that few mysteries are left. Where can a creative artist hope to find inspiration?

> Our novel, all our art, it would seem, has reached a visible end. Music is no longer music, nor painting, painting. The search for novelty becomes a frenzy, like the wild darts of a bird trying to escape from a glassed room. The artist proclaims absurdity and anguish and alienation. He tries anything, he shocks, destroys, befouls. He turns against his kith and kin. He renounces what was called virtue by the generations of men. And he complains—above all he complains: at his personal lot, at the lot of man, at the inevitability of failure and death, at the impotence and folly of effort. . . . The only purpose is to have no purpose. We are all presumed to be rats in the same trap. (*SOF*, p. 19)

While the prospects were grim enough to scare off all but the most dedicated, genuine authors write because they are compelled, and this compulsion assures that creative endeavors will continue no matter how difficult the market or uncertain the times. It is to these dedicated men and women that Brace offered the observations of a lifetime of study.

The Stuff of Fiction shows Brace's breadth of reading though he eschews the heavy seriousness of a university literary critic. He believes that all art since its origin has been primarily play and make believe. "It is song and dance and pantomine and trickery and carnival and spontaneous celebration and worship. It is *Bartholemew Fair* and *Much Ado about Nothing* and *Don Quixote* and *Pickwick* and *The Yeoman of the Guard* and Ringling Brothers and a rain dance."(*SOF*, p. 31) It is story and the revelation of human nature though it may range from documentary to fantasy. The twenties had been a great time for fiction. James Joyce became the pioneer of the subconscious, Sinclair Lewis discovered Main Street and John Steinbeck, the dust bowl, but by the end of the sixties, Brace felt that the only subject left for the modern writer is his own terrifying uncertainty.

Although plot continues to be important in some novels, such as detective stories, the modern artist is more concerned with biography and psychological probing. "Thomas Hardy blamed God for being unaware and indifferent to the woes of the world—God, in his view, had simply dozed off and left mankind in a state of chaotic misery—but today we hardly take the idea of God seriously." (*DTW* II, p. 153) No longer do writers agonize over free will versus determination. But even if the conflict is mainly within, Brace still believed that there must be some kind of moral revelation.

In looking toward the future of novel writing, Brace felt that we were about to enter an age of great satire. He wrote hopefully, "Time for powerful satire is coming, but also time for renewed beliefs and visions. Perhaps the new frontier of our future, the still uncharted wilderness, will be found in the forgotten regions of our own humanity." (*SOF*, p. 150) Great satire, however, requires indignation and a shared belief in right and wrong, goodness and evil. His mistake was not that he was unaware of its requirements, but he had hopes that the winds of change that were destroying the old smug society might lead to a better world. He did not foresee that once the electronic media became the message, humanity would diminish.

William Connor in his doctoral dissertation on Brace at the University of New Brunswick at Fredericton, Canada, criticized the annotated reading list in the Appendix as the weakest part of the *The Stuff of Fiction*. Because it was written in Brace's shaky handwriting and attached to the typed manuscript, he hypothesized that it may have been added at the request of the publisher after Brace became ill. He commented that it is always ill advised to make such a listing because "however reasonable, [it] is bound to satisfy almost no one entirely and will offend many who disagree with it substantially." (Connor, p. 358) Certainly the list is idiosyncratic and old fashioned, but these were the books that had shaped Brace as a writer and his annotations are personal and perceptive. His description of Hardy's *Tess of the d'Urbervilles*, for example, is pure Brace in style. "It clanks along like an old-fashioned steam engine, with pistons and valves and boilers all noisily and visibly at work. But the brute power is immense." Not only does it display Brace's detached way of looking at work as a complicated piece of machinery, but it carries echoes of the mechanical thresher in the novel itself. The listing is not the traditional canon nor apt to be popular with writers today, but the choices are interesting and original.

Even before *The Stuff of Fiction* was in the stores, Jerry had become ill with a circulatory condition that nearly proved fatal. He had a pulmonary embolism from a blood clot in his leg and was rushed to Massachusetts General Hospital Phillips House. There was fear that the blood clots might strike a vital area so surgeons inserted, to quote Jerry's metaphor, a "teflon strainer" and gave him medication to thin his blood. Unfortunately the medicine caused a hemorrhage and he collapsed at home early one morning. Huldah called the Belmont police who sent six burly policemen. They immediately began CPR and undoubtedly saved his life, but the minute or so he had been in cardiac arrest had deprived his brain of blood causing some permanent memory loss. For days his condition remained critical. He was away from teaching for a couple of months and would never be quite the same again.

Refusing to give in to his fears and weakness, Jerry returned to teaching the following year, though it took all his effort. Worried as he was about his intellectual acumen, his memories of the past remained vivid. When Bertha Ruark's young daughter sent him a Halloween picture she had colored for him, its witches and haunted house reminded him of a watercolor he had once painted of the haunted house of Pickering Island. In his playful thank you, he described for her the old house which "wasn't very big, but it was quite weird, with odd turrets and a big chimney with a fishhawk's nest on top of it. There was a ghost in it, and a group of old women, or witches, who tramped about in single file in the fields, all bent over and staring at the ground. We called them Pickers. Strange things used to happen there, but now the house is demolished and gone, and only a few can remember how it used to be." His natural gentleness and kindliness seemed to have been heightened by his increased sense of mortality.

He was pleased when in the spring of 1970 his old Alma Mater, Amherst College, awarded him an honorary Litt. D. at commencement. It was a difficult time with students actively rebelling against the Vietnam War and demanding changes in the colleges. No one ever knew what action they might take. Jerry's health was still frail, but he determined to attend the ceremony. He had hoped to look up his old friend the Amherst poet Robert Francis, whom he had known since Harvard days, but he didn't feel able. Although he was aware that he had to husband his strength, he was disappointed because he had hoped to learn more about the autobiography Francis was writing. Jerry wrote to his old friend Millicent Pettit after the commencement.

> I did feel conspicuously elderly and irrelevant in the presence of the young militants with their beards and red arm bands and their ferocious disdain. They put on a frenzied rock-and-roll performance in the middle of the ceremony—as a sign that they were doing their thing. But nothing else happened & they patiently sat through the speeches and citations. I am happy to be teaching for one more year, but after my recent drop out I really feel irrelevant—I feel like Rip van Winkle. What can I say to young people? What can anyone say for that matter? Is it reasonable to suppose that it must be frustrating to be young in these times and be convinced that the future is an inevitable catastrophe? I can't provide much hope for them.

Gerald's tone is more tolerant and sympathetic to the young than that of many older professors during those disrupting times.

He realized that it was time for him to leave the classroom. As the moment neared he became aware how much he would miss the time spent with fellow teachers and students. A group of his old time colleagues arranged a farewell party at Locke Ober's, an upscale restaurant catering mainly to men. Women were only allowed in a private upstairs dining room out of sight of the public. The presents were carefully chosen: a tide clock for his Deer Isle home and a recording of the Frost reading at Boston University at which he had introduced the poet. Jerry was immensely touched and pleased, especially with the recording. Frost had died in 1963, another break in the friendship chain of those who had meant so much to his life. Jerry had no idea that a recording had been made and he was amazed at the clarity. He wrote that he and Huldah had played it over and over with delight as it brought back that very special evening with extraordinary fidelity. He wrote a thank-you letter to Donald Winslow, who had arranged for the party, in which he expressed what the occasion had meant to him:

> It represents a high point in my life, as you can imagine, and nothing could give me more pleasure and satisfaction. I suppose it is a bad habit to look back at high points, but I'm afraid it becomes inevitable. I am already "looking back" at the delightful last luncheon with my old colleagues, but it is a very happy memory. I can't quite realize that my life at B.U. is over and done with—I shall be really bereft, and shall specially miss the association with my good friends and colleagues. Do please keep in touch—specially you and Charlotte.

Donald Junkins, a former student who had become a professor at the University of Massachusetts at Amherst, sent Jerry a copy of his latest collection of poems, *And Sandpiper She Said*. Jerry's response in February of 1971 is warm and friendly, but reveals something of the confusion of his mind. Having composed a thank you note in his mind, he could not remember whether he had ever actually written it. Once again he expressed concern that he might be losing his mind. He said that he had enjoyed reading the poems for their positive tone in a "day of cynicism and disgust." The enthusiasms of others helped relieve the bleak November of his own soul. He wrote appreciatively: "I think your relish and response to life is wonderful. You love the things you love for what they are (to borrow a Frost line)—and you really love a great deal, your native land and your past, and your present and your people old and new. You love them without sentimentality or delusion—you live with them and are a native part of them. You speak of them with candor, without affectation or self consciousness—with the relish of active participation in them. It is what poetry is or should be, a celebration of life as well as a true experience." Jerry found it difficult to speak of those he loved in the present with candor or those from his past without sentimentality. He envied Junkins his gift. He envied too his youth and enthusiasm, and had enjoyed his account of a sail into Dark Harbor during a heavy gale. It made him feel old. "Those waters are all familiar to me, of course. Actually the hardest wind I ever met with occurred there when a friend and I ran from Bass Harbor to Naskeag in a southeaster—dragging a swamped tender the most part of the way—a half century ago that was."

When Robert Francis' autobiography *The Trouble with Francis* was published, Junkins sent him a copy. Jerry wrote to express his delight.

> It is so like him in every phrase and detail that the effect of it is uncanny. I feel as though I had been with him and heard his voice and followed the working of his mind and had even been able to exchange thoughts with him. His candor is characteristic and wonderful and at times surprising in its depth and perceptions. He has a lot of mind—a good deal more than I do at my time of life. He is like Frost more sure of all he thinks is true. I am glad incidentally, that he writes so warmly about Frost, who is getting such harsh treatment from Thompson and others. His flat statement that he doesn't like modern poetry is sort of good to hear too—it takes nerve for a modern poet to say it so uncompromisingly. I only wish that there had been more of his life and mind in the book. It took courage to put in the chapter on his homosexual trait, but it leaves out so much that we are left with hints and questions—and I'd like to know more about his ideas about writing and reading poetry (which he is so good at!) All that he says is so good that I simply wish there were more."

Don Junkins was at his summer home at Swans Island and Jerry invited him to sail over to Deer Isle. He added that though his boats were in commission, he was not being very adventurous and that he was not "specially happy about the onslaught of old age." When Don arrived he was shocked at the change in his old professor. Though still "endearingly quiet and kindly" he seemed filled with melancholy:

> . . . somehow betrayed by all the gods of strength and health and watcher of hauled boats going punky on deserted shore. I loved him very much and he took energy from my enthusiasms and said so much in what he didn't say. There was kindliness but no sparkle in his eyes, and there was an inimitable softness in his manner that covered, almost, a huge regret that he was old and in a kind of oblivion. I don't know if that's exactly it, but there was a tremendous lovely hurt in his sensibility that he tried to refrain from expressing. There was something of an old elephant in him, and the old sea turtle, something from the tombs of Egypt, all in a different form, of course, but knowing and ageless and helpless in his wisdom. Part of him felt like a ward of his family—Huldah was running around full of capabilities, half oblivious and half all-knowing, and he was so appreciative and kindly and sad, not indulgent but overwhelming and fragile and all present and accounted for."

His condition was heartbreaking for those who had known him as an indefatigable sailor and mentor and friend.

Jerry had given Huldah for Christmas the woodlot next to their Belmont house. It not only assured privacy, but it was a haven for the birds which Huldah enjoyed. He was keeping busy composing the story of his earlier years. Though working on his memoirs brought back happy memories, it increased Jerry's feelings of being a relic of the past. He was full of regrets for the writing he had failed to do. He had long planned to compile a collection of Maine writers which Norton had been willing to publish. He had collected enough Maine poets to give talks on them in Wiscasset and Stonington, but he had never got around to preparing the manuscript. Some of the poets were his good friends: Sam Morse and Phil Booth, and Abbie Huston Evans—who had reached the age of 90 and was still going strong.

He was reminded of his own mortality by the death of his oldest sister Dorothy, the first death of a sibling except for Charlie. She had been like his mother, ladylike and rather prim, quietly arranging flowers and keeping busy in the house while the others sailed. Her husband, John Donaldson, had been one of Jerry's closest, lifelong friends and the couple, with their daughter Julia, had joined the Brace family gatherings in Maine almost every summer.

Jerry was trying to carry on as before. He still used a scythe to cut the long tufts of grass at Deer Isle, and one day when annoyed by a hornet, he swung wildly at it, cutting himself severely. Huldah rushed him to the hospital. Though bleeding profusely, the wound did not prove too serious, but he was embarrassed by his clumsiness. Another time he stepped on a nail and the paramedics had to give him a tetanus shot. Once more he was aware that he was losing his former agility.

On August 18, 1972, he was gratified to receive an honorary degree, a Doctor of Humane Letters, from the University of Maine at Orono in recognition of his faithful rendering of the people and places of the state. It must have been especially pleasing to have Edward Myers, the genuine Down Easterner who composed the citation, compliment his "perfect ear for the rhythm of Maine speech and perfect pitch in portraying the spirit, the long tradition of compatibility with nature, and the unobtrusiveness of fervor of those living their lives truly on this coast." He was honored as well for the five boats he had designed which were still sailing after thirty years—one actually for half a century, and for his watercolors. He was described as a true "renaissance man evoking a reluctant valedictory of the beautiful vanishing world of the downeast coast."

Unfortunately the day of the award it was pouring rain. Huldah already had a touch of bronchitis which worsened. By the time they arrived home, she had a temperature of over 102. He wrote to his friend Mildred Pettit that once

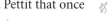

Millicent

also p. 240 →

One of the boats designed by Jerry — the *Williwaw*

he had felt like Paul Bunyan, but no longer. Nothing seemed to have the strength and beauty it had once possessed. Even Eleanor's boat *The Roaring Forties* "alas for the proud name!" had a crack in the keel and was leaking badly.

In September of 1972, the Braces were having lunch when they received a call from their neighbor Phil Shaw that he could see a big boat grounded on the rocks on the far side of Heart Island. The rise of the island hid it from the Braces' view, but forgetting his weakness, Jerry immediately started for the shore with his son Gerry closely following. Rowing with two pairs of oars they rounded the end of the island where they saw a large yawl with the name *Avelinda* on her bow. She had only been saved from destruction by her dragging light anchor which had caught on some rocks. They managed to free the yacht, and son Gerry succeeded in getting the engine to run. They took her to the lee side of the island where she would be more protected from the winds.

The boat turned out to belong to Thomas Cabot, an industrialist who had presided over an international company that turned natural gas into useful by-products. During the Depression, uninhabited islands could be purchased for under a hundred dollars. By the mid-forties Cabot had bought over forty-one of them for a total of less than $5,000. He was a friend of the Porter family of Great Spruce Head and when he had heard from them that nearby Butter Island was for sale following the collapse of the summer resort Dirigo and the death of the Harriman brothers who had owned it, he quickly added it to his collection. As Thomas Cabot recorded in his book, *The Avelinda: Legacy of a Yankee Yachtsman*, (1991) he and his wife had been cutting a trail on the island one day when they noticed that their yawl was not where they had anchored it. Stranded without food or water, the water was too choppy for them to try to row to Great Spruce Head in their dinghy. Fortunately a small knockabout landed on their beach and rescued them. After fruitlessly searching for the missing boat, they were taken to the Buck Harbor Yacht Club where they were given warm food and clothing.

Mr. Cabot commandeered a fishing boat equipped with a radio to search for the missing boat. When they heard from the Coast Guard that the yawl had been found off Heart Island, they misheard the location as Hard Island so wasted time consulting their charts. Meanwhile, Mrs. Cabot was driven by friends to the Braces' house where police and curiosity seekers were already gathering. She quickly and rather peremptorily took charge until her husband finally arrived. He was very grateful to Jerry and delighted to meet the author of *Between Wind and Water*, one of his favorite books. He wrote of Brace in *Avelinda*: "He was my kind of person," and quoted the lines from *Between Wind and Water*: "The Aegean has been called the true realm of gold, but to a sailor of small boats it seems forbidden with its barren heights and depths. In Maine we have what are affectionately called eel ruts and gunk-holes, and those with all the rest, even including the fog, make it the cruiser's true home."

Even a small sloop requires constant care and vigilance. As Jerry grew older he was forced to leave more of the work to the men from the local boat-yards. When the Braces returned to Deer Isle the following summer, Jerry was dismayed to discover that *Festina's* aging mast had been left on swampy ground and improperly covered. It had rotted in the middle and was unusable. At Huldah's urging he bought *Sprite*, a pretty 24-foot plastic Rainbow type sailboat that could sleep four, but he was never happy with it. It came equipped with a Johnson outboard which he did not use, and he complained that the well for it kept filling with water. He could not decide what to do with *Festina*. She was his true love and he could not just carelessly dispose of her. He tried to carry on with his memoirs, but his heart was no longer in it. He wrote to Mildred Pettit that it "makes me sadly aware of the deficiencies of my life and work. And I can't really bring myself to be candid. What I write seems small and pointless though I persist for lack of a better project."

Although retirement meant that Jerry could remain at Deer Isle into October, he felt that he was accomplishing little. Most of the heavy moving of moorings and sawing and chopping was done by his grandson Lincoln. Then Lincoln would run the five miles to Eleanor's house to do the same for her. Jerry was grateful for his help and strength, but he found it difficult not to be resentful that he could no longer take care of such things himself.

When he visited Wiscasset that winter it seemed that everyone there was growing old, too. The Burrages were getting frail and bent, though he admired their spirit. "Mildred has lately been painting pictures for the Rockefellers and—I think—for Kissinger's offices in Washington which I should suppose he spends little time in—anyway tottery or not, she is indomitable." He wrote to me on New Year's day of 1974, "Having written 1974, I pause a moment to reflect anew on the remorseless rush of time (to borrow Conrad's phrase). Perhaps I should be grateful that we have weathered the year in fairly good condition. The less said about that remorseless rush the better, specially when its carrying you pell-mell into your mid-seventies."

Jerry's sister Betty and her husband Huntington moved to Wiscasset to be nearer Eleanor. Jerry and Huldah spent each Christmas with Eleanor. Now the gatherings were enlivened by the addition of Johnnie and Brenda Gilchrist. Though Jerry took little part in the conversation, he enjoyed being surrounded by family. He was reading R. W. B. Lewis's new biography of Edith Wharton, whom he was finding a pretty formidable woman, and he had just finished Richard Sewall's two-volume life of Emily Dickinson. Sewall had been one of his students at Williams, which had added extra interest. It was a constant source of amazement to him that new materials and insights could still be found about someone who had been written about as much as Dickinson.

Jerry was feeling better. Researching his paternal lineage for his autobiography provided a kind of security in the knowledge that he was part of an established line. He began to look at his life from a new perspective. Remembering the "Days That Were" brought back memories of his happy youth.

23
Final Years

Though Jerry in his seventies appeared calm, even withdrawn, he was not prepared to "go gentle into that good night." He resented the infirmities of age and tried to hide them from his family. He had always enjoyed going off into the woods on his old-fashioned skis. Not until his daughter offered to buy him a new pair of the no-wax fiberglass variety did he ruefully confess to her that he no longer went cross-country skiing, because he knew if he fell, he would be too stiff to get up again.

He had also given up cruising far, though he still managed to get in some good sailing. At North Haven, he went ashore to visit the estate of IBM's head, Tom Watson, Jr. He found its size and splendor appalling, though, as he wrote to Millicent Pettit, it was probably as good a way to spend unlimited money as any other. Great Spruce Head Island was more to his taste. "No airfields there or deer parks with elands (or whatever), no pheasant runs—but almost everything the heart really desires." But the visit made him aware of the passage of time. He wrote ruefully to me: "The Porter family are still there, and the place and its life are wondrous as ever, but alas we are all *old*—we being the ones I used to swim with and sail with and play tennis with. There was a June too, whom I fell in love with (she went and married another man)—she is still there and still lovely." For him, Nancy Porter would always remain the heroine of his *Summer's Tale*.

Jerry was never good at speaking about his own work. He told how he had once been interviewed by a young journalist and reviewer for the *New York Times*. "After he had sat and waited for me to say something and I sat and waited for him to ask me something, he got up and walked off. End of interview." This had taught him that if he wanted public recognition, he would have to be more forthcoming. A few other people had approached him, most notably a former student, Joseph Lovering, a professor at Canisius College in Buffalo, who was doing a book on him for the Twayne series. He had visited Jerry when he was so ill at Massachusetts General Hospital, but, of course, everything from that period was hazy in his memory.

In *Between Wind and Water* Brace had written how old men "see times in the mirror of their disillusion." (p. 207) It was a discouraging time. Men continued to fight a fruitless war in Asia, the Watergate scandal had led to the resignation of President Nixon, and people were becoming aware of how seriously the environment was being poisoned and destroyed. Jerry increasingly took refuge in the past. He read the books and papers of his great-grandfather John Pierce Brace and re-read Harriet Beecher Stowe's fictional rendition of him in *Old Town Folks*. He was amazed at the number of parallels between himself and his ancestor. Both men were teachers susceptible to the wiles of pretty female students, both wrote books, and shared an inclination to melancholy. Even more coincidentally, his great-grandfather had once been in love with an auburn-haired girl named Huldah. Huldah Ensign had been his student, and he had written a poem to her which had begun with the lines:

There is not in all Litchfield a damsel so fair
As that girl with the dark eyes & bright auburn hair.

His other students had somehow managed to get hold of the parody and made thirty copies which they distributed to the class, much to his great-grandfather's embarrassment. Jerry was not sure whether his failure ever to propose to her was for want of courage or inclination.

He rather enjoyed two novels by John Brace written in the style of James Fenimore Cooper, but he could make no sense out of an ambitious tale entitled *Tales of the Devil* published at Hartford, Connecticut in 1847. He recognized that it was meant to be a satire on Byronic heroes, especially Ernest Maltravers, a character in a novel by Bulwer-Lytton. What he couldn't accept was its tone of high morality and religion. Not only was Maltravers damned for a sin which Jerry considered innocuous, but he felt that his punishment of having to live for all eternity in the form of a skunk, shunned and reviled by all, maligned the poor, harmless animal. The only explanation Jerry could think of to explain his great-grandfather's moral indignation was that a cousin, Philander Brace, had brought disgrace on the family by being hanged as an outlaw, horse thief, and murderer.

In 1976 W. W. Norton published Jerry's autobiography, *Days That Were*. It covered only up to the age of twenty-one. To his surprise and delight it received excellent reviews. Some people just enjoyed reading about life in earlier times, but others recognized that the book had deeper significance. Jerry was aware how much he had been shaped by his family heritage. He was impressed by the high expectations they had held for the future. During the Victorian era "optimism prevailed not only with the devout and conventional Christians, but with most of the poets and scientists, and philosophers." (*DTW,* p. 26) His grandfather had been certain that a great new day was about to dawn and that he shared a responsibility for its creation. He established the Children's Aid Society. He traveled, read widely, wrote books, was friends with famous people, and worked unceasingly for the betterment of society. Jerry's father, though not as much of a genius as the first Charles Loring Brace, never doubted the rightness of continuing the work his father had begun. Jerry realized how blessed he had been both in his family and his privileged youth.

Writing the memoir of his early life had proved so therapeutic to him that Huldah urged him to continue the story of his life. The popularity of the first volume encouraged him to try, but he found it impossible to be candid when he knew that his wife, children, and friends would be reading his words. Memories blurred details and he no longer had the energy nor will to check dates and facts.

By 1977, Jerry was living increasingly in the past. He wrote how as a youth he had always dreamed of actually experiencing the Roaring Forties and Cape Horn. His reference to the trade winds reminded him of John Donaldson's punning name for Eleanor's boat, *The Roaring Forties*. He added ruefully,

> I don't know how many people were ever aware of the implications of the name but by now it is rather a pathetic joke. Eleanor in her mid-eighties is coming to her end in a nursing home in Penobscot, Maine. Even the R. F. is in rather decrepit condition, though Barbara and her young ones still use her. We are, of course, feeling very sad about Eleanor. She is not quite all there any more, and can't function on her own. The only person she sees is Kathe Wilckens, a wonderfully faithful person: she keeps in touch with us by telephone. My other sister, Betty Gilchrist, six years younger than E. lives in Wiscasset too, but she is in bad shape also.

Jerry recalled how Ray Ewing, the friend for whom back in 1939, he had designed the 22 foot sloop, *Williwaw*, used to mutter "It's hell to be old." Ray had died, but his wife, the artist Louise Ewing was living in the Old Manse at Deer Isle "making like a pioneer woman (with electric heating) full of pleasure in the adventure of it." He and Huldah stayed with her on their short, off-season visits to the island, and it amazed Jerry that she always seemed to be making the most of her life and remained cheerful.

As the boats he had designed grew decrepit and his books went out of print, Jerry began to look at the lives of his past students for proof that his life had been meaningful. He wrote to me: "I like to think of those far-off days when you first came to C.L.A. and we had our freshmen class in Jacob Sleeper Hall—and I never suspected that you would grow up to be a scholar and professor. I don't usually claim credit for the success of my students, but I like to pretend that I had some little necessary part in the making of your career. Anyway I am proud of what you have accomplished." Actually, I was only one of many students for whom he had opened up new worlds of pleasure and opportunity.

All concerns were briefly put aside on December 3, 1977, when Jerry and Huldah celebrated their Golden Wedding anniversary. Friends and relatives sent letters and cards, but the party was limited to immediate family. A picture of the couple was taken which was used for a Christmas card. Loring, Mimi, and their three sons flew to Belmont from Michigan, Gerald flew in from Paris, Barbara and Ralph with four of their children were there, Huldah's sister Jane, and dear friend Kathe Wilckens also came. Barbara organized the party, Mimi planned the banquet for sixteen, and grandchild Diane entertained on the guitar, singing songs of her own composition. The children had planned a very special gift and Jerry was deeply touched. They had commissioned Jack Hemenway, blacksmith at Green Head Forge at Stonington, Maine, to make from plans drawn by Loring, a weathervane designed to look like *Festina* with a tiny figure of a man in a beaked cap at the helm. Sadly, Jerry was never to see it in use. By the time that the compass points were set up on the roof of the boathouse, and Diane climbed a ladder to set the miniature *Festina* on top, Jerry was already seriously ill in Blue Hill Hospital.

The weathervane designed to look like *Festina*

If Jerry never understood modern career women, it was partly because he had not married one. Huldah had allowed her own interests and talents to be subsumed by his in order to provide the protection and nurturing she believed his talent needed. In the final analysis the marriage probably was as successful as most unions between two people of different temperaments and backgrounds. Their son Loring assessed it well when he wrote,

They were a curiously matched couple. To him she represented the strain of competence and self sufficiency that he so admired in rural New England. To her, he was an emissary from a superior and privileged social world as well as an embodiment of literary and artistic talent that transcended what she regarded as her own lesser background and worth. I think she came closer to fulfilling her expectation than vice versa, but she never lost the feeling that he really was a creature from an exalted realm—and in a sense of course he was.

In June of 1977, Eleanor died at age 87. For a long time she had been in pain and lost in a world of her own. Jerry knew her passing was for the best, but he felt he had been deprived of a major support. He wrote sadly to Millicent Pettit, "She has been our family base and center for the last forty years, and we counted on her always to be there, and ready and willing to take us in . . . she has been our stand-by ever since our parents died, and our (my) world seems terribly empty." In August he again wrote to Millicent, "I am staggered by the thought of inheriting the Wiscasset house and am wholly dependent on Huldah's handling of all the complications and dealings with lawyers, appraisers, real estate people etc. etc. The complications of running even a small family operation are staggering indeed, and the larger world of finance is wholly beyond my comprehension. I have been leading a too well protected existence." In the beginning of his married life he had believed that the man is lord of the castle and takes care of business and money matters. Gradually he had turned all that over to Huldah as the more competent of the two—first the checkbook, then the taxes, and now all practical details.

At times he roused himself to activity. He and Huldah went to Wiscasset to check on Betty and to decide what should be done with Eleanor's house and furnishings which included "a century or two of Brace heirlooms—and books. Who was the Victorian poet—was it Tennyson—who used 'property, property, property' as a refrain? Galsworthy quotes it in the Saga."

That summer after Barbara had arrived at Deer Isle to help open the house and get the boats in the water, a family service was held for Eleanor. Jerry, accompanied by Barbara, and nieces Brenda Gilchrist and Julia Barnett, carried Eleanor's ashes aboard the *Sprite*. In front of the house at Dunham's Point where he and Eleanor had once been young and happy together, her ashes were consigned to the waves. While Barbara held the tiller, Jerry read the selections he had carefully chosen as his last gift to her. They were all from his favorite writers. He began with the delicate lines from Frost's "Silken Tent." It was an appropriate choice for he and Eleanor had indeed been "loosely bound by countless silken ties of love and thought." Then he read poems written by two of their friends: "For One Without Fear" by Abbie Hustan Evans and "Last Instructions" by Millicent Pettit. Tears came to his eyes and his voice trembled as he read Millicent's line "Let wind take me away over the side into the tenderness of the blue," but it was when he read the final section of Sarah Orne Jewett's *Country of the Pointed Firs* that he totally broke down into weeping. Even in class he had always been moved by the sheer beauty of that last look of islands and bay. Now he was completely overcome. He himself was surprised and chagrined by the sudden paroxysm of grief and he apologized to the stricken girls who had never seen him cry before. They felt helpless to comfort.

Brenda described that sad August day with its "dark mourning clouds scudding overhead." As they headed back to shore "Eleanor's ashes floated in our wake. Her house (still hers in my mind, though mine now by inheritance) tapped our memories as we sailed by: Eleanor in the *Forties* returning from Eagle Island in a northwest gale wind under only a reefed jib, practically bare poles, entering crammed Sylvester's Cove at breakneck speed, steering made nearly impossible, making the mooring, no problem—a true Brace sailor."

Jerry immediately wrote to Millicent Pettit to let her know how much the lines of her poem had meant to him. He confessed how he had broken down, unable to finish the passage from Jewett. They had always brought tears to his eyes, not because the lines are sad, but because they are so beautiful. He was resolved never to read them aloud again. It was impossible for him to conceive that Eleanor was no longer in her house "still living that serene and faithful life we all depended on for so many years." He had never felt more alone.

Wrapped up in his own sorrows, Jerry seemed barely to notice that Huldah was growing old too and could not handle responsibilities with the ease and efficiency of the past. As usual he left all the problems of settling the estate to her. She wanted to do it as quickly as possible and did not make the effort she once would have done to see that family heirlooms were properly distributed among the nieces and nephews. The contents of the house were sold and the Brace family pieces that had once meant so much to Jerry were scattered. He seemed to assume, perhaps encouraged by her, that none of the younger generation were interested in family property.

In January of 1978, Jerry wrote mournfully that he was disposing of his library with the help of a former student, now a rare book dealer, James Randall. It seemed to Jerry that some of his life went out of the house when his books went. He didn't consult anyone as to what should be sold, assuming that they would be of no interest to his children. It is true that probably none of them would have wanted the many sets of nineteenth-century books, gift of Ellen Coolidge, that had filled his library shelves, but he also sold family treasures such as his great-grandfather's *Tales of the Devil*. He wrote sadly:

> A lot of my books date back to my great-grandfather, J. P. Brace, in the early nineteenth century, and I feel like a traitor to be getting rid of them, but what can I do with them? I doubt if Loring would want to be loaded with the works of Captain Marryat or Gibbon's Decline and Fall or a dozen volumes of Matthew Arnold or Washington

Irving. I've always loved the thought of their being there, and without them I may fade away into the shadows. But I'll be doing that anyway and it might help to get rid of at least some of them. The same problem exists with all the household stuff—or at least with the heirloom stuff like the dining room furniture.

It is sad that he could not have known that Loring would care for such heirlooms, and later would have the dining room furniture and family portraits shipped to his home in Michigan, carrying on the Brace tradition.

Jerry returned to Deer Isle the summer of 1978, though he was feeling weak and suffering from indigestion which he blamed on an ulcer. When the sea air failed to revive him, Huldah urged him to go into Blue Hill Hospital for an examination. They sent him to the larger Bangor hospital where tests revealed that he had a malignant tumor on his liver that had metastasized to other organs. He returned to Blue Hill Hospital, but there was little anyone could do for him. Barbara and and her brother Gerry were already at Deer Isle and Johnnie Gilchrist came. As soon as Lincoln Fairley received word he flew in from California. Jerry was conscious enough to acknowledge his presence, but the next day, the 20th of July, Jerry died. There were no services because he had already made arrangements for his body to be given to Harvard Medical School. It was as if his life were so totally obliterated that not even a stone would mark his existence.

Jerry did not believe in immortality. He found his heaven whenever he sailed the bay or walked alone among the spruce listening to the song of a hermit thrush. Perhaps what he wrote in *Between Wind and Water* about the thrush best expresses his philosophic questionings.

> If you hear him plainly, with the forest silence all about you, you feel the presence of such mystic beauty that your only language for it is the language of divinity. You have inevitably a religious experience. But the bird with that miraculous song, first in one key, then in another, like the notes that innocent people would attribute to God himself, is only a bird like other birds, making his habitual noise for some natural ecological purpose, which may be explained as one of the truths science is in charge of. In the light of that truth, is your glimpse of divine beauty merely a sentimental delusion? Are all your yearnings for some sort of natural felicity the same? (*BWW*, pp. 208, 209)

Intellectually an agnostic, he had the soul of a Transcendentalist.

Jerry's colleagues at Boston University prepared a memorial tribute to be read at faculty meeting and published in the college magazine. Many of those closest to him had died or retired. But his old friend Millicent Pettit's son,

Norman, was teaching there, as were his former chairman, Donald Winslow, and current chair, Morton Berman. Their tribute to him revealed the essence of the man. As a colleague he had seemed "reserved, even forbidding on first meeting. But further acquaintance revealed a man of infinite sympathy and gentleness, a man of great integrity, fair minded, slow to judge people, and as tolerant of his colleagues' foibles as he was of the foibles of his students." But soon even these words of appreciation were buried deep in the archives.

24
L'envoi

Huldah tried to carry on the old pattern of life. Her children and grandchildren made it possible for her to continue summering at Deer Isle, but she independently refused to let them determine her actions. Back at Belmont in the fall, she accepted Barbara's help to settle her in, but she refused to consider a live-in companion or to move to smaller quarters. She still drove her car and volunteered at McLean's, although she was growing forgetful. She had always confessed to a notoriously bad memory, though she had no difficulty in recalling important data such as doctor's appointments, medical dosages, and information vital to her family's health. Loring believes that originally her forgetfulness might have been a sort of domestic ploy to get Jerry to talk. By correcting her errors, he was forced to join into the conversation. Now, the memory lapses were genuine. Fortunately, she had good neighbors to keep an eye on her. She was pleased when son Gerald edited, proof read, and paid to have typed and privately printed the second volume of his father's autobiography which had been turned down for publication by Norton. The manuscript was sketchy, inaccurate, and unpolished, but she wanted family and friends to have it as a last memorial.

In October, George Brockway wrote her a kind letter explaining how much luck and politics have to do with literary reputation. *The Garretson Chronicle* would have assured Jerry fame and fortune if it had not been turned down by the Book of the Month Club, primarily because Amy Loveman thought it made Marquand look bad. He recalled, too, how close Jerry had come to the Pulitzer Prize until James Michener's editor friends had insisted that the award go to *Tales of the South Pacific*. Brockway tried to comfort her by reminding her that Jerry would never have enjoyed being a public figure and a *Time* and *Newsweek* certified sage. This was only partially true, however, for few realized how great his hunger for recognition was. Huldah knew that his old age had been darkened by the public forgetting him. It seemed to her that even Boston University had ignored him in his final years. If his works were forgotten, then the time she had devoted to assuring him the privacy to work uninterrupted, had been in vain.

Though alone much of the winter, she still saw children and grandchildren during the summer. Loring and family could only come for brief stays as his career made heavy demands on his time. Son Gerry visited from France, but he could no longer do heavy work on the Deer Isle place after having a coronary by-pass in 1976 and two artificial hips installed in 1982. By now, however, the grandchildren, especially Barbara's son Lincoln, were able to do the heavy lifting of moorings and clearing of brush. The bunkbeds in the boathouse seemed to be filled continuously with various grandchildren and their young friends.

Jerry's sister Betty died in 1982, the last of her generation. Her ashes too were scattered to the waves on the beach in front of the Dunham Point house where a short service was held by Huldah, Barbara, and Betty's son and daughter, Johnnie and Brenda. When it was over, Johnnie gave Barbara a picture of her father in a silver frame. It had been taken when he was about twenty years old and had stood on Betty's bedside table, in whatever country she happened to be living, throughout her life. She had maintained a lifetime devotion toward her younger brother.

A greater tragedy happened that year when Barbara's daughter Diane, Huldah's only granddaughter, was killed in a motorcycle accident. Her ashes were scattered on the waves in front of the house at Parker's Point. In *Between Wind and Water* Jerry had described the little boat in which he had first learned to row. The lines were read at the service as they scattered Diane's ashes, "if there is a Platonic heaven where the idea of boat exists in divine perfection it will be recognized as the original model for the little tender."(*BWW*, p. 108)

Growing increasingly forgetful, but stubbornly refusing to give up, Huldah was enabled to remain in her Belmont home by the kindly watchfulness of her neighbor, Harriet Karplus, who called each morning to check on her. The morning of August 23, 1986, Huldah mowed the grass and bundled up the brush before stopping to rest in her favorite chair. When she failed to respond to the customary eight A.M. telephone call, Harriet Karplus let herself into the house with her key and found her. She had simply slipped into a permanent sleep. It was exactly the kind of ending that she would have wanted.

Today strangers live in the red brick house in Belmont. At Deer Isle, new cottages have been built along the shore and Heart Island has been privately purchased. But the coastline is as lovely as ever. The house at Parker's Point appears much as it did when the Braces first saw it. Inside, Jerry's watercolors line the walls and his boat models are in their accustomed places. The stuffed loon still stands in the living room, now watching over shelves where all of Gerald Warner Brace's books have been placed along with the volumes written by his sons. Outside the window, the cherry trees offer fruit to birds and humans, and each spring the weather-vane, with its tiny helmsman sailing forever windward, is returned to its perch atop the boathouse. The Brace children, now grey haired and success-ful, along with their various children and grandchildren, including a Charles Loring Brace VI, continue to visit each summer. Jerry's niece, Brenda Gilchrist, a freelance writer, lives year round at Dunham's Point in the old family summer home. Though a win-terized wing has been added, the great living room where the three genera-tions of Braces once gathered is com-paratively unchanged. The Trivet is showing signs of age, but it is still used for guests and writing.

One of Jerry's model boats still in his Deer Isle home

The boats that Jerry so lovingly designed no longer sail the waters of Penobscot Bay. *Festina* was bought by a man from Rockport, Maine, who dreamed of restoring her to sail along the coast, but marriage and a family changed his priorities. Though he sold the lead from her keel and turned her cockpit into a sandbox for his children, he returned her tiller to the Brace fam-ily. There is a another sloop named *Festina*, however, owned by the poet Philip Booth of Castine, Maine, whose parents had proved such good friends to the Braces so many years before when Jerry was ill at Dartmouth College. Although no longer seen in local waters, perhaps somewhere *The Roaring Forties* still sails, for she was restored by Jay Peters in South Blue Hill, Maine, who, after chang-ing her rigging so that she sailed better than before, moved away from the area.

But if the name of Gerald Warner Brace, boat designer and author, is not recognized today, the influence of Brace, the professor lives on. Teaching brings its own form of immortality. He is remembered by former students; not only those whose lives he knowingly touched, but others who studied under him only briefly. Joseph Lovering, who in 1981 published a critical biography, *Gerald Warner Brace*, for the Twayne Series, had been one of the returning G.I.s in Brace's class at Boston University Graduate School. Though he had taken only one course with him, he had been struck by the genuine interest Brace had shown in the stories read and the authors who had written them. Robert B. Slocum had just one course with Brace at Boston University before going off to service in World War II, but a half century later, in 1994, he dedicated his bibliography, *New England in Fiction 1787–1990*:

In Memory of
Gerald Warner Brace
(1901–1978)   *77 yrs*
Inspiring teacher and writer
Whose novels are masterful evocations
of the New England of the first half
of the 20th century

Poets and novelists remember the quiet encouragement he gave to them, and in countless classrooms his words of wisdom have been reiterated by the students who once learned their lessons from him.

The life of Gerald Warner Brace stands as testimony to a time when many shared in an American dream and belief in the future—not based on faster networks of communication—but on hard work and inner strength. His novels may no longer be in print, but the scenes he recreated have not totally disappeared. In spite of encroaching modernization, the islands and mountains of New England remain supremely beautiful. Osprey and eagles are making a comeback and there is increasing awareness of the need for preservation. At Deer Isle, Maine, on foggy days, the spruce covered points of land and islands appear mysterious, and when skies are blue, sails form white patterns against the lavender horizon of the low-lying hills on the mainland. Modern life intrudes, of course, but in the remote hills of New Hampshire and Vermont and along the granite shores of Penobscot Bay, it is still possible to find the rural beauty described in Brace's novels, and to appreciate the "days that were."

Index

A

Allen Stevenson School (NY), 11
Alger, Horatio, 5
Amherst College (MA), xii, 19–27,
    29–31, 37, 46, 59, 113, 118, 170,
    173, 227, 234
Avelinda, 238, 239

B

Bailey's Island (ME), 44
Baird, Theodore, 50
Ball, Miss, 96, 99, 100
Banks, Theodore, 64
Beck, Neva (*see* Sylvester)
Belloc, Hilaire, 25, 35, 37, 113
Belmont (MA), xi, 3, 125–127, 133,
    135–139, 142, 156, 175, 180, 183,
    201, 203, 237, 250
Berman, Morton, 248
Bettina, 9, 14, 15, 22, 43, 46, 94, 112,
    119, 135
Blodgett, Harold, 89, 119
Blue Hill (ME), xiii, 244, 247, 251
Booth, Ed, 90
Booth, Jean, 90
Booth, Philip, 237, 251
Boston University, xi, xiii, 40, 52,
    66, 69, 72, 75, 76, 78, 119–122,
    124, 125, 133, 136–143, 145–148,
    155, 158, 159, 167, 169–173, 176,
    178, 180, 185, 186, 194–196, 199,
    204, 205, 211, 220, 221, 226–229,
    247–249, 251

Brace, Gerald Warner
  Family of:
  Brace, Barbara
    (daughter, *see* Seeley)
  Brace, Bessie (aunt), 6, 17, 68,
    81, 95, 213
  Brace, Betty (sister, *see* Gilchrist)
  Brace, Charles Loring I
    (grandfather), 2, 3, 35, 205, 243
  Brace, Charles Loring II (father),
    1, 3, 10, 13, 39, 73, 117, 126
  Brace Charles Loring III
    (brother), 1, 3, 5, 10, 11, 13–15,
    17, 18, 22, 27, 42, 44, 47, 55, 66
  Brace, Charles Loring IV (son),
    71, 90, 117, 140, 142, 156, 168,
    175, 177, 184, 197, 201, 203,
    212, 244, 247, 249, 250
  Brace, Charles Loring V
    (grandson), 44, 47, 198, 201
  Brace, Charles Loring VI
    (great-grandson), 251
  Brace, Dorothy
    (sister, *see* Donaldson)
  Brace, Eleanor (sister), 3, 5, 9, 13,
    22, 25, 33–37, 42, 44, 45, 56,
    67–69, 73, 81, 82, 93, 117,
    121, 133, 134, 138, 142, 143,
    157, 167, 168, 172, 175, 184,
    207, 208, 213, 238, 240,
    243–246
  Brace, Emma
    (aunt, *see* Donaldson)

Brace, Gerald Warner (son),
91, 117, 122, 140, 143, 156, 171,
174, 177, 184, 238, 244, 249, 250
Brace, Helen Storie (sister-in-law),
47, 66, 73
Brace, Helen Warner, "Elenita"
(Niece), 66
Brace, Huldah Laird (wife),
xi, xiii, 40–43, 51–55, 59–63,
65, 69–79, 81–100, 103–109,
112–119, 121, 125, 133–143, 147,
150–153, 155–157, 168, 174, 175,
178, 183, 184, 201, 212, 213, 215,
220, 227, 233, 236, 237, 239, 240,
243–247, 249, 250
Brace, John Pierce
(great-grandfather), 12, 57, 96,
141, 180, 205, 242, 246
Brace, Leta (aunt, see Croswell)
Brace, Letitia O'Neill
(grandmother), 2, 5
Brace, Louise Warner (mother),
1, 3, 5, 6, 11, 13, 107, 108, 115,
127, 167
Brace, Mimi
(daughter-in-law, see Crozier)
Brace, Robert (uncle), 1, 5, 12, 17,
81
Brace, Roger Crozier (grandson),
201
Writings of:
"Artisans and Models," 102
Bell's Landing, 68, 176, 179, 181,
194, 195
Between Wind and Water, 7, 44,
138, 202, 221–225, 239, 242, 247,
250
Days That Were Vol. I, xii, xv, 7, 9,
12, 29, 35, 38, 114, 151, 242
Days That Were Vol. II, 92, 104,
117, 123, 126, 128, 146, 161, 194,
226
"Deep Water Man," 103, 113, 119
Department (The), 225–229

"Essential Novel," 219
Garretson Chronicle (The), 6, 21,
77, 135, 142, 148–155, 157, 161,
166, 179, 180, 197, 216, 217, 223,
249
Islands (The), xiv, 36, 37, 68, 97,
102, 107–113, 115, 117, 124, 149,
167, 190
Light on a Mountain, 21, 126–131,
157, 170
"Mr. Sandgate and the Mountain,"
51
"Robert Frost's New Hampshire,"
118
Spire (The), 58, 167, 170–172, 175
"Stuff of Fiction," 150, 153, 193,
231–233
Summer's Tale (The), 157, 161,
163–166, 241
"Two Cloudy Stories," 60–62
Wayward Pilgrims (The), 21, 51,
55, 113–117, 154, 167
Wind's Will (The), 38, 213, 215,
216
Winter Solstice, 204–207, 214, 215
World of Carrick's Cove (The), 72,
187–190, 197, 198, 222
"Writer's Talent," 225
Brace Memorial Farm School, 5
Bradley, L. M., 71
Brandt and Brandt, 102
Brearley School for Girls, 8
Brewer, Leighton, 145, 159, 173, 193
Briggs, LeBaron, 26, 47, 50, 51, 54, 57,
58, 79, 92, 178, 194, 231
Brimstone Island (ME), 185
Brockway, George, 149, 150, 153, 157,
166, 173, 175, 191, 214, 215, 249
Brown, Richard, 64
Brown, Wentworth, 64, 65
Bufo Aqua, 43, 67
Buffum, Anne, 26, 28, 40, 54, 69, 90,
96, 114
Buffum, Margaret, 5, 90, 91, 96, 114

Buffum, Walbridge, 23, 26, 90
Bunyan, John, 116, 130, 176
Burrage, Madeleine, 42, 168, 175, 240
Burrage, Mildred, 42, 168, 175, 214, 226, 240
Bush, Douglas, 67, 68
Bushnell, Horace, 2

C
Cabot, Thomas, 238, 239
Cape Rosier (ME), 27, 46, 109
Carter, Bertha, 125, 143, 146, 213, 233, 234
Cartwright, Clermont, 23
Charmian, 56, 67, 123, 135, 149
Chase, Mary Ellen, 111, 198
Chebeague Island (ME), 106, 149, 175
Ches-Knoll, 2, 3, 5, 7, 9, 151
Children's Aid Society, 2, 3, 5, 17, 39, 50, 243
Churchill, Jenny Jerome, 59
City of Bangor, 9
City of Rockland, 9
Cobleigh, Mr. and Mrs., 105
Coffin, Robert Tristram, xiv
Comstock, Ada Louise, 79
Connor, William, 129, 179, 233
Coolidge, Ellen, 26, 42, 68, 73, 79, 110, 127, 130, 246
Coombs, Roy, 55
Cooper, Burton, 211, 228
Cooper, James Fenimore, 204, 242
Corbin Park (NH), 94
Cox, Sidney, 89, 91, 95, 96
Croswell, Jim, 8, 9, 13, 17, 26, 47, 68
Croswell, Leta, 6, 8, 13, 19, 42, 68, 74, 133, 134, 161, 179
Crozier, Jean, 197
Crozier, Mary Louise (Mimi), 197, 198, 201, 212, 244
Crozier, William, 197
Cummington School of Arts (MA), 96, 103

Czalgosz, Leon, 1

D
Dana, Richard Henry, 212
Dangerous Classes of New York, 2
Dartmouth College, xiii, 80, 87, 88, 90, 95, 99, 106, 119, 124, 173, 227, 251
Dartmouth Outing Club, 58, 89
Day, Cyrus, 67, 68, 76, 79, 80
Deer Isle (ME), xi, xiii, 3, 8, 9, 11, 15, 27, 42, 43, 54, 57, 66, 67, 69–71, 74, 90, 92, 103–105, 111–113, 117, 122, 123, 133, 136–138, 140, 141, 148, 161, 174, 183, 184, 187, 197, 199, 201, 207–209, 213, 221, 236, 237, 240, 245–247, 249, 250–252
Deer Isle Historical Society, 213
Delta Tau Delta, 20
Dennett, Carl, xv, 16, 20, 22, 25, 27, 34, 37, 40, 41, 43, 45, 47, 49, 58, 63, 65, 89, 94, 97, 113, 150
Dennett, Catherine, 94, 97, 113
Dewing, Leslie, 106
Dobbs Ferry (NY), 1, 3, 5, 6, 10, 42
Dodd, Anne, 51, 68, 76
Dodd, Jane, 51, 68, 76
Donaldson, Dorothy, 1, 3, 5, 7, 13, 67, 107, 169, 237
Donaldson, Emma, 6, 9, 11, 22, 27, 33, 42, 43, 55, 81, 179
Donaldson, Harry, 9, 11
Donaldson, John, 7, 10–13, 42–45, 56, 67, 92–94, 126, 135, 137–139, 149, 167, 169, 175, 198, 213, 237
Donaldson, Julia, 44, 67, 237
Donaldson, Norman, 10–13, 42, 105, 215
Duck Harbor (ME), 71, 187, 188
Dunham's Point (ME), 8, 9, 17, 75, 92, 104, 134, 137, 176

E

Eagle Island (ME), xi, 46, 92, 93, 143, 163, 185, 246
Edgell, Harold, 47, 50
Edgewood Farm, 9, 74
Evans, Abbie Huston, 237, 245
Ewing, Louise, 243
Ewing Ray, 243

F

Fairley, Rev. James, 27, 52, 72, 109, 155, 179
Fairley, Lincoln, 27, 28, 31, 40, 44, 46, 51, 55, 65, 67, 76, 78, 80, 89, 96, 155, 175, 179, 212
Fairley, Margaret, 76, 108, 175
Faison, Lane, 64, 156
Festina Lente, xi, 56, 123, 135, 142, 146, 157, 184, 188, 193, 198, 203, 213, 223, 239, 244, 251
Fiedler, Arthur, 220
Fitzgerald, Frank, 211
Fling Island (ME), xi, 184
Forsythe, Bob, Jack, and Willie, 6
Francis, Robert, 154, 157, 158, 234, 236
Frost, Robert, xiii, 23, 25, 29, 38, 89, 95, 100, 118, 128, 145, 177, 178, 199, 200, 201, 216, 220, 234–236, 245

G

Gardiner (ME), 214
Garfield, Harry A, 57
Garfield, James A., 57
Gesta Christi, 2
Gilchrist, Betty, 1, 6, 14, 17, 22, 28, 33, 34, 42, 67, 81, 82, 137, 151, 213, 240, 243, 245, 250
Gilchrist, Brenda, xi, 81, 142, 175, 207, 208, 240, 245, 246, 250, 251
Gilchrist, Charles, 81
Gilchrist, Douglas, 35, 36
Gilchrist, Huntington, 17, 28, 33, 34, 42, 81, 82, 85, 151, 213

Gilchrist, John, 33, 81, 84, 137–139, 146, 175, 240, 247, 250
Gilgun, John, 194, 204
Gotshalk, Diane, 197, 244, 250
Gotshalk, Richard, 175, 176, 184, 199, 201, 250
Gotshalk, Lincoln, 178, 184, 240, 250
Gotshalk, Ralph Walter, 199, 225
Grace Church (NY), 19, 28
Graham, Edward K., 185, 199, 205, 212
Great Spruce Head Island (ME), 56, 134, 143, 161–165, 239, 241
Grey, Zane, 12, 14, 16, 41, 165
Guiteau, Charles, 57
Gunnery School (CT), xii, 12, 14
Guthrie, Ramon, 89

H

Hall, Bonnie, 213
Ham, Roswell, 112, 113
Hamlin, Cyrus, 223
Hancock, Mr. and Mrs., 24, 26, 114, 127
Hardy, Thomas, 24, 27, 82, 136, 141, 232, 233
Harris, Arthur S. Jr., 186
Harvard University, xiii, 14, 28, 31, 33, 39, 40, 46, 47, 49, 50, 54, 59, 66–68, 81, 103, 114, 120, 125, 156, 176, 178, 183, 197, 212, 227, 247
Heart Island (ME), xi, 238, 250
Hendrickson, Lincoln, 9, 26, 30, 75, 106, 167
Hendrickson, Marion, 9, 13
Hendrickson, Marion Vaux, 9, 13, 167
Hippocampus, 162
Holman, C. Hugh, 153, 154, 217
Holmes, Doris, 154
Howard, Marion, 185
Howe, George, 33

Hughes, Ted, 196
Hurricane Island (ME), xi, 185, 204

I

Isle au Haut (ME), xi, 46, 71, 111,
    185, 187, 188, 203
Islip (NY), 1

J

Jamaica Plain (MA), 28, 40, 74, 80,
    96, 99, 174
James, Henry, 4, 34, 64, 180
Janncey, Leslie, 76
Jerome, Jenny (*see* Churchill)
Jewett, Sarah Orne, 21, 25, 110, 111,
    150, 154, 158, 164, 180, 198, 245,
    246
J. T. Morse, 9, 56
Johnson, Alice, 154
Johnson, Arthur, 20, 21
Johnson, Carrie, 20, 21, 23, 26, 42,
    73, 127, 150, 151
Joyce, James, 64, 232
Junkins, Donald, 196, 235, 236

K

Karplus, Harriet, 250
Kemble, Fanny, 4
Kemble, Henry, 4
Kipling, Rudyard, 115
Kittredge, Charles Lyman, 49, 80
Kezer, Elizabeth (*see* Otis)
Kossuth, Lajos, 2, 180

L

Laird, Glover, 53
Laird, Huldah (*see* Brace)
Laird, Huldah Blanche Potter, 52,
    53, 73, 85, 174
Laird, Jane, 73, 91, 244
Laird, Noel, 52
Laird, Raymond, 52, 53, 73, 85, 91
Lane, George, 229
Lasell Seminary, 69, 72, 90

Lewis, Millicent, xv, 43, 55, 103,
    109, 116, 234, 237, 239, 241,
    245–247
Licklider, Professor, 58, 64, 66
Lima, Peru, 66
Lincoln County Cultural &
    Historical Society, 214
Little, Dwight, 64, 65, 76, 156
Longfellow, Henry Wadsworth, 37,
    74, 216
Loomis School (CT), xii, 14–19, 27,
    30, 46, 102
Loon, 142
Loring, Katherine, 179, 180
Loveland, Winslow, 120, 147
Loveman, Amy, 249
Lovering, Joseph, 116, 154, 241, 251
Lowell, Robert, 196, 199, 200
Lunt, Storer, 149, 215
Lyon, Mary, 112

M

MacKenzie School, 5
Marks, Jeanette, 100
Marsh, Daniel, 121, 158, 169
Marquand, John, 150, 198, 249
Mary Hitchcock Hospital (NH), 90,
    91, 95
Maryville (TN), 52, 61
Massachusetts General Hospital,
    233, 241
Mather, Merrilee, 140, 143, 147, 148
Mather, Ruth, 139, 140, 147
Mather, Professor Thomas, 120,
    139, 140, 144, 147, 148
Mather, Tom (son), 139, 147
Matinicus (ME), 157, 201–203
Mauritania, 37
Maxcy, Professor, 66, 171
Maynadier, Howard, 50
Mays, Stacy, 92
McCarthy, Mary, 173
McIntosh and Otis (agents), 204,
    215

McKaye, Steele, 3
McLane, Charles B., xv
McLean Hospital, 3, 68, 125, 196, 249
Meiklejohn, Alexander, 23, 29, 30, 170
Melville, Herman, 165, 219
Michener, James 155, 249
Mill Island (ME), 8, 9, 11, 75
Millay, Edna St. Vincent, 202
Miss Master's School (NY), 6
Miss Pierce's Female Academy, 12
Miss Wheeler's School (RI), 6, 73
Moore, Terry, 76
Morse, Sam, 237
Morse, Stearns, 88, 89, 95
Mount Desert (ME), 14, 15, 22, 43
Mount Holyoke College, xiii, 28, 96, 99, 100, 106, 112, 117–120, 124, 125, 170, 175, 176, 199
Mount Greylock (MA), 59, 65, 83
Mount Washington (NH), 76, 77, 89, 96, 123, 151
Murray, John Tucker, 49
Myers, Edward, 237

N

Newsboy Lodging House (NY), 2
North Haven (ME), 7, 15, 43, 56, 103
Norton, Mildred, 76, 121, 122, 184
Norton Publishers, 149, 161, 195, 215, 226, 237, 242, 249
Norton, Richard, 122
Norton, William, 76, 119, 121, 184
Norwich (VT), 80, 87, 90–92, 96, 99

O

Olmsted, Frederick Law, 2, 3, 8, 39
Olmsted, Carol, 70
Olmsted, John, 2
Olmsted, Margaret, 70, 71
Olmsted, Marion, 3
Olmsted, Mary, 3

Olmsted, Richard, 71
Orozco, Jose, 88
Otis, Elizabeth, 148, 149, 204, 207, 208, 215

P

Peck, Lillie, 68, 73, 79
Pettit, Millicent (see Lewis)
Pettit, Norman, 43, 248
Phi Beta Kappa, 31, 159, 186
Philpott, Helen (see Brace)
Piz Nair, Switzerland, 13
Plath, Aurelia, 122
Plath, Otto, 122
Plath, Sylvia, 122, 196
Plath, Warren, 122
Potter, Huldah Blanche (see Laird)
Porcupine Islands (ME), xi, 185
Porter, Eliot, 22, 161–164, 166
Porter, Fairfield, 22, 56, 161, 163, 164
Porter, James Foster, 22, 56, 134, 161, 164
Porter, John, 161, 164
Porter, Nancy, 22, 40, 43, 56, 121, 164, 241
Postlethwaite, Muriel, 73, 81, 117, 134, 141, 142, 167, 168
Pound, Ezra, 106, 200
Pound, Omar, 200
Pressey, Norman, 117, 137
Prides Crossing (MA), 179, 180
Putnam's Publishing, 105, 106, 113, 126, 127, 133, 148

Q

Quabbin Reservoir (MA), 170
Quinn, Bonny, 93, 143, 187
Quinn, Erlund, 93, 143, 187

R

Radcliffe College, 72, 79
Randall, James, 246
Roaring Forties, xi, 93, 238, 243, 246, 251

Edwin

Robinson, Edward Arlington, 30, 214
Robinson, Fred N., 49
Rotterdam, 33
Ruark, Bertha (*see* Carter)

S
Saint Moritz, 13, 35
Santa Barbara (CA), 117, 212
Santayana, George, 149, 150, 198
Scorpion, 10
Scott, Sir Walter, 84, 164
Seeley, Barbara, 95, 117, 121, 140, 175, 178, 184, 199, 201, 203, 224, 225, 245, 250
Seeley, Leah Fletcher, 224
Seeley, Ralph, 224, 225, 244
Sewall, John, 64, 240
Sewall, Richard, 64, 240
Sexton, Anne, 196
Shakespeare, William, 164
Sharp, Dallas Lore, 194
Sharp, Martha, 79
Shaw, Philip, 238
Shell Award, 225
Sherwood, May, 3, 6
Slocum, Robert B., 251
Smith, Henry DeForest 30
Smollett, Tobias, 226
Sneath, George, 120, 171
Snell, Miss, 96, 99, 100
Southeastern Mass. Tech, 220
South Hadley, (MA), 96, 99, 112
Sprite, 239, 245
Sproat, Robert, 159, 228
Starbuck, George, 196
Steinbeck, John, 174, 177, 207–209, 213, 219, 232
Stevenson, R. L., 113, 116
Stewart, George R., 174
Stonington, (ME), 45, 74, 135, 162, 188, 244
Storie, Helen (*see* Brace)
Stowe, Harriet Beecher, 25, 180, 205, 242

Strauss, Nancy (*see* Porter)
Swans Island, (ME), 43, 236
Sylvester, Fred, 9, 42, 74, 75, 123, 128, 134, 140, 189, 190
Sylvester, Lillian, 74, 123, 134, 140, 189
Sylvester, Neva, 189
Sypher, Wylie, 173

T
Tales of the Devil, 242, 246
Taylor, Brodie, 76
Taylor, Ralph Wesley, 119, 185
Texas Quarterly, 207, 219, 220
Thompson "Crock," 30
Thompson, Goodman, 123, 134, 135, 137
Thompson, Josephine, 123, 125, 134, 135, 137
Thoreau, H. D., 207
Travels with Charley, 208, 209, 213
"Trivet," 45, 56, 67, 134, 137, 140, 207, 208, 251
Trollope, Anthony, 173, 207
Tureen, 9
Twayne Series, 116, 251

U
University of Maine (Orono), 237
Unknown God, 2

V
Vaux, Calvert, 2, 39
Vega, 10
Verenis, Betsy, 180
Verenis, Mattina, 180
Vineyard Haven (MA), 9, 10

W
Wagenknecht, Edward, 159, 166, 173, 184, 223
Warburton, Ellen, 15
Warner, May (*see* Sherwood)
Warner, Sarah McKaye, 3
Washburn, Gordon, 64, 67

Washington Square, 4
Waxman, Samuel, 78, 79
Wellesley Hills (MA), 121, 184
Westergaard, Rachel, 175, 212
Whicher, George, 23, 24, 46, 51, 95, 108, 118, 194
White, Irving, 145
Wilckens, Kathe, 197, 243, 244
Williams College, xiii, 28, 57–59, 64, 66, 95, 99, 119, 149, 151, 156, 171, 173, 227, 240
Williams, Gluyas, 94, 122, 137
Williams, John, 119
Williwaw, 243

Winslow, Donald, 136, 145, 169, 184, 229, 235, 248
Wiscasset (ME), 168, 243, 245
Woods Hole (MA), 10, 11, 26, 43
Wooley, Mary Emma, 100, 112
W. W. Norton
    (*see* Norton Publishers)

Y

Yale University, 13, 14, 16, 19, 120, 149
Yale University Press, 215
Young, Stark, 29